The UN Security Council and International Law

The UN Security Council and International Law explores the legal powers, limits, and potential of the United Nations Security Council, offering a broadly positive (and positivist) account of the Council's work in practice. This book aims to answer questions such as when are Council decisions binding and on whom, what legal constraints exist on Council decision-making, and how far is the Council bound by international law? Defining the controlling legal rules and differentiating between what the Council can do, as opposed to what it should do as a matter of policy, this book offers both a tool for assessment of the Council as well as realistic solutions to address its deficiencies, and, most importantly, evaluates its potential for maintaining international peace and security, to the benefit of us all.

Michael Wood is a barrister at Twenty Essex Chambers. He is a member of the UN International Law Commission and a senior fellow at the Lauterpacht Centre for International Law, University of Cambridge. Michael was a legal adviser to the UK Foreign Office between 1970 and 2006. He was also a lawyer in the UK Mission to the UN between 1991 and 1994, working mostly on Security Council matters. He has acted for many governments before the International Court of Justice and other international courts.

Eran Sthoeger is a litigator and a consultant in international law. He is an Adjunct Professor of Law at Brooklyn Law School as well as at Seton Hall Law School. On top of his experience as an international litigator, for nearly a decade Eran monitored and analyzed the work and inner workings of the Security Council as a policy analyst at Security Council Report, NY, an organization that follows and analyzes the work of the UN Security Council.

Hersch Lauterpacht Memorial Lectures

Recent books in the Hersch Lauterpacht Memorial Lecture Series

Michael Wood and Eran Sthoeger *The UN Security Council and International Law*

Tom Ginsburg *Democracies and International Law*

Christine Chinkin *Women, Peace and Security and International Law*

Stephen M. Schwebel, Luke Sobota and Ryan Manton *International Arbitration: Three Salient Problems*

Mary Ellen O'Connell *The Art of Law in the International Community*

Yuval Shany *Questions of Jurisdiction and Admissibility before International Courts*

W. Michael Reisman and Christina Skinner *Fraudulent Evidence before Public International Tribunals: The Dirty Stories of International Law*

Andrés Rigo Sureda *Investment Treaty Arbitration: Judging Under Uncertainty*

Ralph Zacklin *The United Nations Secretariat and the Use of Force in a Unipolar World: Power v. Principle*

John H. Jackson *Sovereignty, the WTO, and Changing Fundamentals of International Law*

Jan Paulsson *Denial of Justice in International Law*

Francisco Orrego Vicuña *International Dispute Settlement in an Evolving Global Society: Constitutionalization, Accessibility, Privatization*

Martti Koskenniemi *The Gentle Civilizer of Nations: The Rise and Fall of International Law 1870–1960*

Thomas M. Franck *Recourse to Force: State Action against Threats and Armed Attacks*

Mohamed Shahabuddeen *Precedent in the World Court*

Antonio Cassese *Self-Determination of Peoples: A Legal Reappraisal*

The UN Security Council and International Law

MICHAEL WOOD
Barrister at Twenty Essex Chambers, London
ERAN STHOEGER
Litigator and Consultant in International Law, New York

Shaftesbury Road, Cambridge CB2 8EA, United Kingdom

One Liberty Plaza, 20th Floor, New York, NY 10006, USA

477 Williamstown Road, Port Melbourne, VIC 3207, Australia

314–321, 3rd Floor, Plot 3, Splendor Forum, Jasola District Centre, New Delhi – 110025, India

103 Penang Road, #05–06/07, Visioncrest Commercial, Singapore 238467

Cambridge University Press is part of Cambridge University Press & Assessment,
a department of the University of Cambridge.

We share the University's mission to contribute to society through the pursuit of
education, learning and research at the highest international levels of excellence.

www.cambridge.org
Information on this title: www.cambridge.org/9781108728737

DOI: 10.1017/9781108692373

© Michael Wood and Eran Sthoeger 2022

This publication is in copyright. Subject to statutory exception and to the provisions
of relevant collective licensing agreements, no reproduction of any part may take
place without the written permission of Cambridge University Press & Assessment.

First published 2022
First paperback edition 2023

A catalogue record for this publication is available from the British Library

ISBN 978-1-108-48349-0 Hardback
ISBN 978-1-108-72873-7 Paperback

Cambridge University Press & Assessment has no responsibility for the persistence
or accuracy of URLs for external or third-party internet websites referred to in this
publication and does not guarantee that any content on such websites is, or will
remain, accurate or appropriate.

Contents

Preface

This book is an updated and expanded version of the Hersch Lauterpacht Memorial Lectures on *The UN Security Council and International Law* given by Michael Wood at the University of Cambridge's Lauterpacht Centre for International Law, 7–9 November 2006.

The text of the three lectures remains available on the Centre's website, and so it is possible to see what has remained constant and what has changed over the last fifteen years. While inevitably there have been many developments over a busy (if not entirely positive) decade and a half of Security Council activity (including some important court pronouncements), the main points made in the lectures remain largely valid. At the same time, Michael is greatly indebted to his co-author for agreeing to join in this publication and for contributing much up-to-date information and introducing some new thinking.

The lectures drew on Michael's experience of Security Council matters while working at the United Kingdom Mission in New York between 1991 and 1994, as well as following the Council closely while in the Foreign and Commonwealth Office between 1994 and 2006. The lectures are rooted in practice, with even, dare one say, a bit of common sense. The many additions and updates have been made together with Eran Sthoeger, who brought a fresh view from his time working for Security Council Report between 2010 and 2020 and thereafter teaching United Nations law. Both authors benefited greatly from their association with the excellent volume *The Procedure of the UN Security Council* by Loraine Sievers and Sam Daws (currently in its 4th edition; Oxford University Press, 2014), with its associated website.

This is a book about the law, not policy. The focus is on what the Security Council can and cannot do as well as its practice over time, not what it should or ought to do with its powers and authority. Unless there are obvious legal issues, we have tried to avoid (except briefly in the conclusions) policy debates such as the eternal questions of Security Council reform, whether concerning the veto or the composition of the Council.

We have sought to retain a style appropriate to lectures: brevity, clarity, and a certain lightness of touch. The text does not aim to be comprehensive or learned; it does not include extensive theoretical digressions or lengthy footnotes.

The authors wish to thank all those working at Cambridge University Press for their assistance with this project. A particular word of thanks is due to Finola O'Sullivan for her great publishing skills, good humour, and patience.

Note on Writings

Writings on the law and practice of the Security Council are extensive. The following are among those that we have found most useful, not least because they reflect actual practice. Further references may be found in the works mentioned here, and in relation to specific points in the chapters that follow.

Sam Daws and Loraine Sievers, *The Procedure of the UN Security Council* (4th ed., Oxford University Press, 2014) is an invaluable resource focusing specifically on procedural aspects. It is the fourth edition of the ground-breaking work by Sydney D. Bailey, first published in 1975. Updates are published online as and when there are significant developments; see www.scprocedure.org/.

The New York-based non-governmental organization Security Council Report has a very useful website, with up-to-date information and analysis on all aspects of the work of the Security Council and links to the principal UN documents; see www.securitycouncilreport.org/.

Monographs and commentaries on the United Nations and the UN Charter, while not all are up-to-date, are usually a good starting point for anyone seeking to investigate a particular area of the law and practice of the United Nations. Sometimes the earlier editions still give important insights, especially where the authors have changed. The following come to mind:

Leland Goodrich, Edvard Hambro, and Anne Patricia Simons, *The Charter of the United Nations: Commentary and Documents* (3rd ed., Columbia University Press, 1969).

Jean-Pierre Cot, Alain Pellet, and Mathias Forteau, *La Charte des Nations Unies: Commentaire article par article* (3rd ed., Economica, 2005).

Bruno Simma, Daniel-Erasmus Khan, Georg Nolte, and Andreas Paulus (eds.), *The Charter of the United Nations: A Commentary* (3rd ed., Oxford University Press, 2012).

Simon Chesterman, Ian Johnstone, and David M. Malone, *Law and Practice of the United Nations* (2nd ed., Oxford University Press, 2016).

Rosalyn Higgins, Philippa Webb, Dapo Akande, Sandesh Sivakumaran, and James Sloan, *Oppenheim's International Law: United Nations* (Oxford University Press, 2017).

Also useful are general works on the law of international organizations, such as:

Philippe Sands and Pierre Klein, *Bowett's Law of International Institutions* (6th ed., Sweet and Maxwell, 2009).

Henry Schermers and Niels Blokker, *International Institutional Law* (6th rev. ed., Brill, 2018).

Among studies focusing on the Security Council, we would mention:

Michael J. Matherson, *Council Unbound: The Growth of UN Decision Making on Conflict and Postconflict Issues after the Cold War* (United States Institute of Peace, 2006).

Edward J. Luck, *UN Security Council: Practice and Promise* (Routledge, 2006).

Niels Blokker, *Saving Succeeding Generations from the Scourge of War: The United Nations Security Council at 75* (Brill/Nijhoff, 2020).

Two useful collections of essays on various aspects of the Security Council are:

David M. Malone (ed.), *The UN Security Council: From the Cold War to the 21st Century* (Lynne Rienner, 2004).

Sebastian von Einsiedel, David M. Malone, and Bruno Stagno Ugarte (eds.), *The UN Security Council in the 21st Century* (Lynne Rienner, 2016).

For the negotiating history of the Charter, a particularly valuable work is:

Ruth B. Russell, *A History of the United Nations Charter: The Role of the United States, 1940–1945* (Brookings Institute Press, 1958).

Finally, the *Max Planck Encyclopedia of Public International Law* and the *Max Planck Encyclopedia of International Procedural Law* contain many entries on aspects of the Security Council and its work; it is available at https://opil.ouplaw.com/home/mpil; see also Peters and Wolfrum in the Bibliography.

Note on Documentation and References

Resolutions and presidential statements adopted by the Security Council are referred to by their official document number, followed by the date adopted. For example, Security Council resolution 1373, adopted by the Security Council at its 4385th meeting, is referred to as S/RES/1373, 28 September 2001. Other Security Council documents, such as meeting records and reports of the Secretary-General to the Security Council, are referred to in the same fashion. For example, the provisional verbatim record of the Security Council's 7354th meeting is referred to as S/PV.7354, 30 December 2014. General Assembly and other UN organs' documents are similarly referenced. The context indicates which organ is referred to.

Shortened references are given in the footnotes to books and articles listed in the Bibliography. Where the same author or authors have more than one entry with the same year, a, b, etc. has been added to indicate the relevant publication. Shortened references are also given to the case law referred to, whereas the full official citations are listed in the Table of Cases.

Table of Cases

Permanent Court of International Justice

The Case of the S.S. 'Lotus', PCIJ, Series A, No. 10 (1927)

International Court of Justice

Admission of a State to the United Nations (Charter, Art. 4), Advisory Opinion, ICJ Reports 1948, p. 57

Reparation for Injuries Suffered in the Service of the United Nations, Advisory Opinion, ICJ Reports 1949, p. 174

Anglo-Iranian Oil Co. Case, Order of July 5th, 1951, ICJ Reports 1951, p. 89

Anglo-Iranian Oil Co. Case (Jurisdiction), Judgment of July 22nd, 1952, ICJ Reports 1952, p. 93

Effect of Awards of Compensation Made by the UN Administrative Tribunal, Advisory Opinion of July 13th, 1954, ICJ Reports 1954, p. 47

Admissibility of Hearings of Petitioners by the Committee on South West Africa, Advisory Opinion of June 1st, 1956, ICJ Reports 1956, p. 23

Case Concerning the Temple of Preah Vihear (Cambodia *v.* Thailand), Merits, Judgment of 15 June 1962, ICJ Reports 1962, p. 6

Certain Expenses of the United Nations (Article 17, paragraph 2, of the Charter), Advisory Opinion of 20 July 1962, ICJ Reports 1962, p. 151

North Sea Continental Shelf, Judgment, ICJ Reports 1969, p. 3

Legal Consequences for States of the Continued Presence of South Africa in Namibia (South West Africa) Notwithstanding Security Council Resolution 276 (1970), Advisory Opinion, ICJ Reports 1971, p. 16

Aegean Sea Continental Shelf, Judgment, ICJ Reports 1978, p. 3

Armed Activities on the Territory of the Congo (Democratic Republic of the Congo *v.* Uganda), Judgment, ICJ Reports 2005, p. 168

Armed Activities on the Territory of the Congo (New Application: 2002) (Democratic Republic of the Congo *v.* Rwanda), Jurisdiction and Admissibility, Judgment, ICJ Reports 2006, p. 6

Accordance with International Law of the Unilateral Declaration of Independence in Respect of Kosovo, Advisory Opinion, ICJ Reports 2010, p. 403

Jurisdictional Immunities of the State (Germany *v.* Italy: Greece Intervening), Judgment, ICJ Reports 2012, p. 139

Request for Interpretation of the Judgment of 15 June 1962 in the Case Concerning the Temple of Preah Vihear (Cambodia *v.* Thailand), Judgment, ICJ Reports 2013, p. 281

Arbitral Award of 3 October 1899 (Guyana *v.* Venezuela), Judgment, Jurisdiction of the Court, December 18, 2020

International Criminal Tribunal for Rwanda

Prosecutor *v.* Joseph Kanyabashi, Decision on the Defence Motion on Jurisdiction, Case No. ICTR-96-15-T, 18 June 1997

International Criminal Tribunal for the former Yugoslavia

Prosecutor *v.* Dusko Tadić a/k/a 'Dule', Decision on the Defence Motion for Interlocutory Appeal on Jurisdiction, Appeals Chamber Decision of 2 October 1995

Prosecutor *v.* Tihomir Blaskić, Request of the Republic of Croatia for Review of the Decision of Trial Chamber II of 18 July 1997, Appeals Chamber Judgement of October 29, 1997

Prosecutor *v.* Tadić, Appeals Chamber Judgment of 15 July 1999

European Court of Human Rights

Application no. 77631/01, Slobodan Milošević *v.* The Netherlands, Decision of 19 March 2002

Application no. 71412/01, Behrami *v.* France and Application no. 78166/01, Saramati *v.* France, Germany and Norway, Decision of 2 May 2007

Al-Jedda *v.* the United Kingdom [GC], App. no. 27021/08, 7 July 2011

Nada *v.* Switzerland [GC], App. no. 10593/08, 12 September 2012

Al-Dulimi and Montana Management Inc. *v.* Switzerland, App. no. 5809/08, 26 November 2013 and 21 June 2016 [GC]

Court of Justice of the European Union

Ayadi *v.* Council of the European Union, Case T-253/02, Judgment of the Court of First Instance (Second Chamber), 12 July 2006
Hassan *v.* Council of the European Union and Commission of the European Communities, Case T-49/04, Judgment of the Court of First Instance (Second Chamber), 12 July 2006
Yassin Abdullah Kadi *v.* Council of the European Union and Commission of the European Communities, Case T-315/01, Judgment of 21 September 2005, [2005] ECR II-3649
Joined Cases C–402/05 P and C–415/05 P, Kadi and Al Barakaat International Foundation *v.* Council and Commission [2008] ECR I–6351

Human Rights Committee

Nabil Sayadi and Patricia Vinck *v.* Belgium, CCPR/C/94/D/1472/2006 (29 December 2008)

Canada

Abousfian Abdelrazik *v.* The Minister of Foreign Affairs and the Attorney General of Canada [2010] 1 FCR 267

The Netherlands

Slobodan Milošević *v.* The Netherlands, 41 ILM (2002) 86–90 (31 August 2001)

United Kingdom of Great Britain and Northern Ireland

R (Al-Jedda) *v.* Secretary of State for Defence [2006] EWCA Civ 327
R (Al-Jedda) *v.* Secretary of State for Defence [2007] UKHL 58, [2008] 1 AC 332

United States of America

Medellín *v.* Texas, 552 US 491 (2008)

Abbreviations

AFDI	*Annuaire français de droit international*
AFISMA	African-led International Support Mission in Mali
AHRLJ	*African Human Rights Law Journal*
AJCR	*African Journal on Conflict Resolution*
AJIL	*American Journal of International Law*
AMIS	AU Mission in Sudan
AMISOM	African Union Mission to Somalia
Am U L Rev	*American University Law Review*
ASEAN	Association of Southeast Asian Nations
ASIL	*American Society of International Law*
AU	African Union
BYIL	*British Yearbook of International Law*
CAR	Central African Republic
CJEU	Court of Justice of the European Union
DPRK	Democratic People's Republic of Korea
DRC	Democratic Republic of the Congo
ECHR	(European) Convention for the Protection of Human Rights and Fundamental Freedoms
ECOWAS	Economic Community of West African States
ECtHR	European Court of Human Rights
EJIL	*European Journal of International Law*
EU	European Union
FCO	UK Foreign and Commonwealth Office
FRY	Federal Republic of Yugoslavia
G8	Group of Eight
IAEA	International Atomic Energy Agency
ICC	International Criminal Court
ICCPR	International Covenant on Civil and Political Rights
ICJ	International Court of Justice

ICTR	International Criminal Tribunal for Rwanda
ICTY	International Criminal Tribunal for the former Yugoslavia
IFOR	International Peacekeeping Force
ILA	International Law Association
ILC	United Nations International Law Commission
ISAF	International Security Assistance Force
ISIL	Islamic State of Iraq and the Levant
JUFIL	*Journal on the Use of Force and International Law*
MAPROBU	African Prevention and Protection Mission in Burundi
MINUSCA	Multidimensional Integrated Stabilization Mission in the Central African Republic
MISCA	African-led International Support Mission in Central Africa
MN	Marginal Note
MNF	Multi-National Force – Iraq
MONUC	UN Organization Mission in Democratic Republic of the Congo (forerunner of MONUSCO)
MONUSCO	UN Organization Stabilization Mission in the DR Congo (the acronym comes from its French name, Mission de l'organisation des nations unies pour la stabilisation en république démocratique du congo)
MPEPIL	*Max Planck Encyclopedia of Public International Law*
MPUNYB	*Max Planck Yearbook of United Nations Law*
NAM	Non-Aligned Movement
NATO	North Atlantic Treaty Organization
NILR	*Netherlands International Law Review*
NPT	Treaty on the Non-Proliferation of Nuclear Weapons (1968)
OAS	Organization of American States
OAU	Organisation of African Unity
OIC	Organisation of Islamic Cooperation (formerly Organization of the Islamic Conference)
OPCW	Organisation for the Prohibition of Chemical Weapons
PCA	Permanent Court of Arbitration
PCIJ	Permanent Court of International Justice
PSC	Peace and Security Council
RBDI	*Revue Belge de Droit International*
RHDI	*Revue Hellénique de Droit International*
SMU Law Rev	*Southern Methodist University Law Review*
UN	United Nations
UNAMID	UN–AU Mission in Darfur

UNAMSIL	United Nations Mission in Sierra Leone
UNASOG	United Nations Aouzou Strip Observer Group
UNCC	United Nations Compensation Commission
UNIIIC	United Nations International Independent Investigation Commission
UNPROFOR	United Nations Protection Force
UNTS	United Nations Treaty Series
VCLT	Vienna Convention on the Law of Treaties
WEU	Western European Union
ZaöRV	*Zeitschrift für ausländisches öffentliches Recht und Völkerrecht*

Introduction

A former British Permanent Representative to the United Nations (UN) in New York, David Hannay, has referred to the Security Council as 'that most mysterious and misunderstood international body'.[1] We are not sure how mysterious it is. But it is certainly misunderstood. If we can make the Council somewhat less mysterious, and somewhat better understood, at least in legal terms, we shall have achieved our purpose.

With honourable exceptions, many writings about the Council pay little regard to actual practice. They introduce domestic law concepts which simply have no place. They confuse legality with legitimacy. They complicate that which is straightforward. There are even those who, in our view, seek to 'demonize' the Council.[2] For them, the members of the Council are rather like the gods of Ancient Greece: they squabble on Mount Olympus; launch the occasional thunderbolt; and intervene in the affairs of mortals with unpredictable – sometimes disastrous – results.

Of course, the Security Council has shortcomings and a track record that is far from perfect. Its structure and composition are criticized. There are five permanent members (reflecting the political realities of 1945) while the other ten are elected for two-year terms. The permanent members also have veto power over the decisions of the Security Council. With these rights come added responsibilities and it is fair to say that the members of the Council – permanent but also elected – have not always risen to the occasion.

[1] Malone (2004), as quoted on the back cover. See also de La Sablière (2015) 19 ('cet organe essentiel des Nations Unies dont les médias parlent beaucoup mais qui est finalement mal connu').

[2] Wood (2004).

At times, the Council was silent when action was called for; at other times, its actions fell short or were too late. From time to time the Council preferred the interests of some over those of others, at the expense, perhaps, of its primary responsibility for the maintenance of international peace and security. It lacks consistency.

Criticism of the Security Council is entirely understandable. Being an organ vested with extraordinary powers, the Council should be closely scrutinized. But, in our view, scrutiny does not serve member states, and the international community at large, if it results in weakening the Council as an institution and undermining respect for the law. Rather, thoughtful criticism, with a proper understanding of the law as it pertains to the Security Council, should aim at improving its efficiency and its ability to carry out its mandate on behalf of the member states.

We shall not deal much with concepts such as 'legitimacy',[3] 'accountability'[4] and 'fairness'.[5] These vague and undefined terms are used rather freely by the Council's critics, but they are general concepts rather than firm legal ones. They are highly subjective notions and can be used to justify almost any conclusion. Nor do we address questions concerning the size and composition of the Council, or the existence of the veto and its use. Discussions on Security Council reform have their place, but involve questions of policy, not law, and are thus outside the scope of this book. This is so even when policy preferences are clothed in pseudo-legal argument (such as the appeal to sovereign equality to oppose permanent membership or the veto). Authors make matters worse by mixing up legal and policy considerations, without making clear which are which.

We cannot, while maintaining the spirit of the Hersch Lauterpacht Lectures, do justice to all the legal issues that relate to the Council. This is in no sense a comprehensive work. We have

[3] Roberts (2008). For other views on 'this rather nebulous term' see Caron (1993) 556. For an early discussion, see Franck (1990). The word 'legitimate' is used by politicians, and even by lawyers, in many ways, sometimes quite nuanced, not to say obscure. As Anthea Roberts (2008, p. 205) has written, '[t]he term "legitimacy" is both overused and under-defined in international law'. One thing seems clear, at least to international lawyers: 'Legitimacy is to be distinguished from legality (lawfulness) . . .' (Wolfrum, 2011, para. 1).

[4] For a consideration of the numerous meanings of this expression, see Tzanakopoulos (2011) 2–6. See also ILA (2004).

[5] Franck (1998).

selected questions which are of topical interest and which often arise in practice. We do not consider some important questions, such as the legal issues that arise in the international administration of territory, which have been dealt with fully elsewhere.[6] We rarely touch on matters of procedure, which are covered extensively by Sam Daws and Loraine Sievers in their excellent book.[7]

If we occasionally sound dogmatic, this is in part because we have deliberately kept this volume succinct, in the spirit of the original lectures. Sir Hersch Lauterpacht might or might not have approved. He praised the Permanent Court for 'avoiding so far as possible a dogmatic manner in stating the law'.[8] But, equally, he praised a League of Nations study of Article 20 of the Covenant for expressing views that were, in his words, 'unusually definite. . . . The answers [he said] were conceived not as a product of academic deliberation concerned with putting both sides of the difficulty, but as an aid to urgent international action of unprecedented significance.'[9] It is in that spirit that we see this volume.

Just as in 2006, when the original lectures were given, so now, in 2022, there is a pressing need to strengthen multilateralism. In this context it is important to support the central role of the Security Council within the Charter's collective security system. The Council remains the only body within the international legal system that can take lawful measures to uphold international peace and security that would otherwise be contrary to international law. Much that is written about the Council is theoretical, negative, and sometimes plain wrong. In its own way, this can threaten the Council's effectiveness as an important expression of multilateralism. Perhaps partly for this reason some politicians, diplomats, and commentators downplay, or even write off altogether, the function of law in the work of the Security Council. They see the Council as a purely political organ, capable of anything – *legibus solutus* (unbound by law).

***

The book is organized as follows. In Chapter 1 we examine the legal nature of the Security Council, including whether it sometimes acts as a legislature or judicial body, and the priority of Charter obligations under Article 103. Chapter 2 considers legal aspects of

[6] Knoll (2008); Wilde (2008). [7] Sievers and Daws (2014).
[8] Lauterpacht (1934) 27. [9] Lauterpacht (1936) 57.

Security Council decisions, such as when they are binding and for whom. Then in Chapter 3 we deal in more detail with the powers and functions of the Council. Chapter 4 considers potential limits on those powers, and the various ways in which the Council may be subject to control. Chapter 5 discusses the Council's resort to measures not involving the use of force. Thereafter, Chapter 6 considers legal issues related to the Council's authorizations to use force. Chapter 7 discusses aspects that are particular to the relationship between the Council and international organizations in the context of the use of force. Chapter 8 examines the relationship between the Security Council and the principal judicial organ of the UN, the International Court of Justice. In Chapter 9, we seek to describe ways in which international law may be developed by and within the Council. The book ends with some short conclusions.

1

The Legal Nature of the Security Council

1.1 Applicable Law

It is not our aim in this chapter to set out the overall legal framework of the UN Security Council, a matter covered throughout the book. But we should say a few words at the outset about the various rules of international law applicable to the work of the Council. Article 38.1 of the Statute of the International Court of Justice is a good place to start:

The Court, whose function is to decide in accordance with international law such disputes as are submitted to it, shall apply:

a. international conventions, whether general or particular, establishing rules expressly recognized by the contesting states;
b. international custom, as evidence of a general practice accepted as law;
c. the general principles of law recognized by civilized nations;
d. subject to the provisions of Article 59, judicial decisions and the teachings of the most highly qualified publicists of the various nations, as subsidiary means for the determination of rules of law.

The Security Council is first and foremost governed by the Charter of the United Nations,[1] including the Statute of the International Court of Justice.[2] The Charter was adopted at San Francisco on 26 June 1945 and entered into force on 24 October 1945. As at present (January 2022), there are 193 member states of the UN.

[1] For detailed information on UN law, see Higgins et al. (2017b); Chesterman et al. (2016); Simma et al. (2012); Cot et al. (2005); Goodrich et al. (1969).
[2] Zimmermann et al. (2019).

The Charter may be amended, though this is not an easy task since the entry into force of amendments requires ratification by all five permanent members.[3] It has been amended three times (1963–5, 1965–8, and 1971–3); the amendments concerned enlargement of the membership of the Security Council (from eleven to fifteen members) and the Economic and Social Council (from eighteen to twenty-seven to fifty-four members). In fact, the law of the United Nations has developed mainly through practice.

Being a multilateral treaty, the Charter falls to be interpreted in accordance with the rules on treaty interpretation reflected in Articles 31 to 33 of the Vienna Convention on the Law of Treaties (VCLT) 'without prejudice to any relevant rules of the organization' (Article 5 of the VCLT).[4]

Acting under Article 30 of the Charter, the Security Council first adopted *Provisional Rules of Procedure* between April and June 1946. They were amended from time to time between 1947 and 1982 (but only occasionally and in minor respects).[5] The Rules continue to be described as 'provisional' some seventy-five years after their adoption. Originally this was because several divisive issues remained outstanding, not least questions related to voting; nowadays perhaps it is also out of a desire to indicate the Council's flexibility on procedural matters.

Since the end of the Cold War much effort has gone into developing the Security Council's working methods;[6] the outcomes are documented in Notes by the President, which since 2006[7] have been consolidated from time to time in '507' documents; at the time of writing, the latest such consolidation is dated 30 August 2017.[8]

It is important to distinguish between meetings of the Council, at which the Council may hold discussions, adopt decisions and make recommendations, and informal meetings of Council members. The latter are not Council meetings and in them Council members

[3] Charter, Arts. 108–9. See Witschel, 'Article 108' (2012); Witschel, 'Article 109' (2012); Winkelmann (2007); Zacklin (1968).

[4] Kadelbach (2012).

[5] S/96/Rev.7, 21 December 1982. On the Provisional Rules of Procedure, see Sievers and Daws (2014) 9–12.

[6] Security Council Report (2007, 2010, 2014, 2017); Sievers and Daws (2014) 12–15, 480–90; Aust (1993); Wood (1996).

[7] Note by the President of the Security Council, S/2006/507, 19 July 2006.

[8] Note by the President of the Security Council, S/2017/507, 30 August 2017.

do not and cannot act on behalf of the Council. They include informal consultations of the members of the Council ('informal consultations of the whole'), which since the 1980s take place very frequently,[9] and the less frequent 'Arria-formula meetings'[10] and 'informal interactive dialogues'.[11]

As of January 2022, the Security Council has adopted more than 2,600 resolutions, many presidential statements, and various other texts (press releases etc.) that may, in a broad sense, be said to form part of the applicable law. Collectively these may be referred to as Security Council 'outcomes'. The interpretation of Security Council resolutions has been the subject of important pronouncements by the International Court of Justice (ICJ).[12]

In addition, there is a considerable number of international conventions that bear on the role of the Security Council. Among the most significant are the Treaty on the Non-Proliferation of Nuclear Weapons (NPT) and the Rome Statute of the International Criminal Court. The NPT requires states withdrawing from the Treaty to notify the Security Council three months in advance.[13] The Security Council has recognized that it has an integral role of ensuring the maintenance of international peace and security as it relates to the use or threat of use of nuclear weapons[14] and that non-compliance with the NPT may be a threat to international peace and security and warrant Council action.[15] The Rome Statute gives the Security Council the authority of both referral[16] and temporary deferral[17] of situations before the Court, as well as a particular role in situations where the crime of aggression is involved.[18]

In addition to such treaty provisions, the rules of customary international law, as well as general principles of law within the meaning of Article 38.1(*c*) of the Statute of the International

[9] Sievers and Daws (2014) 65–74.

[10] The first Arria-formula meeting took place in 1992, Sievers and Daws (2014) 74–92.

[11] The first informal interactive dialogue took place in 2007, Sievers and Daws (2014) 93.

[12] *Namibia* Advisory Opinion, p. 54, para. 116; *Kosovo* Advisory Opinion, p. 442, para. 94; see also Wood (1998); Wood (2016b); Traoré (2020).

[13] Treaty on the Non-Proliferation of Nuclear Weapons, 1 July 1968, Art. X.

[14] S/RES/984, 11 April 1995. [15] S/RES/1887, 24 September 2009.

[16] Rome Statute of the International Criminal Court, Art. 13(b).

[17] Ibid., Art. 16. [18] Ibid., Arts. 15 *bis* and 15 *ter*.

Court of Justice, may also play their part in the work of the Security Council.

Judgments and advisory opinions of the ICJ have been important in explaining and developing UN law, including as regards the Security Council,[19] as have those of other international courts and tribunals.[20]

As a further subsidiary means for the determination of the law, writings have sometimes been cited in Council proceedings.

1.2 The Legal Nature of the Security Council

1.2.1 A UN Organ, without Separate Legal Personality

Blokker has written: 'The Charter closely connects the Security Council to other parts of the United Nations. It is far from a loosely embedded "stand-alone" body within the world organization.'[21] And he goes on to affirm: 'An appreciation of the Security Council is incomplete without at least some evaluation of the larger framework of which it is part.'[22]

The Security Council is one of the six principal organs of the UN. The UN itself has international legal personality, distinct from that of its member states, as the ICJ explained in the *Reparation for Injuries* case.[23] The Council, being an organ of the UN and not a separate organization, does not have international legal personality. Its acts are those of the UN. The separate legal personality of the UN has important implications for matters such as the organization's international responsibility[24] and obligations under treaties to which it is

[19] *Lockerbie*, Provisional Measures; *Admission* Advisory Opinion; *Namibia* Advisory Opinion.

[20] *Prosecutor* v. *Tadić* (1995). [21] Blokker (2020) 162. [22] Ibid., 166.

[23] *Reparation* Advisory Opinion, at p. 179 ('the Court has come to the conclusion that the Organization is an international person, ... it is a subject of international law and capable of possessing international rights and duties, ...').

[24] See the ILC's Draft articles on the responsibility of international organizations (2011) 40–105. The Articles are annexed to UNGA resolution 66/100, 9 December 2011. Art. 6.1 states that the conduct of an organ of an international organization in the performance of functions of that organ 'shall be considered an act of that organization under international law'. Art. 8 states that the conduct of an organ shall be considered an act of the organization under international law 'even if the conduct exceeds the authority of that organ'. The commentaries to the Articles contain many references to the Security Council.

a party[25] and – in so far as they may be applicable – obligations under rules of customary international law[26] and under general principles of law within the meaning of Article 38.1(*c*) of the ICJ Statute. Separate legal personality is also important for international dispute settlement,[27] and for the position of UN members, including when acting as members of the Council.[28]

Those who adopt a 'constitutional perspective' towards the Charter, or indeed towards other areas of international law, seek to import into international affairs legal concepts from domestic legal systems. The Charter, however, is a treaty among states, a multilateral treaty, now virtually universal, with 193 parties. It is, of course, the constituent instrument, or constitution, of the organization known as the United Nations, and as such sets out the composition and powers of its organs. But that does not mean that it has – or should have – the same characteristics as a national constitution. The Charter does embody certain principles of international law, including those on the peaceful settlement of disputes and the non-use of force, as well as the right of self-defence.[29] And it provides, in Article 103, that in the event of a conflict between obligations under the Charter and obligations under any other international agreement, the obligations under the

[25] Vienna Convention on the Law of Treaties between States and International Organizations or between International Organizations, 21 March 1986 (not yet in force).

[26] The extent to which rules of customary international law (for example, customary international human rights law) apply to international organizations remains uncertain. Contrary to the views of some, it was not greatly clarified by the Court's cautious words in the 1980 *WHO* Advisory Opinion, at pp. 89–90, para. 37 ('International organizations are subjects of international law and, as such, are bound by any obligations incumbent upon them under general rules of international law, under their constitutions or under international agreements to which they are parties.').

[27] A topic on the settlement of disputes to which international organizations are parties has been included in the ILC's long-term programme of work (see the ILC's annual report to the General Assembly for 2016, A/71/10, 387–99) but has not yet been included in the ILC's current programme of work.

[28] The ILC's Draft articles on the responsibility of international organizations also apply to the international responsibility of a state for an internationally wrongful act in connection with the conduct of an international organization (Art.1.1 and Part Five).

[29] UNGA/RES/2625 (XXV), 24 October 1970, The Declaration on Principles of International Law concerning Friendly Relations and Co-operation among States in Accordance with the Charter of the United Nations ('Friendly Relations Declaration').

Charter prevail. Article 103 is the Charter's chief 'constitutional' element.

None of this, however, makes the Charter 'the constitution for the international community'. The term 'constitution' has no particular meaning in international law.[30] The 'international community' (itself a much-misused term) has little in common with society within a state. The Appeals Chamber of the International Criminal Tribunal for the former Yugoslavia (ICTY) rightly referred to a flawed 'domestic analogy', which is inappropriate where 'the international community lacks any central government with the attendant separation of powers and checks and balances', and warned that 'the transposition onto the international community of legal institutions, constructs or approaches prevailing in national law may be a source of great confusion and misapprehension'.[31]

1.2.2 A Political Organ, an Executive Organ, a Legislature, a Judicial Body?

According to the Charter, the Security Council is the principal organ of the UN upon which, in order to ensure prompt and effective action, the Members have conferred primary responsibility for the maintenance of international peace and security. Its powers and functions – and their limits – are those set out in the Charter, as developed in practice. In the field of international peace and security, the Council has the power to make recommendations, and to adopt decisions binding on the Members of the UN. By virtue of Article 103, obligations imposed by the Council, being obligations under the Charter, have priority over all other international obligations of states.[32] That is all that needs to be said about the nature of the Council, though some seek to go further.

1.2.2.1 A POLITICAL ORGAN?

The Security Council is often referred to as a 'political' organ. That expression is presumably used to distinguish it from 'legal' organs,

[30] Even within national legal systems, the term is used in many different contexts including, for example, the basic document of a barristers' chambers or a golf club.

[31] *Prosecutor* v. *Blaskić*, para. 40. [32] See Chapter 1.3.

or perhaps technical and administrative ones. The term 'political organ' may carry the unfortunate implication that the Council need pay little attention to the law applicable to its work under the UN Charter, but that is not the case.

1.2.2.2 AN EXECUTIVE ORGAN?

The Appeals Chamber of the ICTY has stated:

> It is clear that the legislative, executive and judicial division of power which is largely followed in most municipal systems does not apply to the international setting nor, more specifically, to the setting of an international organization such as the United Nations. Among the principal organs of the United Nations the divisions between judicial, executive and legislative functions are not clear cut. ... It is clearly impossible to classify the organs of the United Nations into the above-discussed divisions which exist in the national law of States. ... Consequently the separation of powers element of the requirement that a tribunal be 'established by law' finds no application in an international law setting.[33]

Some nevertheless seek to situate the Council within the UN in terms of the separation of powers at the national level. In the early days, the Council was sometimes referred to as the 'executive organ' of the UN (perhaps harking back to the Council of the League of Nations). But, to the extent that it acts like an executive branch of government, this is in only one area of UN activity, the maintenance of international peace and security. It does not routinely act as an executive for the other UN organs. It is not like those organs of certain other international organizations which do in effect act as an executive between meetings of the plenary organ.

1.2.2.3 A LEGISLATURE?

A question often asked, particularly since the adoption of resolution 1373 (2001), is whether the Council may act as a legislature or, as it has sometimes been put, as a 'global legislator'.[34] Perhaps the greatest fear of an all-powerful and unconstrained Council comes when this new move towards 'legislation' is combined with a much-expanded concept of what constitutes a threat to international

[33] *Prosecutor* v. *Tadić* (1995), para. 43.
[34] Rosand (2004); Popovski and Fraser (2014).

peace and security.[35] Here, too, the domestic law analogy is not helpful. The question itself is somewhat abstract. It depends on what is meant by 'legislature'. In practical terms, the real question is whether the mandatory decisions contained in resolution 1373 (2001) (measures against the financing of terrorism), resolution 1540 (2004) (non-proliferation), or resolution 2396 (2017) (foreign terrorist fighters and returnees), or other resolutions creating binding rules, were within the powers of the Council, and thus lawfully adopted. Put that way, the answer is clearly 'yes', so long as the subject -matter of the resolution is within the Council's mandate. These resolutions, as it happens, were adopted unanimously and have been repeatedly reaffirmed. No state has seriously suggested that resolution 1373 (2001) was not lawfully adopted. Such concerns as were expressed about resolution 1540 (2004) seem mostly to have been about the policy question 'Should the Council so act?', not 'Is it within its powers so to act?'. In the case of these resolutions, virtually all states are doing their best to comply. So there is no basis in state practice for suggesting that elements of these resolutions were *ultra vires*, quite the contrary. And the same applies to other 'legislative' resolutions adopted by the Council.

The legal argument seems to boil down to this: that, despite the practice, the Council is empowered to act only in relation to a specific situation or dispute. Back in the 1990s, one of the co-authors of this book wrote that

> [w]hile the Security Council has some of the attributes of a legislature, it is misleading to suggest that the Council acts as a legislature, as opposed to imposing obligations on States in connection with particular situations or disputes ... the Council makes recommendations and takes decisions relating to particular situations or disputes. ... it does not lay down new rules of general application.[36]

This described what was then – in the 1990s – Council practice; it was not a statement of legal constraints on the Security Council.

Nowhere does the Charter state in terms that the Council's Chapter VII powers are limited to specific situations. Is this to be implied, for example from the language of Article 39? While breaches of the peace and acts of aggression are likely to be specific, the same cannot be said of threats to the peace. There is nothing in

[35] See Chapter 3. [36] Wood (1998) 77–8.

the language of Article 39 to suggest that the requirement that the Council determine 'a threat to the peace' refers only to a threat that is specific rather than to one that is more general. Such a restrictive interpretation would be contrary to the object and purpose of the Charter if, in fact, there are now threats of a general nature which require urgent and global action of the kind that the Security Council can best take. Normal treaty-making procedures may be too slow; attempts to speed them up have not met with great success. Furthermore, specific acts that may qualify as breaches of the peace or even acts of aggression may require a more general response.

The adoption of 'legislative' resolutions marked a new development. Resolutions 1373 (2001) and 2396 (2017), and resolutions like them, are qualitatively different from what came before, not least in that they address a general threat, not a specific situation or dispute. But that does not make them *ultra vires.* No one doubts that the Council may impose obligations on states in relation to a particular dispute or situation. It may, for example, require them to impose an arms embargo on a particular state. Such a decision of the Council may also be termed 'legislation'. The question is not whether the Council can legislate – it can and regularly does – but whether it is empowered to do so in a general way in order to address a global phenomenon, unrelated to any specific situation or dispute.

The answer turns on whether a general, unspecific threat to international peace and security is sufficient for the invocation of Chapter VII of the Charter. If the Council determines that international terrorism, or the proliferation of weapons of mass destruction, or a combination of the two, is a threat to the peace – hardly a fanciful conclusion – then it may take such measures as it considers necessary to maintain the peace. Depending on the nature of the threat, such measures may be specific, addressed, for example, to the threat emanating from a particular state, or they may be general, addressed, for example, to the global threat from terrorist groups. There is no great principle involved, though the circumstances in which general measures are considered necessary and appropriate may prove to be rare.

Though the Council has expanded the scope of what can be considered a threat to international peace and security, to what extent various issues and situations are matters that fall under the mandate of the Council remains a divisive issue.[37] Such concerns are understandable. The members of the Council need to exercise caution. If the Council is seen to be acting routinely as a 'world legislator', and is thought to be throwing its weight around in circumstances where this is not justified, states may simply cease to comply with its demands, whatever their legal obligations under the Charter. That would undermine the Council's authority, with very serious consequences for the collective security system across the board.[38]

1.2.2.4 A JUDICIAL BODY?

Some thirty years ago, Elihu Lauterpacht wrote that 'there have been a number of occasions on which ... the Security Council has framed its resolutions ... in language resembling a judicial determination of the law and of the legal consequences said to flow from the conduct of the State that is arraigned'.[39] The examples he gave were those where the Council had held a situation to be unlawful or null and void, and called upon states not to recognize it. They included South West Africa, Southern Rhodesia, Jerusalem and the Occupied Territories, the South African 'Homelands', and the Turkish Republic of Northern Cyprus. He suggested that there was a line to be drawn, 'admittedly imprecise', between 'prescriptions of conduct that are directly and immediately related to the termination of the impugned conduct ... and those findings that ... have a general and long-term legal impact that goes beyond the immediate needs of the situation'. He acknowledged that neither the ICJ (when it had the opportunity in the *Namibia* Advisory Opinion) nor states (other than those directly affected) had objected to such findings. While seemingly still questioning the legality of these 'quasi-judicial' determinations, he conceded that states had acquiesced. His main conclusion was that 'quasi-judicial decisions' should be subject to some kind of judicial review.

[37] See, for example, the various statements made in a debate on 'human rights and prevention of armed conflict' convened by the United States in 2017, PV.7926, 18 April 2017.

[38] Rosand has suggested certain 'safeguards' when the Council legislates (Rosand 2004).

[39] Lauterpacht (1991).

This position is unconvincing, both as a matter of principle and in light of the practice of the Council. The Council made such 'judicial' determinations from the very beginning, for example when it recognized that forces from North Korea (the Democratic People's Republic of Korea (DPRK)) had committed an armed attack against South Korea (the Republic of Korea) in 1950, and recommended that states assist the Republic of Korea to repel the attack.[40] This amounted to a factual and legal determination (the existence of an armed attack), and the consequent legal right stemming from that determination (the right of individual and collective self-defence).

Nothing in the UN Charter or the practice of the Council suggests a distinction between two categories of decisions: prescriptions of conduct as opposed to findings with a general and long-term impact. The Council's action for the maintenance of international peace and security is no longer (if it ever was) confined to immediate steps to restore peace. Much that it does today is longer-term: dispute resolution; protection of civilians; peacekeeping; women and peace and security; peacebuilding; and many more thematic issues. It may deploy a wide range of measures for the peaceful settlement of disputes and the investigation of situations. If it considers it necessary to pronounce upon a legal matter, that surely is within its competence, not least when it calls for the non-recognition of a given situation in order to maintain or restore international peace and security. The real question is how the Council should set about making findings of law, particularly where the factual or legal position is in doubt. That the Council should exercise caution and avoid making factual or legal determinations in haste is undisputed. To argue that if it has done so then it has gone beyond its powers under the Charter is not based on any reasonable interpretation of the Charter. As the ICTY Appeals Chamber has stated: 'Plainly, the Security Council is not a judicial organ and is not provided with judicial powers (though it may incidentally perform certain quasi-judicial activities such as effecting determinations or findings). The principal function of the Security Council is the maintenance of international peace and security, in the discharge of which the Security Council exercises both decision-making and executive powers.'[41] Above all, there is the question of the legal effect of 'quasi-judicial' pronouncements. On rare occasions,

[40] S/RES/82, 25 June 1950; S/RES/83, 27 June 1950; and S/RES/84, 7 July 1950.
[41] *Prosecutor v. Tadić(1995)*, para. 37.

the 'quasi-judicial' determination is a *decision* of the Council and thus must be accepted by all member states, for example when the Council *decided* that Iraq was in material breach of previous Security Council resolutions in 2003,[42] or when the Council *decided* that the continued occupation of Namibia by South Africa constituted a violation of the territorial integrity and a denial of the political sovereignty of the people of Namibia.[43]

More often, the pronouncement of a 'quasi-judicial' matter of law or fact could be inconsequential in terms of Council action against a member state, when it does not lead to any operative consequences, for example when the Council found in resolution 496 (1981) that an act of aggression had been committed against Seychelles without taking further action against the aggressor, which it refrained from naming.

That said, if one were to take the Council's assertion at face value, it would entail the international legal responsibility of the state involved, exposing it to legal consequences such as reparation.

The Council itself said as much when, following an attack against Tunisia in 1985, in resolution 573 (1985) it condemned 'the act of armed aggression perpetrated by Israel'.[44] In this instance, it added that it considered that 'Tunisia has the right to appropriate reparations as a result of the loss of human life and material damage which it has suffered and for which Israel has claimed responsibility.'[45] While this assertion was not binding, it was a legal determination by the Security Council based on its assessment of the facts and Israel's admission.

It is important to note that 'quasi-judicial' determinations that are not *decisions* of the Council are not binding as such. What is binding is any enforcement action taken by the Council in its decisions, whether based on these facts and legal determinations or not. The factual and legal assertions, on the other hand, in these instances remain a matter of objective assessment. While such a statement by the Council may carry much weight, for example before a court or tribunal, the latter may still reach factual and legal conclusions different from those reached by the Council, which on many occasions has to act very swiftly.

[42] S/RES/1441, 8 November 2002, para. 1.
[43] S/RES/269, 12 August 1969, para. 3. [44] S/RES/573, 4 October 1985, para. 1.
[45] Ibid., para. 4.

This seems to be the balance struck in the Kampala amendments to the Rome Statute with respect to the role of the Security Council in relation to the crime of aggression.[46] Under the new Article 15 *bis*, the practical effect of a Security Council determination that an act of aggression has occurred is that it enables the International Criminal Court (ICC) Prosecutor to proceed immediately with an investigation.[47] Otherwise, the Prosecutor must wait for six months and obtain the authorization of a pretrial chamber as is required in all other circumstances.[48] Article 15 *bis* clarifies, however, that a determination that an act of aggression has occurred by any 'organ outside the Court' – including, of course, the Security Council – is without prejudice to the Court's independent judgment.[49] Here, the Council's legal determination carries some weight and has practical effect, but is ultimately subject to the independent determination of the Court itself.

It is true that the Council does not always pronounce itself on the facts and their legal consequences for other member states. But there is no legal reason preventing the Council from doing so. In some instances, these 'quasi-judicial' determinations enhance, rather than detract from, the authority of the Council since determining that a breach of international law occurred could provide legitimacy and justification for consequent measures taken by the Security Council. On the other hand, if one were to accept the argument that the Council is not the correct UN organ to make such determinations, that would mean that the organ with the primary responsibility for the maintenance of international peace and security should remain silent when illegal uses of force occur. Furthermore, collective security measures under Article 42, it is recalled, are to be taken only when the Council considers that measures not involving the use of armed force would be inadequate. The Council thus has the power, under Article 41, to take any measures not involving the use of armed force in order to avoid resort to Article 42. These measures must include the ability to make legal determinations which, though of potential serious consequence, are not more imposing on states than other enforcement measures available to the Council that fall short of the use of force.

[46] Resolution RC/Res. 6, 11 June 2010. [47] Rome Statute, Art. 15 *bis*, para. 7.
[48] Rome Statute, Art. 15 *bis*, para. 8. [49] Rome Statute, Art. 15 *bis*, para. 9.

1.3 Priority of Charter Obligations (Article 103)

Article 103 is the cornerstone of the Charter's collective security system; it is an essential component in ensuring that the Security Council is able to exercise effectively its primary responsibility for the maintenance of international peace and security and thus ensure prompt and effective action by the UN.[50] Article 103 provides:

> In the event of a conflict between the obligations of the Members of the United Nations under the present Charter and their obligations under any other international agreement, their obligations under the present Charter shall prevail.

Together with Article 25, this means that the Council has the authority to take legally binding decisions with which all member states must comply. 'This extraordinary power . . . gives the Council the ability to alter the international legal landscape instantaneously.'[51]

Article 30 of the VCLT recognizes the absolute priority of the rule in Article 103.[52] Article 103 has occasionally been referred to expressly, often implicitly, in other international agreements.[53] While perhaps a useful reminder, the inclusion of such a reference is not, of course, necessary in order for Charter obligations to prevail, at least among members of the UN. The same goes for explicit or implicit references to Article 103 in resolutions of the Security Council.

The International Law Commission (ILC) has noted the significance of Article 103 when considering topics other than the law of treaties.[54] Its Study Group on Fragmentation considered the effect of Article 103 in some detail, which the Group's report explained as

50 Wood (2011); Paulus and Leiß (2012); Kolb (2014). 51 Ratner (2004) 592.

52 Art. 30(1) of the VCLT begins: 'Subject to Article 103 of the Charter of the United Nations, . . .'. See also Art. 30(6) of the Vienna Convention on the Law of Treaties between States and International Organizations or between International Organizations, 21 March 1986: 'The preceding paragraphs are without prejudice to the fact that, in the event of a conflict between obligations under the Charter of the United Nations and obligations under a treaty, the obligations under the Charter shall prevail.'

53 For example, the Convention on International Civil Aviation Art. 3 *bis* (a), states that the 'provision shall not be interpreted as modifying in any way the rights and obligations of States set forth in the Charter of the United Nations', implicitly acknowledging their supremacy. See Convention on International Civil Aviation as amended by Protocol relating to an amendment to the Convention on International Civil Aviation (Art. 3 *bis*), 2122 UNTS 337.

54 See text from note 59 on for the relationship between Art. 103 and *jus cogens*.

follows: 'What happens to the obligation over which Article 103 establishes precedence? Most commentators agree that the question here is not one of validity but of priority. The lower ranking rule is merely set aside to the extent that it conflicts with the obligation under Article 103.'[55] The Study Group's conclusion 35 reads:

> The scope of Article 103 of the Charter of the United Nations extends not only to the Articles of the Charter but also to binding decisions made by United Nations organs such as the Security Council. Given the character of some Charter provisions, the constitutional character of the Charter and the established practice of States and United Nations organs, Charter obligations may also prevail over inconsistent customary international law.[56]

Article 103 has been considered in a number of court decisions.

In its 1984 *Nicaragua* v. *US* Judgment on jurisdiction and admissibility, the ICJ observed that 'all regional, bilateral, and even multilateral, arrangements ... must be made always subject to the provisions of Article 103 of the Charter of the United Nations'.[57]

In its *Lockerbie (Provisional Measures)* Orders, the ICJ held that the obligations of the members of the UN under the Charter, which prevailed over other obligations by virtue of Article 103, included obligations imposed by mandatory decisions of the Security Council:

> 39. Whereas both Libya and the United Kingdom, as Members of the United Nations, are obliged to accept and carry out the decisions of the Security Council in accordance with Article 25 of the Charter; whereas the Court, which is at the stage of proceedings on provisional measures, considers that prima facie this obligation extends to the decision contained in resolution 748 (1992); and whereas, in accordance with Article 103 of the Charter, the obligations of the Parties in that respect prevail over their obligations under any other international agreement, including the Montreal Convention.[58]

[55] A/CN.4/L. 682, 13 April 2006, paras. 328–60, at 333. Art. 103 contrasts with Art. 20 of the Covenant of the League of Nations, under which the Members of the League agreed that 'this Covenant is accepted as abrogating all obligations or understandings inter se which are inconsistent with the terms thereof'. The Study Group's analytical report was finalized by its Chair, Martti Koskenneimi. The UN General Assembly took note of both the conclusions and the analytical study, UNGA/RES/61/34, 4 December 2006, para. 4.

[56] A/CN.4/L. 682, 13 April 2006, paras. 182–3.

[57] *Nicaragua* v. *US* (1984), at p. 440, para. 107.

[58] *Lockerbie Provisional Measures (Libya* v. *UK)*, at p. 15, para. 39; *Lockerbie Provisional Measures (Libya* v. *US)*, at p. 126, para. 42.

This has been described as 'an extensive interpretation of the powers of the Security Council when acting under Chapter VII'.[59] Few would agree with that. The Court's interpretation reflects a fundamental aspect of the Charter's collective security system, and follows from the ordinary meaning of the language of Articles 25 and 103. It represents the constant practice and understanding of the Council and of states.

More recent case law on the relationship between Article 103 and other international obligations, from other international courts and bodies, has addressed a different issue: the relationship between obligations under the Charter and *jus cogens* norms. The *Yusuf* and *Kadi* cases before the Court of First Instance of the European Communities concerned the compatibility of European Community regulations restricting assets with various provisions of the European Convention on Human Rights (ECHR). The Court of First Instance held that the obligations of the member states of the European Union (EU) to enforce sanctions required by a Chapter VII Security Council resolution prevailed over fundamental rights protected by the European legal order. The Court also held that it had no jurisdiction to inquire into the lawfulness of a Security Council resolution – other than to check, indirectly, whether it infringed *jus cogens*. Higgins has remarked that '[t]his raises a whole series of different issues, including whether it is the Luxembourg Court that holds any power of judicial review of Security Council resolutions, if such power indeed exists'.[60]

The Court of Justice of the European Union (CJEU), however, took an entirely different approach. Rather than trying to assess how states are to uphold fundamental rights under EU law in light of an overriding obligation imposed by the Security Council, the Court took what may be described as a 'dualist' approach,[61] reviewing regulations taken to implement the Security Council resolutions solely under EU law, independently of whether another international legal obligation prevailed.[62]

[59] *Genocide* case, Separate Opinion of Judge *ad hoc* Lauterpacht, at p. 439, para. 99.
[60] Higgins (2006) at 801. [61] Kokott and Sobotta (2012).
[62] *Yusuf and Kadi* v. *European Council*. See also Advocate General Poiares Maduro's Opinion, holding that 'obligations imposed by an international agreement cannot have the effect of prejudicing the constitutional principles of the EC Treaty' (para. 24).

The Human Rights Committee adopted essentially the same approach in *Sayadi* v. *Belgium*, a complaint under the Optional Protocol to the International Covenant on Civil and Political Rights (ICCPR), concerning the imposition of sanctions by the Security Council on a married couple at the behest of Belgium and their implementation under Belgian and EU law.[63] Disregarding Article 103 altogether, the Committee took the view that

> [w]hile the Committee could not consider alleged violations of other instruments such as the Charter of the United Nations, or allegations that challenged United Nations rules concerning the fight against terrorism, the Committee was competent to admit a communication alleging that a State party had violated rights set forth in the Covenant, regardless of the source of the obligations implemented by the State party.[64]

In taking this siloed approach, including on the merits of the complaint, it also dismissed the relevance of Article 46 of the ICCPR, which states that the ICCPR shall not 'be interpreted as impairing the provisions of the Charter of the United Nations', opining that what was at issue was Belgium's actions, not the UN Charter.[65] This allowed it simply to ignore Article 103 and focus exclusively on the ICCPR.[66]

The jurisprudence of the European Court of Human Rights (ECtHR) is more nuanced, though, in practice, it also serves to limit the significance of Article 103. The case of *Al-Jedda* concerned a person detained in 2004 by British forces acting as part of the Multi-National Force – Iraq (MNF), under a mandate conferred by the Security Council, on the ground that his detention was necessary for imperative reasons of security in Iraq. The Council resolution specifically provided the MNF with 'authority to take all necessary measures to contribute to the maintenance of security and stability in Iraq in accordance with the letters annexed to this resolution ... setting out its task'. The annexed letters stated that the MNF 'was prepared to undertake a broad range of tasks, ... including ... internment where this is necessary for imperative reasons of security'. Al-Jedda challenged his detention, arguing that it was unlawful under Article 5 of the ECHR.

63 *Sayadi* v. *Belgium*. 64 Ibid., para. 7.2. 65 Ibid., para. 10.3.
66 For more, see Milanovic (2009b).

In the domestic proceedings in London, the Court of Appeal accepted the overriding effect of the obligations under the Security Council resolutions. The relevant Security Council resolutions on Iraq were adopted under Chapter VII of the Charter, in particular Article 42. Under Article 103 of the Charter, obligations upon member states created by the Charter prevailed over their obligations under any other international agreement.[67]

The House of Lords agreed with the lower court.[68] Like the Court of Appeal, it rejected Al-Jedda's argument that the resolution authorized certain actions but placed no obligation on the United Kingdom to act, so Article 103 was not applicable. Lord Bingham referred to 'a strong and to my mind persuasive body of academic opinion which would treat Article 103 as applicable where conduct is authorized by the Security Council as where it is required'.[69] He then quoted from the Simma commentary on the UN Charter, stating that the opposite conclusion would compromise 'the very idea of authorizations as a necessary substitute for direct action by the SC'.[70]

With respect to the specific action, Lord Bingham opined:

> It is of course true that the UK did not become specifically bound to detain the appellant in particular. But it was, I think, bound to exercise its power of detention where this was necessary for imperative reasons of security. It could not be said to be giving effect to the decisions of the Security Council if, in such a situation, it neglected to take steps which were open to it.[71]

Lord Bingham did recognize that there are certain boundaries or limitations to the applicability of Article 103: first, when the UK exercises its powers under the Security Council resolution, 'it must ensure that the detainee's rights under Article 5 are not infringed to any greater extent than is inherent in such detention';[72] and second, Article 103 results in the prevalence of obligations under the UN Charter for all treaty obligations, including human rights obligations, 'save where an obligation is *jus cogens*'.[73]

The ECtHR did not opine on the legal implications of conflicting obligations under the UN Charter and the ECHR. Nor did it opine on whether Article 103 applies to conduct based on Security

[67] *R (Al-Jedda)* v. *Secretary of State for Defence* (2006), paras. 76–84.
[68] *R (Al-Jedda)* v. *Secretary of State for Defence* (2007). [69] Ibid., para. 33.
[70] Ibid., quoting Frowein and Krisch (2002) 729. [71] Ibid., para. 34.
[72] Ibid., para. 39. [73] Ibid., para. 35.

Council authorizations. Instead, the Court introduced the notion of harmonious interpretation between Security Council resolutions and human rights:

> [T]he Court considers that, in interpreting its resolutions, there must be a presumption that the Security Council does not intend to impose any obligation on Member States to breach fundamental principles of human rights. In the event of any ambiguity in the terms of a Security Council Resolution, the Court must therefore choose the interpretation which is most in harmony with the requirements of the Convention and which avoids any conflict of obligations. In the light of the United Nations' important role in promoting and encouraging respect for human rights, it is to be expected that clear and explicit language would be used were the Security Council to intend States to take particular measures which would conflict with their obligations under international human rights law.[74]

The Court found that resolution 1546 (2004) did not 'explicitly or implicitly' require 'the United Kingdom to place an individual whom its authorities considered to constitute a risk to the security of Iraq in indefinite detention without charge' and that, therefore, the UK violated article 5 of the ECHR.[75]

In *Nada* v. *Switzerland*, concerning a resident of Campione d'Italia, a Swiss enclave surrounded by Italy, the ECtHR conceded that the travel ban imposed on Nada – which meant that he could not leave the enclave for years – under the Security Council's 1267 sanctions regime could not be solved by harmonious interpretation as in *Al-Jedda*.[76] The Court nevertheless found that 'Switzerland enjoyed some latitude, which was admittedly limited but nevertheless real, in implementing the relevant binding resolutions of the United Nations Security Council'.[77] Accordingly, it examined whether, within this 'limited latitude', Switzerland's actions were necessary and proportionate, that is, 'the possibility of recourse to an alternative measure that would cause less damage to the fundamental right in issue whilst fulfilling the same aim must be ruled out'.[78] The Court concluded that Switzerland failed to strike the right balance as it notified the 1267 Sanctions Committee that its

[74] *Al-Jedda* v. *United Kingdom* (2011), para. 102. [75] Ibid., para. 109.
[76] *Nada* v. *Switzerland*, para. 172. Resolution 1267, para. 7 itself was explicit that the sanctions regime was to be implemented 'notwithstanding the existence of any rights or obligations conferred or imposed by any international agreement'.
[77] Ibid., para. 180. [78] Ibid., para. 183.

domestic investigations concluded that the suspicions against Nada were unfounded only four years after the fact and did not apply for potential humanitarian exceptions from the sanctions on his behalf.[79]

In a third case, *Al-Dulimi* v. *Switzerland* of 2016, the ECtHR appears to have stretched 'harmonious interpretation' to its limits.[80] The case concerned Switzerland's application of an assets freeze pursuant to the Security Council mandated Iraq sanctions regime. The Court noted that resolution 1483 (2003) did not contain any explicit language on limiting respect for human rights[81] and, moreover, since the resolution

> does not contain any clear or explicit wording excluding the possibility of judicial supervision of the measures taken for its implementation, it must always be understood as authorising the courts of the respondent State to exercise sufficient scrutiny so that any arbitrariness can be avoided . . . In such cases, in the event of a dispute over a decision to add a person to the list or to refuse delisting, the domestic courts must be able to obtain – if need be by a procedure ensuring an appropriate level of confidentiality, depending on the circumstances – sufficiently precise information in order to exercise the requisite scrutiny in respect of any substantiated and tenable allegation made by listed persons to the effect that their listing is arbitrary. Any inability to access such information is therefore capable of constituting a strong indication that the impugned measure is arbitrary, especially if the lack of access is prolonged, thus continuing to hinder any judicial scrutiny.[82]

The Court did not accept the Swiss Federal Court's approach, which merely verified the identity of the applicants before approving the implementation of the assets freeze.[83] It took the view that '[t]he applicants should, on the contrary, have been afforded at least a genuine opportunity to submit appropriate evidence to a court, for examination on the merits, to seek to show that their inclusion on the impugned lists had been arbitrary'.[84] This, despite the fact that 'the Court accepts that the Federal Court was unable to rule on the merits or appropriateness of the measures entailed by the listing of the applicants', which was at the Security Council's discretion.[85]

[79] Ibid., paras. 181–99. For a critique of the judgment, see Milanovic (2012).
[80] *Al-Dulimi* v. *Switzerland*, see Milanovic (2016).
[81] *Al-Dulimi* v. *Switzerland*, para. 140. [82] Ibid., paras. 146–7.
[83] Ibid., para. 150. [84] Ibid., para. 151. [85] Ibid., para. 150.

In her dissenting opinion, Judge Nußberger described the Court's basing itself on 'harmonious interpretation' as 'a "fake harmonious interpretation" that is not in line with basic methodological requirements of international treaty interpretation'.[86] She took the view that decisions of the Security Council prevail 'unless the arbitrariness of a measure ordered by the Security Council is so plain to see that no State governed by the rule of law could agree to implement it', and explained that the Swiss courts met this standard when they ensured the applicants' identity and that the assets frozen were, indeed, theirs.[87]

In the authors' view, Article 103 cannot be interpreted in a way that would deprive it of the practical effect intended by the drafters of the Charter; the jurisprudence of the CJEU – and of the ECtHR – goes too far in that direction. At the same time, Jenks was right when he said that 'Article 103 cannot be invoked as giving the United Nations an overriding authority which would be inconsistent with the provisions of the Charter itself'.[88]

The following points aim to summarize the basic position in law.[89]

First, the effect of Article 103 is not to invalidate the conflicting obligation but merely to set it aside to the extent of the conflict.[90] Any other position, for example that the conflicting obligation is or becomes void, is not borne out in practice and in most cases would make no sense. Thus, for example, if a sanctions regime is incompatible with rights of navigation under the Danube Convention, it is obvious that the effect of Article 103 is not to void provisions of the Danube Convention, even for the target state, but merely to give priority to the Charter obligations while they subsist.

Second, Article 103 applies to obligations imposed by the mandatory provisions of Security Council resolutions, since by virtue of Article 25 (and Article 48) such obligations are 'obligations … under the present Charter'.[91]

Third, in order to be effective Article 103 must apply equally to action taken under Council authorizations, as was rightly concluded by the House of Lords in the *Al-Jedda* case.[92]

[86] Ibid. See also the separate opinion of Judge Keller.
[87] Ibid. For further critique, see Milanovic (2016). [88] Jenks (1953) 439.
[89] Wood (2011) 253–4. [90] A/CN.4/L. 682, 13 April 2006, para. 333.
[91] *Lockerbie* Provisional Measures (*Libya* v. *UK*), at p. 15, para. 39.
[92] *R (Al-Jedda)* v. *Secretary of State for Defence* (2007), para. 33.

Fourth, it is generally accepted that the priority which Article 103 affords to the Charter over international agreements is equally applicable to rules of customary international law (general international law).[93] This is indeed essential if the purposes of the Charter in the field of the maintenance of international peace and security are to be achieved.

Fifth, there are no exceptions to the obligations under treaty and customary international law over which Charter obligations prevail, other than (according to a widely held but by no means unanimous view) *jus cogens* norms (peremptory norms of general international law).[94] Any such *jus cogens* exception is, in any event, more theoretical than real,[95] and the matter remains open.[96]

Hersch Lauterpacht wrote an article in 1936 entitled 'The Covenant as the "Higher Law"'. It is about Article 20 of the Covenant of the League of Nations, the Covenant equivalent of Article 103. He points out that prior to September 1935 (when sanctions were applied against Italy), Article 20 'was seldom mentioned'. Article 103 was likewise seldom mentioned until the Council became more active at the end of the Cold War. Hersch Lauterpacht says of Article 20, in powerful language, that it 'is a perpetual source of legal energy possessed of a dynamic force of its own and calculated to ensure the effectiveness of the Covenant unhampered by any treaties between Members'. The same may be said of Article 103 of the Charter. Like so much of Lauterpacht's writing, his words are as relevant today as when they were written.

***

Our overall conclusion on the nature of the Security Council is as follows. The use of domestic law analogies in international law is often misleading. It is not particularly helpful to seek to encapsulate the nature of the Council in a short phrase, especially one derived from domestic systems. Those who do so often go on to deduce further legal or political consequences: that as an executive it is

93 A/CN.4/L. 682, 13 April 2006, paras. 182–3; Paulus and Leiß (2012), MN 68, and sources quoted therein.

94 *Genocide* case, Separate Opinion of Judge *ad hoc* Lauterpacht, at p. 440, para. 100; Paulus and Leiß (2012) MN 19, 70, and sources quoted therein.

95 But see Lemos (2020) for a different conclusion.

96 Costelloe (2021).

uncontrolled; that as a legislature it lacks democratic legitimacy; that as a quasi-judicial body it should follow certain 'rule of law' principles and be subject to judicial review. These lines of argument start from a false premise.

Rather, the Security Council is the UN organ with the primary responsibility for the maintenance of international peace and security. Its powers and functions are those set out in the Charter, as developed in practice. Its aim is to ensure 'prompt and effective action by the United Nations'. As explained later in this book, in these regards it has a broad discretion not subject to judicial review.

2

Decisions of the Security Council

The present chapter looks at legal aspects of decisions of the Security Council. It addresses certain aspects of voting in the Security Council; it then considers when Council decisions are binding and who is bound by Security Council decisions, and finally whether binding decisions may be included in presidential statements.

2.1 Certain Legal Questions Concerning Voting in the Security Council

As already indicated, we do not in general intend to address procedural matters, even when these raise important legal questions,[1] since they are already well covered elsewhere. There are, however, three legal points relating to voting in the Security Council that do need to be mentioned: the distinction between procedural matters and all other matters, the circumstances under which a party to a dispute shall abstain from voting, and whether there are any other legal constraints on the use of the veto.[2]

Article 27 of the Charter reads:

1. Each member of the Security Council shall have one vote.
2. Decisions of the Security Council on procedural matters shall be made by an affirmative vote of nine members.

[1] For example, the practice under abstention, non-participation, or absence was not regarded as excluded by the words 'including the concurring votes of the permanent members', *Namibia* Advisory Opinion, at p. 22, para. 22.

[2] Sievers and Daws (2014) 295–372 (ch. 6); Zimmermann (2012); Higgins et al., (2017b) 10.33–10.60.

3. Decisions of the Security Council on all other matters shall be made by an affirmative vote of nine members including the concurring votes of the permanent members; provided that, in decisions under Chapter VI, and under paragraph 3 of Article 52, a party to a dispute shall abstain from voting.[3]

2.1.1 Procedural Matters / All Other Matters

The distinction between procedural matters and all other matters is important because, under Article 27(2), the veto does not apply when the Council is voting on procedural matters. It applies only in the case of voting on 'non-procedural matters' (the 'Yalta formula').[4]

There is usually no difficulty nowadays in deciding whether a matter is procedural or non-procedural. The Council has built up a considerable practice on this question. For example, the inclusion of an item on the agenda of the Council is procedural.[5] When a difference does arise, and cannot be resolved, it is now well established that the decision on whether the question is procedural or non-procedural (the 'preliminary question') is itself non-procedural and thus subject to the veto (the 'double veto').[6]

2.1.2 When Must a Party to a Dispute Abstain from Voting?

The circumstances under which a party to a dispute (including a permanent member) must abstain from voting seem clear enough from the last part of Article 27(3): 'provided that, in decisions under Chapter VI, and under paragraph 3 of Article 52, a party to a dispute shall abstain from voting'.[7] However, in practice Council members seem largely to ignore this provision. Cases of obligatory abstention have been very rare, and it may be thought that the

[3] For a discussion on the special provision for Council voting in connection with the election of the members of the ICJ set forth in the ICJ Statute, see Chapter 8.2.4.

[4] The term 'veto' does not appear in the Charter. It is used to refer to cases where a non-procedural proposal receives enough positive votes to pass (nine votes), but fails to be adopted because of the negative vote of one or more permanent members.

[5] Stalin personally needed to be persuaded of this while the San Francisco Conference was in session, see Luck (2006) 14.

[6] Sievers and Daws (2014) 318–27. [7] Ibid., 338–50.

practice of the Council is such that the provision no longer applies.[8] That would be an adjustment of the Charter through practice not dissimilar to the interpretation of 'concurring votes' in the same paragraph[9] (though, unlike the latter, it is not a development that has been expressly endorsed by the ICJ).

2.1.3 *Other Legal Constraints on the Use of the Veto?*

'Facts are better than dreams.'[10] In recent years, some elaborate theories have been developed by writers arguing that permanent members are required to abstain from casting a veto under certain circumstances, such as when the effect of the veto would be to block action against the commission of mass atrocities. Such theories have perhaps been encouraged by the stated willingness of certain permanent members to voluntarily commit to such abstention, and to call on other permanent members to do the same.[11] At least one leading politician has referred to the casting of an 'unreasonable' veto, which could somehow be ignored.[12]

One author has recently put forward the thesis that the use or threat of the veto in a way that 'contravenes' fundamental norms of international law or the Purposes and Principles of the United Nations is unlawful and falls outside the proper exercise of power by the Security Council and each of its members.[13] It has also been suggested that a veto resulting in a failure to act may lead to the UN incurring international responsibility, giving rise to the right

[8] For a survey of the Council's practice on this issue, see Sievers and Daws (2014) 341–50.

[9] Sievers and Daws (2014) 339–40; in a recent example, when Russia vetoed a draft resolution under Chapter VI on Ukraine (S/2014/189, 15 March 2014), Council members did not raise any objection to Russia's participation, see S/PV.7138, 15 March 2014.

[10] Churchill (1949). [11] Security Council Report (2015) 4–6.

[12] British Prime Minister Blair in the lead-up to the invasion of Iraq in 2003; the suggestion was rejected outright by the Attorney General, Lord Goldsmith, in his advice of 7 March 2003:

> I do not believe that there is any basis in law for arguing that there is an implied condition of reasonableness which can be read into the power of veto conferred on the permanent members of the Security Council by the UN Charter. So there are no grounds for arguing that an "unreasonable veto" would entitle us to proceed on the basis of a presumed Security Council authorization. (77 BYIL (2003) 819)

[13] Trahan (2020), ch. 4.

to take countermeasures.[14] Such theories are legally unconvincing; there is all the difference in the world between a voluntary commitment to restraint in the use of the veto, and acceptance of a legal obligation not to cast a veto.

2.2 When Are Council Decisions Legally Binding?

The Council may adopt legally binding decisions or make non-binding recommendations.[15] When considering resolution 1244 (1999) in its *Kosovo* Advisory Opinion, the ICJ began by saying:

> Within the legal framework of the United Nations Charter, notably on the basis of Articles 24, 25 and Chapter VII thereof, the Security Council may adopt resolutions imposing obligations under international law. The Court has had the occasion to interpret and apply such Security Council resolutions on a number of occasions and has consistently treated them as part of the framework of obligations under international law.[16]

Article 25 of the Charter provides:

> The Members of the United Nations agree to accept and carry out the decisions of the Security Council in accordance with the present Charter.[17]

As we shall see in Section 4.2, there has been some debate over the effect of the concluding words, 'in accordance with the present Charter'. It has sometimes been suggested that member states need not carry out decisions of the Council if they consider that the decision has not been taken in accordance with the Charter. Such a reading would go directly against the intention of the drafters to avoid the position under the Covenant of the League whereby each member could decide for itself whether there was a breach of the Covenant; this was seen as a great weakness of the League, effectively depriving it of any powers in the field of international peace and security beyond recommendations, which member states were free to ignore.

[14] Tzanakopoulos (2009).

[15] Sievers and Daws (2014) 380–93; Security Council Report (2008).

[16] *Kosovo* Advisory Opinion, at p. 439, para. 85.

[17] This provision is reinforced by Article 48(1): 'The action required to carry out the decisions of the Security Council for the maintenance of international peace and security shall be taken by all the Members of the United Nations or by some of them, as the Security Council may determine.'

To determine whether the Council has taken a decision that is mandatory under Article 25, it is necessary to interpret the resolution or series of resolutions in question. Three common misconceptions need to be avoided.[18]

First, it is not the case that a resolution adopted under Chapter VII of the Charter is thereby legally binding – though it has been argued that the converse may be true, that is, a resolution not adopted under Chapter VII will (in any event, generally) not be legally binding. The Council's powers under Chapter VII are expressly stated as being to 'make recommendations, or decide what measures shall be taken'. The Council may make recommendations which, while they may be of great significance (such as resolution 242 (1967) on the situation in the Middle East) and impose political obligations, are not legally binding as such.

Second, it is not the case that when the Council acts under Chapter VII, this invariably, or even commonly, involves or implies the immediate or probable use of military force. The taking or authorizing of armed force is only one of a range of measures that may be taken under Chapter VII; these include investigations, recommendations to the parties, economic sanctions, establishing *ad hoc* international criminal tribunals, and administering territory. In fact, the Chapter VII measures to which the Council most commonly resorts are those under Article 41 of the Charter not involving the use of force. But this misconception, the political association of Chapter VII with the use of force, often lies behind the reluctance of some states to refer explicitly to Chapter VII even where this would be desirable in the interests of clarity. Examples will be discussed later in this section.

Third, even when the Council adopts a resolution or other outcome document which contains legally binding decisions, it does not mean that the entirety of the resolution or document is legally binding. A lengthy resolution may contain just one legally binding provision. Determining the legal obligations contained in a given resolution requires meticulous reading of its text, distinguishing the non-legally binding provisions – which can still carry much political significance – from the legal obligations imposed by the Security Council.

[18] See Security Council Report (2008).

There may be cases where it is politically convenient, if only to achieve a consensus, not to be entirely clear whether provisions of a Security Council resolution are legally binding or not, or on the scope of any legal obligation.[19] Ambiguity is often the price of consensus, with Security Council resolutions as with treaties. In any event, even nonbinding resolutions of the Council may have considerable political weight. And they are not always without legal significance, particularly if repeated, even if one would not necessarily go as far as Judge Sir Hersch Lauterpacht, who said: 'A Resolution recommending to an Administering State a specific course of action creates *some* legal obligation which, however rudimentary, elastic and imperfect, is nevertheless a legal obligation .... The State in question, while not bound to accept the recommendation, is bound to give it due consideration in good faith.'[20]

As will be explained, it may be important, and not only for lawyers, to be able to distinguish between provisions of Security Council resolutions and other outcome documents that are legally binding – that is, contain binding decisions – and those that are not. The Charter itself makes a clear distinction between mandatory and non-mandatory acts of the Council, between decisions and recommendations. There was, and perhaps still is, a divergence of views among states as to whether binding decisions may be taken exclusively under Chapter VII of the Charter (as the United Kingdom and France said in the Security Council debate following the *Namibia* Advisory Opinion),[21] or whether they may be taken under other provisions of the Charter, and notably by virtue of a general empowerment under Article 24 (as the Court opined in *Namibia*).[22]

[19] Consider, for example, the ambiguous scope of S/RES/1973, 11 March 2011, authorizing the use of force 'to protect civilians and civilian populated areas under threat of attack in the Libyan Arab Jamahiriya, including Benghazi'; or the legal effect of S/RES/2165, 14 July 2014, authorizing cross-border and cross-line access for the UN and its partners to deliver humanitarian aid in Syria.

[20] *Voting Procedure* Advisory Opinion, Separate Opinion of Sir Hersch Lauterpacht, at pp. 118–19.

[21] As Sievers and Daws (2014) explain (386–7), the *Namibia* Advisory Opinion (at pp. 52–3, paras. 111–13) provoked a sharp difference of views in this regard, see S/PV.1588, 5 October 1971, paras. 15–19 (France); S/PV.1589, 6 October 1971, paras. 51–3 (UK).

[22] The ICJ rejected the view that it was only under Chapter VII that the Security Council could take binding decisions, *Namibia* Advisory Opinion, at pp. 52–3, para. 113.

The significance of this debate should not be overstated; in practice, the Council almost always acts under Chapter VII (whether explicitly or not) when it intends to impose obligations. If it is agreed that a resolution contains legally binding elements, then the question of whether it is a Chapter VII resolution or not is essentially academic.

One clear provision for binding decisions outside Chapter VII is Article 94, though this has hardly ever been invoked. A decision taken under Article 94 is binding Council action taken outside of Chapter VII:

1. Each Member of the United Nations undertakes to comply with the decision of the International Court of Justice in any case to which it is a party.
2. If any party to a case fails to perform the obligations incumbent upon it under a judgment rendered by the Court, the other party may have recourse to the Security Council, which may, if it deems necessary, make recommendations or *decide upon measures* to be taken to give effect to the judgment.[23]

It seems clear that a Council decision regarding non-compliance with an ICJ judgment which imposes legally binding obligations is based on the Council's authority under this Article, not Chapter VII. The argument that any such binding decision still requires the Council to exercise its enforcement powers under Chapter VII (with the exception of an authorization to use of force under Article 42) is not tenable, given the clarity of the text of Article 94. Indeed, the ability of the Security Council to adopt binding measures to enforce ICJ judgments when deemed necessary is not in question, and asking under which provision of the Charter the Council is exercising its authority is perhaps interesting, but of little practical consequence.

It should, nevertheless, be possible for outsiders (and indeed those on the Council) to be able to ascertain whether a provision of a resolution is binding or not. The distinction can be important in practice for many reasons. First and foremost, governments need to know whether they are under a legal obligation to do or abstain from doing something, or whether they have a more or less free hand. And that can also be relevant in international or domestic

[23] Emphasis added.

court cases, or for what they say in Parliament. Equally, they need to know whether other states are under a legal obligation to act in a certain way. Another context in which it can be critically important to know whether a provision of a resolution is mandatory is in the application of Article 103 (which operates to give priority to obligations – but not recommendations – under the Charter).[24] Knowing whether a provision is binding may also be important for domestic law implementation. In monist legal systems, binding obligations may automatically become domestic law.

The Court of First Instance of the European Union drew attention to the distinction between recommendations and decisions in the cases of *Hassan* and *Ayadi*:

> Article 39 of the Charter of the United Nations draws a distinction between 'recommendations', which are not binding, and 'decisions', which are. In this case, the sanctions provided for by paragraph 8(c) of Resolution 1333 (2000) were indeed adopted by way of 'decision'. Likewise, in paragraph I of Resolution 1390 (2002) the Security Council 'decide[d]' to continue the measures 'imposed' by that provision.[25]

There are three main elements to look for when assessing whether the Council has made a legally binding decision:

1. a determination by the Council, under Article 39, of the existence of a threat to the peace, breach of the peace, or act of aggression. Only when it has identified the existence of a threat to the peace, breach of the peace, or act of aggression may the Security Council proceed to adopt binding enforcement measures under Chapter VII. By far the most common is a determination of a threat to the peace, which can be expressed in varying language: key are the words 'determining/determines' and 'threat to ... peace' (which may be expressed in different ways, including 'threat to international peace and security' or 'threat to regional peace');[26]
2. evidence that the Council is indeed acting under Chapter VII. This is commonly stated in the final preambular paragraph, but

[24] See Chapter 1.
[25] *Ayadi* v. *Council of the EU*, para. 156; *Hassan* v. *Council of the EU*, para. 92.
[26] S/RES/2165, 14 July 2014, for example, determined that the 'humanitarian situation in Syria constitutes a threat to peace and security in the region'. For more on this, see Chapter 3.

equally there may be express reference to particular provisions within Chapter VII (Article 40, 41, or 42);

3. that the Council has taken a 'decision' within the meaning of Article 25. An express reference to Article 25 is not needed or even common, but such reference sometimes appears in lieu of an express reference to Chapter VII; its presence points strongly to an intention to adopt a legally binding decision.[27]

The clearest case is when the Council expressly includes each of these three elements in the resolution, that is to say, when the resolution in question (or an earlier closely related one referred to in the resolution) states that the Council has determined that such-and-such is, or continues to be, a threat to the peace; that it is 'acting under Chapter VII' or under a specific provision in Chapter VII, such as Article 41; and that it 'decides' that something shall be done. An example where all three elements were present is resolution 1718 (2006) on the DPRK.

That said, determining whether the Council is imposing legally binding obligations is not simply a matter of ascertaining whether these three elements of 'best practice' are present or not in the text under consideration. Security Council resolutions are not drafted by professional legislative drafters. There is no equivalent in New York of the legislative drafters you find in a national system, or indeed of the kind of legal drafting specialization present in Brussels (including *juristes-linguistes*). It is left entirely to the members of the Council, including those who have legal advisers on their delegations, to do the best they can, often under severe time and political pressure. The UN Secretariat lawyers are not generally involved, and the Council's own Secretariat (the Security Council Affairs Division) is unlikely to become involved in drafting. As a result, while some drafting practices are apparent, they are liable to change without warning or explanation. And, regrettably, the Council is often inconsistent in its practice and use of language.

As one commentator has explained:

At the UN, we have international lawyers and non-international lawyers working side by side on draft resolutions. And even international lawyers

[27] For an informed view on how to determine whether a resolution imposes binding obligations, see Bellinger (2013) discussing S/RES/2118, 27 September 2013.

do not necessarily share the same opinions. ... [T]he wording of UN resolutions also reflects the purely political, non-legal, views of the delegates who draft them (e.g., condemn, renounce, implore, deplore[,] etc.) and the final outcomes are usually achieved after a long process of drafting changes to try to accommodate the political stances of every delegation in the room (i.e., toning down versus heating up the language; plus the divergent goals of the negotiators). International lawyers do not always have the final say.[28]

Drafting in the Security Council may become highly politicized or even personal. One former insider has explained:

In general, the absence of one of the "best practice" elements means that one or more of the P-5 members has resisted inclusion of an element in order to retain constructive ambiguity regarding the effect of the resolution. After the use of force by the U.S. in Iraq and Libya, both Russia and China have been particularly reluctant to include any reference to Chapter VII in order to avoid giving the U.S. any cover at all to use force.[29]

When it comes to the interpretation of Security Council resolutions, there are no agreed rules like the customary rules of treaty interpretation reflected in Articles 31–3 of the VCLT.[30] But there has been some guidance from the ICJ. Precisely on the question of when decisions may be legally binding, in the *Namibia* Advisory Opinion the Court said:

It has ... been contended that the relevant Security Council resolutions are couched in exhortatory rather than mandatory language and that, therefore, they do not purport to impose any legal duty on any State nor to affect legally any right of any State. The language of a resolution of the Security Council should be carefully analysed before a conclusion can be made as to its binding effect. In view of the nature of the powers under Article 25, the question whether they have been in fact exercised is to be determined in each case, having regard to the terms of the resolution to be interpreted, the discussions leading to it, the Charter provisions invoked and, in general, all circumstances that might assist in determining the legal consequences of the resolution of the Security Council.[31]

Thus, there are only elements in the text, as already discussed, that give greater or lesser clarity. In addition, there is a wide range of

[28] Kriangsak Kittichaisaree commenting on Joyner (2017).
[29] Bellinger (2013). [30] Wood (1998); Wood (2016b); Traoré (2020).
[31] *Namibia* Advisory Opinion, at p. 53, para. 114.

elements external to the text that may aid clarity and provide evidence of the intention of the Council and its members, such as statements made by members of the Council before or after the adoption of a resolution, in which they may indicate whether they consider the resolution to give rise to legal obligations, shedding light on the intent behind its wording. As stated by the ICJ in the *Kosovo* Advisory Opinion:

> Before continuing further, the Court must recall several factors relevant in the interpretation of resolutions of the Security Council. While the rules on treaty interpretation embodied in Articles 31 and 32 of the Vienna Convention on the Law of Treaties may provide guidance, differences between Security Council resolutions and treaties mean that the interpretation of Security Council resolutions also require that other factors be taken into account. Security Council resolutions are issued by a single, collective body and are drafted through a very different process than that used for the conclusion of a treaty. Security Council resolutions are the product of a voting process as provided for in Article 27 of the Charter, and the final text of such resolutions represents the view of the Security Council as a body. Moreover, Security Council resolutions can be binding on all Member States (*Legal Consequences for States of the Continued Presence of South Africa in Namibia (South West Africa) notwithstanding Security Council Resolution 276 (1970), Advisory Opinion, I.C.J. Reports 1971*, p. 54, para. 116), irrespective of whether they played any part in their formulation. The interpretation of Security Council resolutions may require the Court to analyse statements by representatives of members of the Security Council made at the time of their adoption, other resolutions of the Security Council on the same issue, as well as the subsequent practice of relevant United Nations organs and of States affected by those given resolutions.[32]

A key element in determining the binding nature of a provision is the operative word. As it is the 'decisions' of the Security Council that impose legal obligations according to Article 25 (and Article 48) of the Charter, the verb 'decides' is commonly used by the Council to indicate in the clearest possible terms that it is imposing a legally binding obligation in a given outcome document, for example when imposing sanctions under Article 41[33] or other types of enforcement measures, such as no-fly zones.[34]

[32] *Kosovo* Advisory Opinion, at p. 442, para. 94.
[33] See, for example, S/RES/2507, 31 January 2020, on the CAR; S/RES/2498, 15 November 2019, on Somalia.
[34] S/RES/1973, 17 March 2011, on Libya, para. 6.

The Security Council may use other operative words when adopting a binding decision, but in such cases the legal nature of the action is not always clear.

One word that is clear is 'authorize'. Article 42 speaks of necessary 'action' taken by the Council to implement its decisions. So, for example, when the Council 'authorizes' the use of force, it permits (or requires) states to take action that would otherwise be contrary to international law. The Council *authorized* the use of force against Libya in 2011 in order to protect civilians and enforce the no-fly zone;[35] it *authorized* states to use force to repel Iraq from Kuwait in 1990;[36] and so on. Similarly, it *empowered* the UK to detain a vessel that was in violation of sanctions against Southern Rhodesia.[37]

There are certain terms that the Council uses – calls upon, urges, encourages – that are generally considered to indicate non-binding recommendations. But even here there may be some ambiguity, especially with 'calls upon', the term found in Article 41 itself. It may be necessary to consider the word used in official languages other than English since all six language versions are authentic. Comparing the English with the French can be illuminating.

In the *Namibia* Advisory Opinion, the ICJ found that when the Council *called upon* South Africa to withdraw immediately from Namibia this imposed a legal obligation on South Africa.[38] The Council's *declaration* that the continued presence of South Africa in Namibia was illegal and invalid and its *call upon* member states to refrain from any relations with South Africa in contravention of this declaration were also found to be legally binding.[39] Indeed, the Council itself had expressed its frustration with South Africa ignoring its *decisions*.[40] Even if some may question the ICJ's conclusion in this case, its interpretation demonstrates that there can be instances where the use of seemingly non-binding language may nevertheless lead some to conclude that a resolution imposes legally binding obligations.

To conclude, however, that the Council *calling upon* a state to do or refrain from doing something is legally binding will be the

[35] Ibid., paras. 4, 6. [36] S/RES/678, 28 November 1990, para. 2.

[37] S/RES/221, 9 April 1966, para. 5.

[38] *Namibia* Advisory Opinion, p. 83, para. 115. [39] Ibid.; Joyner (2017).

[40] S/RES/276, 30 January 1970, para. 3. Though the Council did *decide* that the continued presence of South Africa in Namibia was illegal in S/RES/269, 12 August 1969, it used *decisions* in the plural.

exception, not the rule. And the use of certain other operative words by the Council is even harder to interpret, the verb 'demand' being a case in point.

The texts adopted by the Council indicate that a demand may be binding. In resolution 283 (1970) on Namibia, for example, the Council expressed its grave concern that South Africa had not complied with its *decisions* 'demanding the immediate withdrawal of South Africa',[41] thus acknowledging that its demands were Council *decisions* and required compliance.

It may be argued that when the Council 'demanded' something it was considered a way for the Council to sound assertive without actually adopting binding language. Or that *demand* is used by the Council to remind states and others to abide by their obligations existing independently in international law.[42] But the Council's practice has evolved in a way that leads to the conclusion that a 'demand' may be (though is not necessarily) legally binding.

That, at the very least some Council members are of the view that the 'demands' of the Security Council can impose legal obligations is evident. A series of resolutions adopted by the Council in response to the Iraqi invasion of Kuwait in 1990 reflected evolving Council practice. Resolution 660 (1990) determined that the invasion was a breach of international peace and security and demanded that Iraq withdraw from Kuwait. This was presumably a provisional measure adopted under Article 40. Four days later, in resolution 661 (1990), the Council reaffirmed resolution 660 (1990) and 'determined' that Iraq had failed to comply with that resolution, and then took certain action as a consequence. Then, in resolution 662 (1990) three days later, it repeated its demands of Iraq to withdraw from Kuwait. In response to the annexation of Kuwait by Iraq, it 'decided' that the act had no legal validity and then 'demanded' that Iraq rescind its decisions.

This series of resolutions indicates an understanding that *demands* can be binding on member states. Council members at the time also understood that the demand for Iraqi withdrawal was of a legally binding nature. France opined: 'Iraq is now required to implement without delay or condition Security Council resolution 660 (1990) which, adopted under Chapter VII of the Charter, is binding on all States.'[43] Canada stated: 'The decisions of the Council are binding

[41] S/RES/283, 29 July 1970, preamble. [42] Joyner (2017).
[43] S/PV.2933, 6 August 1990, p. 21.

on all Member States, including Iraq. Failure to comply with the terms of resolution 660 (1990) leaves this Council with no alternative but to consider what further measures can be applied to give effect to the resolution.'[44] China said that 'resolution 660 (1990) must be implemented immediately, effectively and in real earnest'.[45] Russia referred to 'immediate and full implementation of the requirement that Iraq withdraw its forces from Kuwait'.[46] The Democratic Republic of the Congo (DRC), then Zaire, demanded 'strict respect, immediately, for the provisions of resolution 660 (1990), particularly its paragraph 2 [demanding withdrawal]'.[47] Ethiopia referred to the 'requirements' of resolution 660 (1990).[48] At least certain Council members were thus convinced that the Council's demand for Iraqi withdrawal was legally binding.

There are other, more recent instances of demands of the Council that were considered obligatory. For example, the demand that the DPRK suspend its ballistic missile programme in 2006[49] or that Iran suspend its nuclear programme from the same year.[50] In addition, the ICJ considered that the 'demands' of the Council contained in resolution 1244 (1999) imposed legal obligations.[51]

As mentioned, there could be situations where, due to political compromises, the Security Council is imposing legal obligations while making use of 'constructive ambiguity' in a legally binding text. A decision could, therefore, be binding without explicitly containing some or all of the three elements mentioned earlier in this section, though this is hardly satisfactory and may lead to bitter disagreement later.

Resolution 743 (1992) establishing UNPROFOR in Croatia[52] was adopted unanimously; it contained a preambular paragraph recalling the provisions of Article 25, but – for political reasons – did not state expressly that the Council was 'acting under Chapter VII'. However, immediately before the adoption of the resolution, the

44 Ibid., p. 23. 45 Ibid., p. 28. 46 Ibid., p. 32. 47 Ibid., pp. 34–5.
48 Ibid., p. 37.
49 S/RES/1695, 15 July 2006, para. 2; S/PV.5490, 15 July 2006, p. 7 (France); p. 4 (USA); Bellinger (2013).
50 S/RES/1696, 31 July 2006, para. 2; S/PV.5500, 31 July 2006, statement of the USA, p. 3, statement of the UK, p. 4, statement of China, p. 4; Joyner (2017).
51 *Kosovo* Advisory Opinion, at pp. 449–50, para. 115. For more examples of binding 'demands', see Chapter 5.
52 S/RES/743, 21 February 1992.

President of the Council stated, with the agreement of all Council members, that 'Article 25 will apply to the decisions the Council will be taking in this resolution'.[53] The ICJ had paid particular attention to a similar reference to Article 25 in the *Namibia* Advisory Opinion.[54]

Resolution 2165 (2014), also unanimously adopted, concerned cross-border and cross-line access for the UN and its partners to deliver humanitarian aid in Syria; it was adopted against the backdrop of Syria blocking such access across conflict lines.[55] Due to objections by China and Russia, the final text did not include an explicit reference to Chapter VII but, instead, underscored in a final preambular paragraph that member states were obligated under Article 25 to accept and carry out the Council's decisions.[56] The Council then went on to *decide* that UN humanitarian agencies and their partners were authorized to deliver humanitarian assistance in Syria, upon notification to the government but without the latter's consent, and that all parties in Syria shall allow and ensure the safety of those delivering such assistance.[57] All Council members viewed the resolution as creating legal obligations.[58]

Another example that raised similar questions was resolution 1695 (2006) on the DPRK, which imposed certain requirements on member states to 'prevent missile and missile-related items, materials, goods and technology being transferred to DPRK's missile or WMD programmes'.[59] While it is understood that this resolution contains legally binding elements,[60] it does not refer to Chapter VII or identify a threat to the peace; rather, it states that the Council is acting 'under its special responsibility for the maintenance of international peace and security', a reference to Article 24 of the Charter. But, regardless of how it relates to Chapter VII, it is considered binding.

[53] S/PV.3055, 21 February 1993, p. 3.
[54] *Namibia* Advisory Opinion, at pp. 52–3, para. 113.
[55] S/RES/2139, 22 February 2014.
[56] S/RES/2165, 14 July 2014, preamble; cf. S/RES/2118, 27 September 2013.
[57] Ibid., paras. 2–8.
[58] S/PV.7216, 14 July 2014, e.g., statement of Luxembourg, p. 3, statement of Australia, p. 4, statement of Russia, p. 5, statement of the USA, p. 7.
[59] S/RES/1695, 15 July 2006, paras. 3–4.
[60] S/PV.5490, 15 July 2006, statement of Japan, pp. 2–3, statement of the UK, p. 6; Bellinger (2013); Milanovic (2009a).

Furthermore, what powers exactly under the Charter the Security Council can exercise as part of its general empowerment is also difficult to answer.[61] Chapter VI concerns the Council's mandate to make recommendations for the peaceful settlement of disputes, the exception being its power of inquiry under

> Article 34: 'The Security Council may investigate any dispute, or any situation which might lead to international friction or give rise to a dispute, in order to determine whether the continuance of the dispute or situation is likely to endanger the maintenance of international peace and security.'

It is difficult, however, to find a clear example of a commission of inquiry established by the Council under Article 34 which creates legal obligations for member states, such as an obligation to co-operate. The reason for this is that often this measure is taken in situations that the Council has already identified as a threat to international peace and security; it may be, in fact, a measure taken by the Council under Article 41.

A frequently cited example of the Council's use of Article 34 is the establishment, by resolution 1595 (2005), of the UN International Independent Investigation Commission (UNIIIC) to assist the Lebanese authorities in their investigation of the assassination of Prime Minister Hariri.[62] Though this was done in co-operation with the Lebanese government, because of the internal infighting in Lebanon the Council further obliged Lebanon to fully co-operate with the Commission.[63] Though it is, perhaps, possible to interpret the establishment of the Commission as being implicitly under Article 41, this seems unlikely. There is no indication that this resolution was adopted under Chapter VII, particularly as compared to a resolution adopted some six months later, under Chapter VII, which obliged Syria to co-operate with the Commission.[64]

This case seems to be the exception, not the rule. Take, for example, the international commission of inquiry for Darfur, which was established by a Chapter VII resolution and may well be a measure taken under Article 41.[65] Or the more complicated case of resolution 2235 (2015) authorizing the Secretary-General, in co-ordination with the Organisation for the Prohibition of Chemical Weapons (OPCW)

[61] See, in this context, the discussion about Article 94 in this section.
[62] S/RES/1595, 7 April 2005, para. 1. [63] Ibid., para. 3.
[64] S/RES/1636, 31 October 2005. [65] S/RES/1564, 18 September 2004.

Director-General, to establish the Joint Investigative Mechanism for identifying perpetrators of chemical weapons attacks in Syria.[66] At first sight, this resolution was not adopted under Chapter VII and can be said to be an example of the establishment of a commission of inquiry under Article 34. However, the Council recalled that 'in its resolution 2118, [the Security Council] decided that the Syrian Arab Republic and all parties in Syria shall cooperate fully with the OPCW and the United Nations and stresses that this includes an obligation to cooperate with the ... Joint Investigative Mechanism'.[67] Resolution 2118 (2013), which decided that Syria shall co-operate with the measures taken by the Council to address the use of chemical weapons in Syria, was adopted under Chapter VII. Thus, the establishment of the Joint Investigative Mission seems to have been a measure taken under Article 41 of the UN Charter.

To conclude on this point, it would of course be helpful, and of practical significance, if the Security Council were to adopt consistent and transparent practices with respect to its legally binding decisions. This would have considerable merit in terms of clarity and certainty, but the reality is that diplomats are often likely to see at least short-term advantage in a degree of ambiguity or flexibility. If they do, it is important that they are at least aware of the ambiguities, which may lead to problems for the future.

2.3 Who Is Bound by Security Council Decisions?

2.3.1 UN Member States and Non-Member States

The obvious answer to the question who is bound by Security Council decisions is that all UN member states (or the member state or states specifically addressed by the decision) are bound. This is clear from Articles 25 and 48 of the Charter (the latter with respect to Council resolutions under Chapter VII). Council decisions may also be binding internally for the different bodies of the UN, including the Secretariat. The more difficult questions concern non-member states, international organizations, non-state actors, and individuals.[68]

[66] S/RES/2235, 7 August 2015, para. 5.

[67] Ibid., para. 7. Though the resolution does not refer to Chapter VII as such, it identifies the use of chemical weapons in Syria, and more generally, as a threat to international peace and security and takes certain measures under Article 41.

[68] Krisch, 'Introduction to Chapter VII' (2012) MN 65–9.

UN membership has become virtually universal, and it is highly unlikely that a UN member state will cease to be a member.[69] The question of the binding effect of Council decisions for non-member states is thus nowadays more theoretical than practical. That said, there are still a few cases where it might be of practical significance. For example, what is the binding force of Council decisions for 'observer states' such as the Holy See and the State of Palestine, or other entities not yet admitted to membership, such as Kosovo and Western Sahara.[70]

Article 2.6 of the UN Charter imposes an obligation on the Organization to ensure that non-member states act in accordance with the Principles of the Charter 'so far as may be necessary for the maintenance of international peace and security'. This obligation cannot be said to apply to non-member states themselves.[71] Rather, it is an obligation of the UN (and presumably therefore of its member states) in its relations with non-member states. Notably, in accordance with Article 103 of the UN Charter, for member states this obligation may supersede obligations owed towards non-member states.

As explained in Chapter 1, the argument, in this context and elsewhere, that the Charter is a form of 'constitution' of the international community is misguided and based on an attempt to apply domestic legal doctrines to the international sphere. It cannot alter the basic fact that the Charter is a treaty that binds only the parties themselves.[72] The practice in relation to non-members in the past, in particular Switzerland, which voluntarily complied with UN sanctions, confirms that Council decisions do not bind non-member states.

The content and language of Council decisions may sometimes suggest otherwise. The increasingly common practice of addressing provisions of resolutions – including those containing binding obligations – to 'all States' might be interpreted as suggesting an assumption by the Council that imposing obligations on non-member states is within its powers. On the other hand, it may reflect a belief that the obligations in question are anyway binding

[69] Higgins et al., (2017b), ch. 8. [70] Talmon (2012) MN 12–13.
[71] Ibid., MN 5.
[72] Ibid., MN 28, 73–4. For an opposing view, see Fassbender (2009) 147–8; Peters (2012) MN 44.

on all states under international law, for example in the case of obligations under customary international humanitarian or human rights law. Or the drafting may simply be a matter of political rhetoric.

From early on, the Council has dealt with certain situations and disputes concerning non-member states (and other entities) in the exercise of its functions to maintain international peace and security.[73] In none of these situations was the issue of non-membership raised as an impediment to the Council's authority to issue binding decisions on non-member states.[74] In addition, several non-member states have officially acted to implement more general Council resolutions, such as sanctions, perhaps indicating an understanding that resolutions addressed to 'all States' are applicable to them.[75]

The ICJ has not been clear on this issue. In the *Reparation* case, it concluded that UN member states can create an international organization with an objective international legal personality, which can bring claims against a non-member state.[76] This, however, falls short of maintaining that they can also create obligations for that state, opining only that states can create a new subject of international law.

In the *Namibia* Advisory Opinion, the Court stated that non-member states are not bound by Security Council resolutions; however, at the same time, it concluded that since the mandate of South Africa was declared illegal by the UN General Assembly, the body that vested South Africa with the mandate, non-member states are 'to act in accordance with those decisions'[77] and to assist the UN with respect to its actions against South Africa concerning Namibia.[78]

In *Kosovo*, the Court moved further in the direction of recognizing that it is possible for resolutions to bind persons other than member states when it said: 'The Court recalls in this regard that it has not been uncommon for the Security Council to make demands on actors other than United Nations Member States and inter-governmental organizations .... When interpreting Security Council resolutions, the Court must establish, on a case-by-case basis, considering all

[73] See, for example, S/RES/54, 15 July 1948 ordering Jordan, not yet a member state, along with other Arab League members, to lay down its arms amid the Israeli–Arab war.

[74] Talmon (2012) MN 51. [75] Ibid., MN 57–8.

[76] *Reparation for Injuries* Advisory Opinion, at p. 185.

[77] *Namibia* Advisory Opinion, at p. 56, para. 126. [78] Ibid., at p. 58, para. 133.

relevant circumstances, for whom the Security Council intended to create binding legal obligations.'[79] This might be read as suggesting that there are no limits on whom the Council can bind in its decisions. But it is difficult to see on what legal basis that could be so; the Court did not explain.

On the other hand, the case of Switzerland conveys a different understanding of the legal position on this issue. Prior to joining the UN in 2002, Switzerland was clear that it did not consider its own voluntary implementation of Council sanctions as legally required.[80] This was also the view of the Federal Republic of Germany.[81]

It has been suggested that state practice indicates that a rule of customary international law has emerged that Council decisions imposing obligations on all states regarding matters of international peace and security are, indeed, binding on non-member states.[82] However, it is hard to find any general practice to that effect, particularly that of non-member states, which would be required for such a rule to emerge. If, on the other hand, a non-member state had developed a practice of implementing Security Council decisions addressed to 'all States' as a legal obligation, it could be considered to have generally accepted the binding force of such decisions and be estopped from refusing to implement future Council decisions, or from picking and choosing which ones to implement.

2.3.2 *International Organizations*

Beyond states, assessing who is bound by Security Council decisions is not an issue of consent per se since states can, in principle, decide upon the rights and obligations of other subjects of international law, as they do in various international legal fields such as international human rights law, international humanitarian law, international criminal law, investment law, and so on. But that is not the same as saying that the Security Council can directly impose

79 *Kosovo* Advisory Opinion, at pp. 450–1, paras. 116–17.

80 Peters (2012) MN 33; for a different view on Switzerland, see Talmon (2012), MN 59–62.

81 See UN Doc. S/7781, 21 February 1967; Talmon (2012) MN 57.

82 Talmon (2012) MN 74–5, noting that the last time the Security Council referred explicitly to non-member states was in 1996.

obligations on non-state actors, who are by definition not parties to the Charter. Most indicative in this context are Council resolutions authorizing the use of force.

Under Chapter VIII of the Charter, the Security Council 'shall, where appropriate, utilize . . . regional arrangements or agencies for enforcement action under its authority'.[83] This makes it clear that the Council may authorize certain organizations, that is, give them the right, to use force. The Charter also makes it clear that international organizations, with the exception of the UN acting through the Security Council, cannot themselves authorize the use of force.[84] That legal restraint is, of course, addressed to the member states that are members of a given international organization.

Historically, Council practice on this issue has been such that the Council would authorize the use of force by member states, whether individually or through international organizations of which they are members.[85] For example, resolution 1031 (1995) which followed the Dayton Accords authorized 'Member States acting through or in cooperation with the organization referred to' in the Accords to establish an International Peacekeeping Force (IFOR) and take all necessary measures to implement the Accords; it did not in terms authorize NATO, as such, to use force. When the EU decided to intervene in the DRC in 2003, the Council authorized 'the Member States participating' in a multilateral force to take all necessary measures to fulfil its mandate.[86] A similar approach was taken in resolution 1497 (2003) later that year establishing a multinational force in Liberia, rather than authorizing the Economic Community of West African States (ECOWAS) as such. When the Council established the African Union Mission to Somalia (AMISOM), it authorized 'the Member States of the African Union' to establish the mission and take all necessary measures to carry out their mandate.[87] The authorization to use force in Libya in 2011 to protect civilians was addressed to 'Member States that have notified the Secretary-General, acting nationally or through regional organizations or arrangements'.[88]

[83] UN Charter, Art. 53(1). [84] Ibid.
[85] Higgins (1998); Talmon (2012) MN 50. [86] S/RES/1484, 30 May 2003.
[87] S/RES/1744, 20 February 2007. For the latest language of the Council on AMISOM, see S/RES/2568, 12 March 2021.
[88] S/RES/1973, 17 March 2011.

However, some more recent resolutions have adopted different language, apparently authorizing the international organization itself to use force, rather than its member states acting through it. For example, resolution 2085 (2012) authorized the deployment of an African-led International Support Mission in Mali (AFISMA) 'which shall take all necessary measures ... to carry out' its tasks, including 'to support the Malian authorities in recovering the areas in the north of Mali under the control of terrorist, extremist and armed groups'.[89] AFISMA was established by an AU Peace and Security Council (PSC) communiqué authorizing the decision taken by ECOWAS to deploy forces in Mali to assist the government.[90] And in 2013 the Council welcomed the decision of the African Union (AU) to establish the 'African-led International Support Mission in Central Africa' (MISCA), and proceeded to authorize its deployment and MISCA to take all necessary measures to contribute towards certain tasks.[91] Also in the Central African Republic (CAR), in 2014, the Council authorized 'the EU operation to take all necessary measures'.[92]

If the Council lacked the legal capacity to create rights and obligations for international organizations, it could be said that it necessarily followed that the authorizations granted did not, in fact, authorize the organizations to use force. At the same time, the Council did not in these instances explicitly authorize states themselves to use force as it had previously done when it authorized member states to use force individually or as members of an international organization. If this were the correct legal position, it could further follow that these interventions were an illegal use of force. However, in none of these cases was the relevant organization perceived as acting without the proper authorization.

It could very well be that recent Council resolutions reflect less than perfect drafting by Council members, and that the intention was to authorize the use of force by the member states establishing or participating in the force, as was the case in previous decisions of the Council. After all, multinational forces authorized to use force by the Council are, by their nature, a compilation of states' forces. In any event, the difference in drafting is not of practical

[89] S/RES/2085, 20 December 2012, para. 9.
[90] PSC/PR/COMM.(CCCXXIII), 12 June 2012.
[91] S/RES/2127, 5 December 2013. [92] S/RES/2134, 28 January 2014, para. 44.

consequence because, while the Council cannot impose *obligations* on international organizations, the member states have agreed that the Council can give international organizations the *right* to use force under Article 53(1) of the Charter.

2.3.3 The International Criminal Court

While the question whether Council decisions may bind international organizations seems largely theoretical, it could have consequences for the binding force of certain Council decisions, including Council referrals and deferrals to the ICC. Article 13(b) of the Rome Statute enables the ICC to exercise jurisdiction if a 'situation in which one or more crimes appears to have been committed is referred to the Prosecutor by the Security Council acting under Chapter VII of the Charter of the United Nations'.[93] The idea behind Article 13(b)'s reference to a 'situation' at large seems to have been not to discriminate between warring parties in a dispute.

Nevertheless, on the two occasions when the Council has referred a situation to the ICC, it added a clause excluding personnel from a state not party to the Rome Statute from the jurisdiction of the ICC.[94] These clauses arguably contradict the language of the Rome Statute which refers to 'situations', by discriminating between parties to the same conflict.

It is important to note that if such a contradiction exists, this binding decision of the Council supersedes the obligations that member states which are parties to the Rome Statute owe to the ICC.[95]

However, international organizations as such are not bound by Council decisions, and there is nothing in the Rome Statute that obligates the ICC itself to accept the exclusion of jurisdiction over certain nationals in considering situations referred to it by the Security Council.

Of course, all situations under the jurisdiction of the ICC are ultimately, by their very nature, confined both in scope and in time in some way. Substantive and temporal jurisdiction cannot be

[93] Lentner (2018).
[94] S/RES/1593, 21 March 2005; S/RES/1970, 26 February 2011.
[95] See the discussion of Article 103 in Chapter 1.

unlimited. For example, in the draft resolution vetoed by China and Russia referring the situation in Syria to the ICC, the situation was described as 'the widespread violations of human rights and international humanitarian law by the Syrian authorities and pro-government militias, as well as the human rights abuses and violations of international humanitarian law by non-State armed groups, all committed in the course of the ongoing conflict in the Syrian Arab Republic since March 2011'.[96] This definition of the conflict was thought to address US concerns about establishing jurisdiction over other actors (mainly relating to the Israeli occupation of the Golan Heights).[97] In contrast to the previous examples, this definition would not have distinguished between parties to a conflict, or between their actions. It would, however, have excluded other possible actors or conflicts by confining the situation to a particular conflict.[98]

To date, the ICC has yet to consider the consequences of such limitations upon its jurisdiction. Ultimately, it will be up to the ICC to decide in each case if the jurisdictional limitations imposed in Council referrals are part of the definition of the situation or not. If they are not, they are not legally binding on the ICC even if they are binding on the member states, thus superseding their obligation to co-operate with the ICC concerning cases covered by this jurisdictional limitation.

Article 16 of the Rome Statute makes provision for the Council, acting under Chapter VII of the Charter, to defer investigations or prosecutions for periods of one year, a request which must be complied with. The deferral may be renewed at will.[99] The language of this provision is more specific than that concerning referrals. Here, it seems, the Council has the authority to defer specific investigations or cases, not situations. The Council has done so several times, though not without controversy.

[96] S/2014/348, 22 May 2014, paras. 1 and 2. The draft resolution was not adopted, having received thirteen votes in favour and two against (China, Russian Federation), S/PV.7180, 22 May 2014.

[97] Security Council Report (2015) 35.

[98] The draft resolution separately included the jurisdictional limitation contained in the other referrals, for nationals, current or former officials or personnel from a state not party to the Rome Statute.

[99] Article 16 reads: 'No investigation or prosecution may be commenced or proceeded with under this Statute for a period of 12 months after the Security Council, in a resolution adopted under Chapter VII of the Charter of the United Nations, has requested the Court to that effect; that request may be renewed by the Council under the same conditions.'

At a time when the relationship between the USA and the ICC was tenuous, the Council adopted three resolutions providing immunity for twelve months to nationals of states not parties to the Rome Statute participating in Council-mandated or Council-authorized peacekeeping operations.[100] Resolution 1422 (2002) requested,

> consistent with the provisions of Article 16 of the Rome Statute, that the ICC, if a case arises involving current or former officials or personnel from a contributing State not a Party to the Rome Statute over acts or omissions relating to a United Nations established or authorized operation, shall for a twelve-month period starting 1 July 2002 not commence or proceed with investigation or prosecution of any such case, unless the Security Council decides otherwise.

This was extended for a further twelve months by resolution 1483 (2003), but was not further extended.

In resolution 1497 (2003), the Council did not make a binding request in accordance with Article 16 of the Rome Statute, but simply decided that current or former officials or personnel from a contributing state not a party to the Rome Statute shall be subject to the exclusive jurisdiction of the contributing state.[101]

Critics viewed this as a misuse of Article 16, which was not meant to be used as a blanket immunity for certain nationals in a given situation, but rather as a tool to allow for political resolution of a conflict that might be jeopardized by criminal prosecution. Here, too, as the ICC is not bound by Council decisions, if the situation ever arose, the ICC would have to determine for itself whether such elements of a Council decision fall within the confines of Article 16 or not.

2.3.4 Non-State Actors

Finally, can the Council impose legally binding obligations on non-state actors, such as rebel groups, private companies, or individuals? Here one needs to distinguish between imposing legal obligations on non-state actors directly, and indirectly regulating their conduct through legally-binding obligations imposed on states. When the Council imposes sanctions on individuals, for example, it does so by obligating states to implement sanctions against individuals. In such

[100] S/RES/1422, 12 July 2002; S/RES/1487, 12 June 2003.
[101] S/RES/1497, 1 August 2003, para. 7.

instances, the issue of imposing obligations on non-state actors does not arise.[102]

The ICJ has accepted that the Security Council can impose legal obligations on non-state actors. In *Kosovo*, it examined whether the declaration of independence was a violation of resolution 1244 (1999), which suggests that the resolution could have imposed legal obligations on the non-state actors that made the declaration.[103] It took as a given that the Security Council intended to oblige the 'KLA and other armed Kosovo Albanian groups' to lay down their arms and co-operate with the ICTY.[104]

The Council frequently addresses non-state actors in its outcome documents, making recommendations or urging them to take certain action. That the Council can address non-state actors is not contentious, but it does not provide guidance on the issue of imposing legal obligations on them. In fact, the Council has addressed such actors from early on. In the case of the situation in Palestine in 1947, for example, the Security Council invited representatives of both the Arab and the Jewish communities in Palestine to interact with it directly, even while the British Mandate over Palestine was still in existence.[105] The President of the Council then met with the representatives and called upon both sides to implement certain measures including a ceasefire.[106]

Council practice from the very beginning demonstrates an intention by the Council to impose legal obligations on non-state actors. Going back to the example of Palestine, after the British ended their presence in Palestine and the Arab League States joined the conflict, the Security Council ordered a ceasefire and threatened further enforcement action under Chapter VII against both the states and the 'authorities concerned'.[107] It then decided that each party had a series of *obligations* concerning violations of the truce, including to use all means at their disposal to prevent violation of the truce in the areas under their control.[108] In a later resolution, the Council reminded 'the Governments and authorities concerned that all the obligations and responsibilities of the parties set forth [in earlier resolutions] are to be

102 See the discussion in Peters (2012).
103 *Kosovo* Advisory Opinion, at pp. 448–52, paras. 110–19.
104 Ibid., at p. 350, para. 115. 105 S/RES/43, 1 April 1948, para. 2.
106 S/RES/46, 17 April 1948, para. 1. 107 S/RES/54, 15 July 1948.
108 S/RES/56, 19 August 1948.

discharged fully and in good faith' and determined that they had 'duties' imposed on them by the previous resolution.[109]

Indeed, the Council has regularly demanded that non-state actors act or refrain from certain actions, often addressing them together with states.[110] For example, in resolution 2514 (2020) on South Sudan, it made several demands of non-state actors, including 'that all parties to the conflict immediately end the fighting throughout South Sudan and engage in political dialogue, and further demands that South Sudan's leaders implement the permanent ceasefire declared in the Revitalised Agreement'.[111] In a thematic resolution on the 'protection of civilians', the Council demanded 'that parties to armed conflict comply strictly with the obligations applicable to them under international humanitarian, human rights and refugee law, *as well as to implement all relevant decisions of the Security Council*' without distinguishing between states and non-state actors.[112]

It has been noted that the Council tends to address non-state actors more frequently where there is no apparent state with control over these actors and that some Council members sometimes try to limit Council interaction with non-state actors.[113] But this goes to political preferences, such as considerations of the importance of state sovereignty, not the inability of the Council to bind non-state actors.[114]

This practice, that goes beyond the language in the UN Charter, seems necessary if the Council is successfully to perform its functions of maintaining international peace and security in a world where non-state actors are regularly parties to conflicts.[115]

2.4 May Binding Decisions Be Included in Presidential Statements?

A presidential statement is a statement made by the President of the Security Council on behalf of the Council, read out at a formal

[109] S/RES/59, 19 October 1948, paras. 3 and 5. [110] Boon (2019).
[111] S/RES/2514, 12 March 2020, particularly para. 1.
[112] S/RES/1894, 11 November 2009, para. 1. [113] Boon (2019).
[114] See, for example, negotiations over resolution 2395 (2017), found in Security Council Report, What's in Blue, Counter-Terrorism Committee Executive Directorate: Mandate Renewal, 20 December 2017, available at www.whatsinblue.org/2017/12/counter-terrorism-committee-executive-directorate-mandate-renewal.php#.
[115] Peters (2012).

meeting of the Council and issued as an official document of the Council. Such statements are generally regarded as having less political weight than resolutions. Unlike resolutions, however, statements require consensus among the members of the Council since they are not adopted by vote. Hence, occasionally, it has become necessary to turn a draft statement into a resolution so that it can be adopted by vote.

The legal standing of presidential statements, whether they may and do include binding obligations, is a matter on which the Council's practice has evolved over the years. It is now not to be excluded, though it remains very rare, that such statements may include language with legal force. As Sievers and Daws rightly say, 'there is no *a priori* reason why a presidential statement or other decision format cannot convey a mandatory decision by the Council'.[116]

Over the years, presidential statements have changed in form, style, and frequency. What were first summary statements of the views of Council members or general points of discussion, and later statements summarizing discussions held in informal consultations, eventually became statements made by the President 'on behalf of the Council'. In addition, the way in which presidential statements have been documented has also evolved. As with resolutions during the Council's early years, presidential statements were first simply part of the meeting records; then they were issued as separate 'S' documents; and then, from January 1994 onwards, they were issued in a special document series (S/PRST/1994/1, *et seq.*), thus distinguishing them from other Council documents.

This 'institutionalization' over time reflects the growing importance and possibly enhanced legal standing of presidential statements. From what were originally statements of secondary political significance, without legal consequence, their political importance as voicing the consensus view of all Council members on a particular issue has increased considerably. In one or two cases they now even include language with apparent legal force, though the fact that such language is included in a presidential statement may leave the Council's intention unclear. The rise in significance of presidential statements may explain why, nowadays, they are less frequently

[116] Sievers and Daws (2014) 374–80; see also Tavernier (1993); de La Sablière (2015) 46–7.

adopted. In 1994, when they were first issued as S/PRST documents, there were eighty-two such statements made, while only twenty-four were made in 2021.[117]

Article 25 of the Charter speaks of 'decisions' of the Council, not resolutions. The term 'decisions' applies to presidential statements and resolutions alike, as it is not form specific. It was the Security Council, in its practice, which proceeded to adopt resolutions as the form of its 'decisions'. In the same vein, the Council may very well change or add other forms for its 'decisions'. However, this does not in itself answer the underlying question whether presidential statements may and occasionally do include legally-binding decisions of the Council.

If presidential statements may include decisions of the Council, and one were to apply the means of interpretation indicated by the Court in the *Namibia* Advisory Opinion, one would need to assess the language, context, and all circumstances relevant to the issuance of each presidential statement in order to determine whether it – or some of its language – had binding force.

On the other hand, over the years several states have expressed their view that a presidential statement is inherently a Council document that does not impose legal obligations on states.[118] On one occasion, however, a United Kingdom representative said that a presidential statement was 'a formal and binding position of the Council'.[119] Other states have taken similar positions on individual occasions.[120]

This relates to the view that only resolutions under Chapter VII are legally binding. Writing in 2003, Talmon observed:

> the presidential statements adopted to date have neither made reference to Chapter VII nor have they contained a formal determination pursuant to Article 39. A mere allusion by the Security Council to a threat to the peace is not sufficient in this respect. It is therefore suggested that none of these presidential statements falls under Chapter VII. It is already for this reason that most States and the majority of the literature would, it is suggested correctly, deny them any binding legal force.[121]

[117] See also Security Council Report, In Hindsight: The Security Council in 2019, 31 January 2020, available at www.securitycouncilreport.org/monthly-forecast/2020-02/in-hindsight-the-security-council-in-2019.php.

[118] Talmon (2003) 452–3.

[119] Milanovic (2009a).

[120] E.g., S/PV.7116, 22 February 2014, statement of Argentina, p. 9 on the 'binding character' of S/PRST/2013/15.

[121] Talmon (2003), 450.

The author surveyed various presidential statements to demonstrate that they had never imposed, terminated, or suspended sanctions, or established peace operations.[122] And, indeed, most presidential statements do not contain any language that would normally be seen as binding, or they make 'demands' of non-state actors and are meant to send a political, rather than a legal, message.[123]

In 2007, the non-governmental organization Security Council Report concluded that

> Council practice has evolved in response to practical needs with resolutions as the primary instrument and, increasingly in recent times, statements as a secondary instrument. Council decisions have no prescribed format required by the Charter. However, an analysis of Council practice suggests a remarkably consistent pattern of adopting resolutions as the sole vehicle for Council decisions intended to bind parties to a conflict.[124]

At the same time, it seems clear that presidential statements may include organizational decisions, such as establishing a Security Council subsidiary body[125] or requesting a report from the Secretary-General.[126]

However, as with the issue of binding resolutions other than under Chapter VII, one must distinguish between possible legal limitations and the political realities. In principle, there is no reason why a presidential statement that deems the Afghan conflict 'a serious and growing threat to regional and international peace and security'[127] or a presidential statement that expresses the Council's concern 'about the situation in Liberia and the threat it constitutes to international peace and security in the region'[128] cannot be considered as adopted under Chapter VII, even without an explicit reference to Chapter VII in the text.

122 Ibid., 442–3.

123 See, for example, S/PRST/2012/15, 21 April 2012, calling on the leaders of the military coup perpetrated in Guinea-Bissau to release the interim president, the prime minister and all other detained officials. See also S/PRST/2015/10, 24 April 2015; S/PRST/2015/25, 16 December 2015; S/PRST/2016/7, 13 May 2016; S/PRST/2015/4, 19 January 2015.

124 Special Research Report (2008).

125 S/PRST/2001/2, 31 January 2001.

126 S/PRST/2015/12, 11 June 2015. On at least one occasion, a report was even requested by the Council in an unofficial document, a press statement, see SC/10335, 21 July 2011.

127 S/PRST/2000/12, 7 April 2000.

128 S/PRST/2002/36, 13 December 2002.

While it remains the case that the Council has never established or terminated a sanctions regime in a presidential statement, it has adjusted a sanctions regime pursuant to a presidential statement. In a presidential statement of 13 April 2009, on the North Korea sanctions regime, the Security Council 'agree[d] to adjust the measures imposed by paragraph 8 of resolution 1718 (2006) through the designation of entities and goods, and direct[ed] the Committee established pursuant to resolution 1718 (2006) to undertake its tasks to this effect'.[129] 'Pursuant to the aforementioned presidential statement', to quote the Security Council's Sanctions Committee, the goods subject to the sanctions regime were adjusted and three entities were added to the sanctions list, modifying the legal obligations of member states.[130]

Two conclusions may be drawn. *First*, that member states are themselves often unclear as to whether presidential statements may contain words with legal force. No doubt, from a political standpoint, resolutions carry more gravitas and are perceived by states and others as weightier and bring with them legal clarity and certainty. *Second*, for the sake of clarity and effectiveness, the Council should strive to make legally binding decisions only in resolutions under Chapter VII. The political need for clarity is, perhaps, more important than the question of whether or not presidential statements can, in principle, be legally binding.

[129] S/PRST/2009/7, 13 April 2009.

[130] S/2009/222, 24 April 2009. Similar provisions in S/PRST/2012/13, 16 April 2012, were also acted upon by the Committee, see S/2012/287, 2 May 2012.

3

The Powers of the Security Council

This chapter assesses the powers of the Security Council in three stages. *First*, it introduces the scope of the Council's powers. They are potentially far-reaching, although within a particular field – the maintenance of international peace and security. The chapter then examines the Council's practice and discretion with respect to determining the existence of a threat to the peace, breach of the peace, or act of aggression. Finally, it addresses whether such determinations are subject to judicial review. Possible limitations on the powers of the Security Council are considered in Chapter 4.

3.1 General Considerations

One author has stated that 'a favourite of many legal academics but considered rather irrelevant by government officials and political scientists[] is the concern that the Council might act either beyond its powers in the Charter or in violation of other norms of international law'.[1] These concerns are often – but by no means always – without foundation. They need to be taken seriously if the Council is to remain effective. Most of the more serious concerns are, in our view, political rather than legal.

It is generally accepted that the Security Council, like any organ of the UN, is bound by law. It acts within a legal framework, under a constituent instrument that defines its powers and functions. The ICJ said as long ago as 1948 in the *Conditions of Admission*

[1] Ratner (2004) 603.

case: 'The political character of an organ cannot release it from the observance of the treaty provisions established by the Charter when they constitute limitations on its powers and criteria for its judgment. To ascertain whether an organ has freedom of choice for its decisions, reference must be made to the terms of the constitution.'[2] The Appeals Chamber of the Yugoslav Tribunal put it this way in *Tadić*:

> The Security Council is ... subjected to certain constitutional limitations, however broad its powers under the constitution may be. Those powers cannot, in any case, go beyond the limits of the jurisdiction of the Organization at large, not to mention other specific limitations or those which derive from the internal division of power within the Organization. In any case, neither the text nor the spirit of the Charter conceives of the Security Council as *legibus solutus* (unbound by law).[3]

It does not follow from the fact that the Council is bound by law that the exercise of its powers is subject to judicial review, at least in the sense in which the term is used in domestic legal systems. But even if its acts are not normally justiciable, that does not mean that the Council is absolved from complying with the law applicable to it. The ICJ has repeatedly made the point in relation to states. Thus, in *Democratic Republic of the Congo* v. *Rwanda*: 'Whether or not States have accepted the jurisdiction of the Court, they are required to fulfil their obligations under the Charter of the United Nations and other rules of international law ... and they remain responsible for acts attributable to them which are contrary to international law.'[4] That said, as will be discussed in Chapter 4, a common misconception is that the Security Council is bound by international law, as such.

The Council's powers were intended, by the drafters of the Charter, to be broad and flexible. The powers of the Council within its core field of activity are 'open textured and discretionary'.[5] But they cannot, as a matter of principle, be unlimited, even within that core field. It is widely accepted that the Council is to act in accordance with the Purposes and Principles of the United Nations, and – though this is perhaps less clearly established – that the Council

[2] *Conditions of Admission* Advisory Opinion, at p. 64.
[3] *Prosecutor* v. *Tadić* (1995), para. 35.
[4] *Democratic Republic of the Congo* v. *Rwanda*, at p. 53, para. 127. [5] Lamb (1999).

cannot contravene peremptory norms of international law *(jus cogens)*.[6]

The terms of the Charter and the established practice of the Council are sufficiently flexible that it is difficult to conceive of circumstances actually arising that could raise serious doubts about the legality of the Council's actions or whether it abused its discretion. That is as it should be. A Security Council that was constantly looking at the 'judge over its shoulder'[7] might not always be willing and able to take prompt and effective action for the maintenance of international peace and security.

3.2 The Powers of the Security Council

The starting point for considering the powers of the Security Council is Article 24, paragraph 1, of the Charter, which reads:

> In order to ensure prompt and effective action by the United Nations, its Members confer on the Security Council primary responsibility for the maintenance of international peace and security, and agree that in carrying out its duties under this responsibility the Security Council acts on their behalf.

Article 24, paragraph 2, second sentence, provides that '[t]he specific powers granted to the Security Council for the discharge of [its duties under its primary responsibility for the maintenance of international peace and security] are laid down in Chapters VI, VII, VIII and XII'. Chapter VI of the Charter addresses the pacific settlement of disputes, with the intention that the Security Council shall concern itself with a dispute well before it materializes into a situation that threatens peace and security.[8] Its scope is very broad; it allows states to bring their disputes to the attention of the Council;[9] if they have failed to settle a dispute that is 'likely to endanger the maintenance of international peace and security', it

[6] See Chapter 4.

[7] The expression is taken from a British Government Legal Department publication entitled *The Judge Over Your Shoulder – A Guide to Good Decision Making*, first published in 1987. This publication is intended to give British civil servants 'both a good understanding of the legal environment in which decisions in central government are made and an ability to assess the impact of legal risk on their work'.

[8] Goodrich and Hambro (1946) 146.

[9] Charter, Art. 35.

requires them to refer it to the Council.[10] The Security Council then calls upon states that have failed to settle their disputes peacefully to do so.[11] In addition, Chapter VI empowers the Council to investigate situations that may endanger international peace and security.[12] It grants the Council the authority to recommend to states specific dispute settlement procedures to settle their disputes, including referring their legal disputes to the ICJ.[13] In order to settle a dispute the continuance of which is likely to endanger international peace and security, the Security Council is vested with the power to recommend to states the terms of settlement it deems appropriate.[14] Furthermore, as part of its interaction with regional organizations, the Security Council 'shall encourage the development of pacific settlement of local disputes through such regional arrangements or by such regional agencies either on the initiative of the states concerned or by reference from the Security Council'.[15]

In acting to settle disputes before they become situations that endanger international peace and security, the Security Council contributes to the fulfilment of one of the Purposes of the UN Charter, '[t]o maintain international peace and security, and to that end: to take effective collective measures *for the prevention and removal of threats to the peace*'.[16] Linked to the Security Council's mandate to assist states in settling disputes peacefully is the Security Council's focus on conflict prevention and mitigation.

On the occasion of the 2005 World Summit, the Security Council adopted resolution 1625 (2005) in which it reaffirmed 'the need to adopt a broad strategy of conflict prevention, which addresses the root causes of armed conflict and political and social crises in a comprehensive manner',[17] and expressed 'its determination to enhance the effectiveness of the United Nations in preventing armed conflicts'.[18] The Security Council further stressed 'the importance of establishing effective comprehensive strategies of conflict prevention, focused on averting negative developments in the security, economic, social and humanitarian sectors'.[19] Over the years, conflict prevention

[10] Ibid., Art. 37.1. [11] Ibid., Art. 33.2. [12] Ibid., Art. 34. [13] Ibid., Art. 36.
[14] Ibid., Art. 37.2. [15] Ibid., Art. 53.3.
[16] UN Charter, Art. 1.1 (emphasis added); Goodrich and Hambro (1946) 40; Security Council Report (2017) 2.
[17] S/RES/1625, 14 September 2005, preamble. [18] Ibid., para 1.
[19] Ibid., para 4.

elements have been part and parcel of the Security Council's consideration of a wide range of issues.[20]

3.3 Determining the Existence of a Threat to the Peace, Breach of the Peace, or Act of Aggression

While the role of the Council under Chapter VI is particularly broad, action under Chapter VII is limited to threats to the peace, breaches of the peace, and acts of aggression; this is clear both from the title of Chapter VII and from its opening provision, Article 39, which is the gateway to the Chapter.

There are two main issues concerning the scope of the Security Council's powers under Article 39: *first*, the Council's power to determine the existence of a threat to the peace, breach of the peace, or act of aggression; and *second*, having made such a determination, the Council's power to make recommendations, or decide what measures shall be taken in accordance with Articles 40, 41, and 42, to maintain or restore international peace and security. The second issue will be addressed in subsequent chapters. Both main issues are essentially for political assessment, with the Council having very broad discretion; they are not decisions which can reasonably be subjected to judicial review.

[20] E.g., S/PV.8546, 12 June 2019, a briefing on 'Conflict prevention and mediation'; S/PV.7857, 10 January 2017, a ministerial-level open debate on conflict prevention and sustaining peace; S/PV.7561, 17 November 2015, a ministerial-level open debate on 'Security, development and the root causes of conflict'; S/RES/2150, 16 April 2014, calling on states to prevent and fight against genocide and other serious crimes under international law, reaffirming the principle of responsibility to protect populations from genocide, war crimes, ethnic cleansing, and crimes against humanity; S/PRST/2013/4, 15 April 2013 on 'Prevention of conflicts in Africa: addressing the root causes'; S/PRST/2011/18, 22 December 2011 on preventive diplomacy. Prevention has also been a theme in the Security Council's attention to terrorism, for example S/PV.7690, 11 May 2016, an open debate focusing on countering the narratives and ideologies of terrorism. On youth and violent extremism, S/PRST/2019/15, 12 December 2019; on the role that African youth can play in the prevention and resolution of conflicts, S/RES/2419, 6 June 2018, reaffirming the important role that youth and youth-led civil society can play in peacebuilding and sustaining peace; S/PV.7432, 23 May 2015, a high-level open debate on the role of youth in countering violent extremism and promoting peace. Prevention was also a theme in the Council's discussion on conflict in the Middle East, S/PV.8600, 20 August 2019, for example in the Statement of the Chef de Cabinet of the Secretary-General Maria Luiza Ribeiro Viotti, p. 3, Peru, p. 15, Kuwait, p. 16, Côte d'Ivoire, p. 23; see also Security Council Report (2017) 8–9.

Article 39 reads:

> The Security Council shall determine the existence of any threat to the peace, breach of the peace, or act of aggression and shall make recommendations, or decide what measures shall be taken in accordance with Articles 41 and 42, to maintain or restore international peace and security.

It is not always clear whether the Council is acting under Chapter VII or under other provisions of the Charter; this needs to be borne in mind when seeking to assess the Council's practice as regards the scope of the three terms used in Article 39.

The scope of the three terms found in the title of Chapter VII and in Article 39 as well as the Council's discretion when it makes what is referred to as an 'Article 39 determination' have given rise to much debate among commentators.[21] There has been less controversy within the Council itself, at least recently, although there are still occasional assertions that the Council is intervening in matters which are essentially within the domestic jurisdiction of member states.[22] It was already clear in 2006 that 'an expansive view of the Council's jurisdiction and mandate is now well established, and is available wherever its members are prepared to act'.[23] As Judge *ad hoc* Sir Robert Jennings put it in the *Lockerbie* case, it is widely accepted that 'there is no power of judicial review of Security Council decisions under Chapter VII of the Charter'.[24]

Of the three expressions found in Article 39, by far the most often used in the practice of the Security Council is 'threat to the peace'.[25] It is open-ended and has been given an extended meaning in the practice of the Council. But caution is required in assessing the Council's practice. The precise terms used by the Council need to be carefully examined, including to understand whether it is acting under Chapter VII or not. As we saw in Chapter 2, when considering which Council decisions are legally binding, when the Council acts under Chapter VII in relation to a threat to the peace it should mirror the basic

[21] Krisch, 'Article 39' (2012); Matheson (2006) 41–64; de Wet and Wood (2022).

[22] The domestic jurisdiction principle in Article 2(7) is, of course, without prejudice to the application of enforcement measures under Chapter VII.

[23] Matheson (2006) 41.

[24] *Lockerbie, Preliminary Objections (Libya* v. *UK)*, Dissenting Opinion of Sir Robert Jennings, p. 111.

[25] Krisch, 'Article 39' (2012) MN 12; de Wet and Wood (2022) para. 7.

language of Article 39 ('determining', 'threat', and 'peace'). In practice, it generally does so, though various expressions are used for 'peace' (including 'peace', 'international peace and security', 'peace and security in the region'[26]) as well as verbs such as 'affirming'[27] or 'concerned that'[28] certain situations are a threat, instead of 'determining'. Deliberate avoidance of Article 39 language may signal an intention not to act under Chapter VII.

Over time, the practice of the Security Council, particularly since the end of the Cold War, has expanded the scope of what is considered a threat to the peace and, more broadly, what may be considered relevant for the Council's mandate as a body entrusted with the maintenance of international peace and security, for example in the context of thematic debates.[29] It remains, however, important to distinguish between cases where the Council makes an explicit (or occasionally implicit) determination under Article 39 of a 'threat to the peace' and hence is acting under Chapter VII, and cases where it discusses matters that relate to or may endanger international peace and security and is operating under other provisions of the Charter, including Chapter VI, whether it is considering a particular dispute or situation or conducting a thematic debate.

When the Council acts under Article 39, the terms it uses to describe the circumstances that amount to a threat to the peace can be revealing. In the hope of avoiding setting a precedent, or appearing to be intervening in the domestic affairs of states,[30] the Council has often strained to bring out the international implications of an essentially internal situation, as well as its exceptional nature, and has sometimes emphasized the request of the territorial state.[31] Some examples follow.

The presidential statement issued at a Council meeting held at heads of state and government level on 31 January 1992 is often

[26] S/RES/2165, 14 July 2014, for example, determined that the 'humanitarian situation in Syria constitutes a threat to peace and security in the region'.

[27] In S/RES/1540, 28 April 2004, and S/RES/2118, 27 September 2013, the operative words were, respectively, '*Affirming*' and '*Reaffirming*'.

[28] S/RES/733, 23 January 1992.

[29] See generally de Wet and Wood (2022); Matheson (2006) 6–7.

[30] Though Article 2(7) of the Charter makes clear that enforcement measures adopted under Chapter VII are not considered to be in violation of the principle of non-intervention.

[31] Österdahl (2005) 1–20.

seen as a watershed; Council members adopted an expansive view of international peace and security:

> The absence of war and military conflicts amongst States does not in itself ensure international peace and security. *The non-military sources of instability in the economic, social, humanitarian and ecological fields have become threats to peace and security.* The United Nations membership as a whole, working through the appropriate bodies, needs to give the highest priority to the solution of these matters.[32]

Even before the end of the Cold War there was Council practice that regarded internal matters as threats to international peace and security,[33] notably in the Congo,[34] Southern Rhodesia,[35] and South Africa.[36]

By now, beyond the classic interstate armed conflicts which were in the minds of the drafters of the Charter,[37] international peace and security is seen as engaged, inter alia, by situations internal to a single territory or state,[38] international terrorism,[39] including the refusal to hand over terrorist suspects,[40] proliferation of weapons of mass destruction and their means of delivery,[41] violations of human rights law,[42] protection of civilians and violations of international humanitarian law,[43] piracy,[44]

[32] S/23500, 31 January 1992. The statement included a long passage on disarmament, arms control, and weapons of mass destruction, in which, inter alia, Council members said that '[t]he proliferation of all weapons of mass destruction constitutes a threat to international peace and security'.

[33] Fifoot (1992). [34] S/RES/161, 21 February 1961.

[35] S/RES/216, 12 November 1965.

[36] S/RES/417, 31 October 1977; S/RES/418, 4 November 1977.

[37] Krisch, 'Article 39' (2012) MN 13.

[38] E.g., S/RES./713, 25 September 1991; S/RES/918, 17 May 1994; S/RES/1132, 8 October 1997.

[39] E.g., S/RES/1368, 12 September 2001; S/RES/1373, 28 September 2001; S/RES/2178, 24 September 2014; S/RES/2462, 28 March 2019.

[40] E.g., S/RES/748, 31 March 1992 regarding Lockerbie; S/RES/1044, 26 April 1996 on Sudan; S/RES/1267, 15 October 1999 regarding Afghanistan's refusal to hand over Osama bin Laden.

[41] E.g., S/23500, 30 January 1992; S/RES/1441, 8 November 2002; S/RES/1540, 28 April 2004; S/RES/2105, 5 June 2013; S/RES/1467, 18 March 1993; S/PRST/2006/41, 6 October 2006.

[42] E.g., S/RES/688, 5 April 1991; S/RES/713, 25 September 1991; S/RES/1325, 31 October 2000.

[43] E.g., S/RES/767, 24 July 1992; S/RES/918, 17 May 1994; S/RES/1208, 19 November 1998; S/RES/1314, 11 August 2000; S/RES/2165, 14 July 2014.

[44] E.g., S/RES/2500, 4 December 2019.

organized crime,[45] illicit trafficking in small arms and light weapons,[46] overturning of democratic principles,[47] health crises,[48] and the effects of climate change on conflict.[49]

Carefully drafted Article 39 determinations include:

- resolution 748 (1992) ('*Determining*, in this context, that the failure by the Libyan Government to demonstrate by concrete actions its renunciation of terrorism and in particular its continued failure to respond fully and effectively to the requests in resolution 731 (1992) constitute a threat to international peace and security');[50]
- resolution 794 (1992) ('*Determining* that the magnitude of the human tragedy caused by the conflict in Somalia, further exacerbated by the obstacles being created to the distribution of humanitarian assistance, constitutes a threat to international peace and security');[51]
- resolution 841 (1993) ('*Considering* that the above-mentioned request of the Permanent Representative of Haiti, made within the context of the related actions previously taken by the Organization of American States and by the General Assembly of the United Nations, defines a unique and exceptional situation warranting extraordinary measures by the Security Council within the framework of the Organization of American States, *Determining* that, in these unique and exceptional circumstances, the continuation of this situation threatens international peace and security in the region');[52]

[45] E.g., S/PRST/2018/9, 8 May 2018; S/RES/2482, 19 July 2019.

[46] E.g., S/PRST/2004/7, 25 March 2004; S/PRST/2006/38, 9 August 2006; S/PRST/2010/6, 19 March 2010.

[47] E.g., S/RES/841, 16 June 1993; S/RES/1132, 8 October 1997; S/RES/2337, 19 January 2017.

[48] E.g., S/RES/2177, 18 September 2014, determining that the unprecedented extent of the Ebola outbreak in Africa constitutes a threat to international peace and security; S/PRST/2014/24, 21 November 2014; and also S/PV.4087, 10 January 2000, which was an open debate on the impact of AIDS on peace and security in Africa; S/RES/1308, 17 July 2000 encouraged voluntary HIV/AIDS testing and counselling for peacekeeping troops; S/RES/2565, 26 February 2021 and S/RES/2532, 1 July 2020 considered 'that the unprecedented extent of the COVID-19 pandemic is likely to endanger the maintenance of international peace and security', thus using Article 34 (Chapter VI) language and not in express terms determining a threat to the peace.

[49] S/PRST/2011/15, 20 July 2011.

[50] S/RES/748, 31 March 1992.

[51] S/RES/794, 3 December 1992.

[52] S/RES/841, 16 June 1993.

- resolution 1373 (2001) ('*Reaffirming further* that such acts [as the attacks of 9/11], like any act of international terrorism, constitute a threat to international peace and security');[53]
- resolution 1540 (2004) ('*Affirming* that proliferation of nuclear, chemical and biological weapons, as well as their means of delivery, constitutes a threat to international peace and security');[54]
- resolution 2177 (2014) ('*Determining* that the unprecedented extent of the Ebola outbreak in Africa constitutes a threat to international peace and security').[55]

Cases where the Council made no Article 39 determination, and was not acting under Chapter VII, include:

- resolution 2482 (2019), paragraph 1 ('linkages between international terrorism and organized crime, whether domestic or transnational, which constitute a serious challenge and a threat to international security');[56]
- resolutions 2532 (2020) and 2565 (2021) ('*Considering* that the unprecedented extent of the Covid-19 pandemic is likely to endanger the maintenance of international peace and security').[57]

3.4 The Justiciability of Council Determinations under Article 39

A much debated question among writers, particularly since the *Lockerbie* cases, is whether the Security Council's Article 39 determinations are justiciable. The ICJ has not itself expressed a view on the matter. Individual judges have. In his dissenting opinion at the Provisional Measures stage of the *Genocide* case, Judge *ad hoc* Elihu Lauterpacht rightly said that it was not for the Court 'to substitute its discretion for that of the Security Council in determining the existence of a threat to the peace, a breach of the peace or an act of aggression, or the political steps to be taken following such a determination'.[58] In *Tadić*, the Yugoslav Tribunal said that whereas

[53] S/RES/1373, 28 September 2001. [54] S/RES/1540, 28 April 2004.
[55] S/RES/2177, 18 September 2014. [56] S/RES/2482, 6 August 2019.
[57] S/RES/2532, 1 July 2020; S/RES/2565, 26 February 2021.
[58] *Genocide* case, Separate Opinion of Judge *ad hoc* Elihu Lauterpacht, at p. 439, para. 99.

'the act of aggression is more amenable to a legal determination, the threat to the peace is more a political concept'.[59]

Most writers share the view that the Council's determinations under Article 39, and especially as regards a 'threat to the peace', are essentially political, and that courts and tribunals should not seek to substitute their own views for those of the Council.[60] Some, however, adopt a 'constitutionalist' approach, and a few have even suggested that the Council has regularly exceeded its powers. That view has little, if any, support in state practice.

As for the scope of the Council's power, having made the necessary determination under Article 39, to make recommendations and adopt measures under Chapter VII, here again the Appeals Chamber of the ICTY had something to say: 'Article 39 leaves the choice of means and their evaluation to the Security Council, which enjoys wide discretionary powers in this regard; and it could not have been otherwise, as such a choice involves political evaluations of highly complex and dynamic situations.'[61] Judge *ad hoc* Lauterpacht also covered the point in the passage just cited from the *Genocide* case.[62]

The specific powers of the Council to call upon the parties to comply with provisional measures (under Article 40), to decide on measures not involving the use of force, including so-called 'sanctions' (under Article 41), and to take enforcement measures (under Article 42) will be addressed in later chapters.

59 *Prosecutor* v. *Tadić* (1995), para. 29.
60 E.g., Krisch, 'Article 39' (2012) MN 4–6; de Wet and Wood (2022) paras. 29–33.
61 *Prosecutor* v. *Tadić* (1995), paras. 31, 39; see also *Prosecutor* v. *Kanyabashi*, paras. 21–6; see also Schabas (2014) 178–9.
62 Note 58.

4

Limits on the Powers of the Security Council

4.1 General Considerations

Following our discussion of the powers of the Security Council in Chapter 3, this chapter considers some of the limitations on these powers, real or imagined. In particular, it examines limits deriving from the Purposes and Principles of the United Nations and the norms of *jus cogens*. It then briefly explores some checks and balances on the actions of the Council.

Some legal scholars have devoted great efforts to devising a series of sweeping limits on the powers of the Council, and to suggesting that the acts of the Council are or should be subject to judicial review in the same ways as the acts of national authorities. Yet to do so runs counter to the Council's purpose: in the words of Article 1, 'to take effective collective measures for the prevention and removal of threats to the peace', and in the words of Article 24, 'to ensure prompt and effective action' to that end. What these writers tend to overlook is that the principal restraints on the Council are political, not legal.

Perhaps the chief limitation in practice is that, with very few exceptions, the Council's actions fall within its primary responsibility for the maintenance of international peace and security. In other words, is the particular issue a matter for the Council to deal with under the UN Charter? Legally speaking, this may be often overlooked nowadays because of the flexibility of the Charter and the expansion of the concept of peace and security over the years, as described in Chapter 3.

It is difficult to envisage the limitation to its core field being justiciable as a legal matter, except perhaps in a most extreme case, which is highly unlikely to arise in practice; but it remains a very real limitation nonetheless, due to the differing political positions of the member states, including the permanent members. To what extent various issues and situations – including those already discussed in the Council – are matters that fall under the mandate of the Council remains a divisive issue. For example, in the first Council meeting on human rights as a stand-alone issue in April 2017, some Council members took the view that 'systematic violation of human rights is inherent to conflicts, which, in turn, can threaten international peace and security'.[1] Others, such as Russia, took the view that

> the Council cannot serve as a forum for discussions about human rights situations, wherever they may be ... We cannot agree with the assertion made in the concept note prepared for the meeting, according to which violations of human rights should be considered as an issue related to the primary responsibility of the Security Council for maintaining international peace and security, in accordance with the Charter.[2]

These differing views, essentially on policy, will no doubt continue to be aired in the Council in the years to come.

4.2 'in accordance with the present Charter'

Article 25 provides:

> The Members of the United Nations agree to accept and carry out the decisions of the Security Council in accordance with the present Charter.

It has sometimes been suggested that the words 'in accordance with the present Charter' in the English text of Article 25 are ambiguous. Either they might refer to the decisions being carried out in accordance with the Charter or they might mean that it is only decisions that are in accordance with the Charter that have to be accepted and carried out.[3] The latter reading could lead to a situation in

[1] S/PV.7926, 18 April 2017, statement of Uruguay, p. 9, and also the statements of the USA, p. 4, the UK, p. 19, and Senegal, p. 18.

[2] S/PV.7926, 18 April 2017, p. 12; see also the statements of Kazakhstan, p. 8, Egypt, p. 9, and Bolivia, pp. 22–3.

[3] See Peters (2012) MN 56. This reading finds some support in the *Namibia* Advisory Opinion, where the Court stated that the decisions of the Council 'adopted in conformity with the purposes and principles of the Charter ... are consequently binding on all States Members of the United Nations', at p. 53, para. 115.

which individual states decide for themselves which Council decisions are, and which are not, in accordance with the Charter.[4] That would place the Charter system of collective security at the mercy of individual states, and thus render it potentially toothless, as the League system proved to be when things got tough. That is what the drafters of the Charter were determined to avoid.[5]

The better reading of Article 25, the more natural and grammatical reading, and the one more in line with the intention that the Council be effective, is that the words 'in accordance with the present Charter' qualify the manner in which members of the UN are to carry out the Council's decisions. Indeed, any ambiguity in the English text is resolved when one looks at the text in the other equally authentic languages. This interpretation does not mean that a resolution of the Council cannot be *ultra vires* or adopted by a procedure not in accordance with the Charter; it means that a member of the UN cannot rely on these words in Article 25 to claim the right unilaterally to decide that it will not comply with a decision of the Council.

4.3 'in accordance with the Purposes and Principles of the United Nations'

Those who would bind the Council within a legal straitjacket often point to the first sentence of Article 24, paragraph 2: 'In discharging these duties [that is to say, the Council's duties under its primary responsibility for the maintenance of international peace and security] the Security Council shall act in accordance with the Purposes and Principles of the United Nations.' It is somewhat artificial to extrapolate from this sentence a whole series of specific limits on the Council's powers. The Purposes of the United Nations, set out in Article 1 of the Charter, have been described as 'very loosely formulated, reflecting a political programme rather than strictly defined legal rules'.[6] As one author

[4] A less far-reaching version of this latter argument is that the words refer to relevant Charter provisions that give the Council the power to adopt binding decisions, see Goodrich et al. (1969) 208; see also *Namibia* Advisory Opinion, Dissenting Opinion of Judge Fitzmaurice, at p. 293, para. 113.

[5] Krisch, 'Introduction to Chapter VII' (2012) MN 2–3.

[6] Schweigman (2001) 167.

has put it, '[t]he Purposes and Principles are very general statements that are not defined and are subject to a wide range of interpretation, and some by their nature do not seem to have specific legal content'.[7] Their fulfilment and the relative importance to be attached to them are essentially matters for policy choice, not for courts or lawyers.

The maintenance of international peace and security is placed first among the Purposes of the United Nations set forth in Article 1 of the Charter. The list of Purposes begins:

1. To maintain international peace and security, and to that end: to take effective collective measures for the prevention and removal of threats to the peace, and for the suppression of acts of aggression or other breaches of the peace, and to bring about by peaceful means, and in conformity with the principles of justice and international law, adjustment or settlement of international disputes or situations which might lead to a breach of the peace.

The other Purposes in Article 1 are particularly broad. They include:

2. To develop friendly relations among nations based on respect for the principle of equal rights and self-determination of peoples, and to take other appropriate measures to strengthen universal peace;
3. To achieve international co-operation in solving international problems of an economic, social, cultural, or humanitarian character, and in promoting and encouraging respect for human rights and for fundamental freedoms for all without distinction as to race, sex, language, or religion.

The Principles in Article 2 are – for the most part – somewhat more specific, the main relevant one in the present context being Article 2, paragraph 7, on domestic jurisdiction. But even here we find very broad concepts such as 'the principle of the sovereign equality of all [the] Members [of the United Nations]' and the fulfilment 'in good faith of the obligations assumed ... in accordance with the Charter'.

Some of the Purposes and Principles set out in Articles 1 and 2 will now be addressed.

[7] Matheson (2006) 35.

4.3.1 *'in conformity with the principles of justice and international law'*

The second of the Purposes set out in Article 1, paragraph 1, of the Charter, reads: 'to bring about by peaceful means, and in conformity with the principles of justice and international law, adjustment or settlement of international disputes or situations which might lead to a breach of the peace'. Some commentators have suggested that this means that the Security Council is bound always to act in accordance with international law. They overlook the fact that, and this was quite deliberate at San Francisco, the reference to justice and international law applies only in relation to bringing about, by peaceful means, adjustment or settlement of disputes or situations which might lead to a breach of the peace. It does not apply to action under Chapter VII.[8] And even in the case of action under Chapter VI, the reference is to the 'principles' of justice and international law, not international law itself. Moreover, juxtaposition of justice and international law – which are not the same, as the Charter makes clear – makes the application of this clause, even in the context of the Council's recommendations under Chapter VI, a matter for political appreciation. It could only be in extreme cases – if at all – that it might be said that the Council had not acted in accordance with 'the principles of justice and international law' and, as explained, this would apply only to recommendations under Chapter VI – and not to binding decisions under Chapter VII or under any general powers that may exist.

4.3.2 *Domestic Jurisdiction*

Article 2, paragraph 7 provides expressly that the principle of non-intervention set out in that paragraph 'shall not prejudice the application of enforcement measures under Chapter VII'. There is therefore no scope for an argument limiting the powers of the Security Council to adopt enforcement measures under Chapter VII by reference to the principle of non-intervention in the domestic affairs of a state.

Article 2, paragraph 7 could impose limits on the Security Council's powers except where it is taking enforcement measures

[8] Wolfrum, 'Article 1' (2012) MN 21–2.

under Chapter VII. But the interpretation of this provision, both by the General Assembly and by the Council, and the expansion of international law into fields previously thought to be within the reserved domain (and not only in the field of human rights) mean that its importance as a restriction is much reduced. In addition, it is difficult to imagine how the Council, in making recommendations under its Chapter VI powers (or recommendations under Chapter VII for that matter), could be said to be 'intervening' in matters that are essentially within the domestic jurisdiction of any state. Recommendations do not involve coercion. Nor is it easy to see how such recommendations by the Council could be said to infringe the rather neglected second limb of Article 2, paragraph 7 and 'require the Members to submit [matters which are essentially within the domestic jurisdiction of any state] to settlement under the ... Charter'.

4.3.3 Self-Determination

Article 1, paragraph 2 of the Charter refers to 'the principle of equal rights and self-determination of peoples'. It has been suggested that the Security Council would infringe the right of self-determination if, for example, it imposed a government against the wishes of the people of a territory, or without their consent. Yet it might well need to do this temporarily in order to secure the peace and even, in the longer term, to enable a people to exercise their right of self-determination, as its practice demonstrates. The modes of exercising the right of self-determination are many, and the choices essentially political. It is hard to see that any action that might be taken by the Council could seriously be said to infringe self-determination.

4.3.4 Human Rights

As a matter of policy, the Security Council will doubtless not wish to override the human rights of individuals, except where it is necessary and proportionate so to do in order to carry out its primary responsibility to maintain international peace and security. The circumstances in which the Council may act under Chapter VII – threat to the peace, breach of the peace, act of aggression – may be likened, at the international level, to a 'public emergency threatening the life of the nation' or to a 'war or other emergency threatening the life of the nation', which are the conditions for derogations under human rights treaties. Yet it has sometimes been suggested that the Council is legally bound to respect international human rights law, either because of the inclusion of cooperation in promoting and encouraging respect for human rights among the Purposes in Article 1 of the Charter, or because rules of international human rights law are *jus cogens*. These arguments will now be addressed.

The attempt to show that the Council is, as a matter of law, constrained generally by human rights usually relies on the cross-reference in Article 24 of the Charter to the Purposes of the United Nations. Paragraph 3 of Article 1 provides that the Purposes of the United Nations include '[t]o achieve international co-operation . . . in promoting and encouraging respect for human rights and for fundamental freedoms for all without distinction as to race, sex, language, or religion'. But the specific reference to human rights in Article 1 of the Charter is not a strong hook upon which to hang a weighty theory. Nor are the other Charter references to human rights.

Though some of its recent jurisprudence has resulted in narrowing the scope of the Council's ability to override rights protected by the ECHR in practice,[9] the ECtHR has rightly acknowledged that

> [w]hile it is equally clear that ensuring respect for human rights represents an important contribution to achieving international peace (see the Preamble to the Convention), the fact remains that the UNSC has primary responsibility, as well as extensive means under Chapter VII, to fulfil this objective, notably through the use of coercive measures. The responsibility of the UNSC in this respect is unique and has evolved as a counterpart to the prohibition, now customary international law, on the unilateral use of force.[10]

A separate line of argument is to the effect that as the members of the Security Council are individually bound by human rights obligations, both conventional and customary, the Council itself is so bound. However, this ignores the separate legal personality of the UN, the effect of Article 103 of the Charter, and basic notions of international responsibility.

Yet another line of argument is that individual Council members remain bound by their respective human rights obligations and

[9] See Chapter 2. [10] *Behrami* v. *France*, para. 148.

remain liable under their respective conventional and customary law obligations when exercising their responsibilities as Council members. They cannot, or should not, do through the Council that which they could not do individually, so the argument goes. Thus, it has been suggested that a member of the Security Council that is also a member of the Council of Europe could be in violation of the ECHR in respect of its actions in the Council, such as voting in a certain way or committing troops to a mission which allegedly violates human rights.[11] Presumably, the same could be argued in respect of other human rights systems. This argument was rejected by the ECtHR, which noted that such actions are 'crucial to the effective fulfilment by the UNSC of its Chapter VII mandate and, consequently, by the UN of its imperative peace and security aim' and that to rule otherwise 'would be to interfere with the fulfilment of the UN's key mission in this field including, as argued by certain parties, with the effective conduct of its operations'.[12]

4.3.5 Good Faith and Abuse of Rights

Another possible restriction deriving from the Purposes and Principles of the Charter is good faith. A requirement to act in good faith seems unexceptional. But what does it mean in the context of action by the Security Council, and who could decide whether the Council has acted in good faith or not? One author concludes that it means 'that it may neither abuse its powers, nor act arbitrarily' and that 'the measures decided upon in order to restore the peace should be necessary and proportional'.[13] But that is to read a great deal into a few general words and, as explained earlier, considering the wide discretion of the Council to decide when it is appropriate to act and how, it is hard to imagine a situation where it could reasonably be argued that the Council exceeded that discretion by acting arbitrarily.

The Council is sometimes accused of inconsistency in its approach to comparable situations. Accusations of double standards are understandable, but they overlook the political nature of the Council. The Council may well act in one situation but not, for

[11] As opposed to being liable for its domestic implementation of Security Council resolutions.

[12] *Behrami* v. *France*, para. 149.

[13] Schweigman (2001); see also de Wet (2007).

political or other reasons, in another that may be considered comparable. Occasionally, the argument has been put forward in legal terms. In *Tadić*, it was argued that the Council had been inconsistent in not setting up tribunals in other situations where there were violations of international humanitarian law, but the Tribunal was not impressed.[14] It is difficult to see how any persuasive legal argument could be devised that would impose a requirement of consistency upon a body with a remit as wide and political as that of the Security Council. Edward Luck expressed the position well in his book on the Council: 'The Council . . . is given wide latitude to pick the cases, the timing, and the tools for its interventions. There is no language in Chapter VII urging the members of the Council to be consistent, fair, or equitable in their judgments about when and how to get involved.'[15]

4.4 Limits Inherent in *Jus Cogens* Norms

A norm of *jus cogens* (otherwise known as a peremptory norm of general international law) is defined in Article 53 of the VCLT as 'a norm accepted and recognized by the international community of States as a whole as a norm from which no derogation is permitted and which can be modified only by a subsequent norm of general international law having the same character'. Is the Security Council bound to respect *jus cogens* norms? In his Separate Opinion at the Provisional Measures stage of the *Genocide* case, Judge *ad hoc* Lauterpacht said:

> The concept of *jus cogens* operates as a concept superior to both customary international law and treaty. The relief which Article 103 of the Charter may give the Security Council in case of conflict between one of its decisions and an operative treaty obligation cannot – as a simple hierarchy of norms – extend to a conflict between a Security Council resolution and *jus cogens*.[16]

It is widely considered that this is a correct statement of the position. Nowadays, it seems almost to be taken for granted among writers that obligations under the Charter cannot prevail over a *jus cogens* obligation, and that Article 103 is to be read as implicitly but

[14] *Prosecutor* v. *Tadić* (1995), paras. 26–7. [15] Luck (2006) 23.
[16] *Genocide* case, Separate Opinion of Judge *ad hoc* Lauterpacht at p. 440, para. 100.

necessarily subject to this exception.[17] The ICTY took this view in the *Tadić* case.[18] In the *Kadi* case, the Court of First Instance of the European Communities said:

> International law . . . permits the inference that there exists one limit to the principle that resolutions of the Security Council have binding effect: namely, that they must observe the fundamental peremptory provisions of *jus cogens*. If they fail to do so, however improbable that may be, they would bind neither the Member States of the United Nations nor, in consequence, the Community.[19]

Assuming that the priority given to Charter obligations does not extend to peremptory norms of general international law (*jus cogens*), the next step is to be clear about what are, and what are not, peremptory norms, and how they might limit the Council's freedom of action. The problem, of course, is that, in the words of Professor Brownlie, '[m]ore authority exists for the category of *jus cogens* than exists for its particular content'.[20] And as Judge Higgins has said, '[t]he examples [of norms having the character *of jus cogens*] are likely to be very, very few in number'.[21]

This is one of those areas of international law where there is a good deal of wishful thinking. One monograph, for example, relies heavily on writings, downplays the consensual element, and appears to assert the existence of an extraordinarily wide range of *jus cogens* norms, including the whole of human rights law, the principle of *non-refoulement*, and norms prohibiting the large-scale pollution of the environment.[22]

In its *Kadi* judgment, the Court of First Instance in Luxembourg also appeared to adopt an expansive view of *jus cogens*. Using various terms for the notion, the Court referred to 'the mandatory provisions concerning the universal protection of human rights, from which neither the Member States nor the bodies of the United Nations may derogate because they constitute "intransgressible principles of international customary law"'.[23] Turning to the

[17] Paulus and Leiß (2012) MN 19. [18] *Prosecutor* v. *Tadić* (1995), para. 296.

[19] *Kadi* v. *Council* (2005), para. 230; see also *Al-Jedda* v. *Secretary of State* (2007), para. 35, in which the House of Lords also referred to *jus cogens* as overriding the primacy of obligations under the UN Charter, though there was no question of a breach of a *jus cogens* norm on the facts of that case.

[20] See also Swiss Federal Court, as discussed in *Behrami* v. *France*.

[21] Higgins (2006) 801. [22] Orakhelashvili (2006).

[23] *Kadi* v. *Council* (2005), para. 231.

human rights at issue in the case, the Court said (somewhat obscurely) that 'in so far as the right to property must be regarded as forming part of the mandatory rules of general international law, it is only an arbitrary deprivation of that right that might, in any case, be regarded as contrary to *jus cogens*'.[24] As regards the right to a fair hearing, the Court found that 'no mandatory rule of public international law requires a prior hearing for the persons concerned in circumstances such as those in this case . . .'. As regards the right of access to a court, the Court similarly found that the limitations imposed by the Security Council were 'inherent in that right as it is guaranteed by *jus cogens*'.[25]

In its commentary to Article 26 of the 2001 Articles on State Responsibility, the ILC pointed out:

> Article 53 of the Vienna Convention requires not merely that the norms in question should meet all the criteria for recognition of a norm of general international law, binding as such, but further that it should be recognised as having a peremptory character by the international community of States as a whole. So far, relatively few peremptory norms have been recognised as such. But various tribunals, national and international, have affirmed the idea of peremptory norms in contexts not limited to the validity of treaties. Those peremptory norms that are clearly accepted and recognised include the prohibition of aggression, genocide, slavery, racial discrimination, crimes against humanity and torture, and the right of self-determination.[26]

The Study Group of the International Law Commission on Fragmentation included a similar list in its final report of April 2006.[27]

In 2015, the ILC decided to take up a topic on 'Peremptory norms of general international law (*jus cogens*)', and, in 2019, it adopted a set of twenty-three draft conclusions on first reading (with commentaries).[28] The second and final reading is expected in 2022. The Commission's work has focused on the methodology for identification and the legal consequences of *jus cogens*; the question whether to include a list of peremptory rules proved controversial both in the Sixth Committee and within the Commission. Ultimately, the draft conclusions adopted on first reading in 2019 included in an Annex a non-exhaustive list of peremptory rules previously identified by the ILC: the prohibitions

[24] Ibid., para. 242. [25] Ibid., para. 288. [26] ILC (2001) 85.
[27] A/CN.4/L.682, 13 April 2006, para. 374.
[28] A/74/10, 10 December 2019, paras. 147–208.

of aggression, genocide, slavery, torture, racial discrimination and apartheid, and crimes against humanity, as well as the right of self-determination. Added to previous lists are 'basic rules of international humanitarian law'.[29] The fourth report of the Special Rapporteur had included a discussion of other rules, such as the right to life, which have been mentioned as possible peremptory rules, but these were not included.[30]

The ILC's first reading draft conclusions included a draft conclusion 16 entitled 'Obligations created by resolutions, decisions or other acts of international organizations conflicting with a peremptory norm of general international law (*jus cogens*)'. This reads: 'A resolution, decision or other act of an international organization that would otherwise have binding effect does not create obligations under international law if and to the extent that they conflict with a peremptory norm of general international law (*jus cogens*).' The commentary, somewhat obscurely, notes that decisions of the Security Council

> require additional consideration since, pursuant to Article 103 of the Charter of the United Nations, obligations under the Charter prevail over other rules of international law. For this reason, considering the hierarchical superiority of peremptory norms of general international law (*jus cogens*), the Commission considered it important to highlight that draft conclusion 16 applies equally to binding resolutions, decisions and acts of the Security Council.[31]

We now look briefly at some of the *jus cogens* norms listed by the ILC in 2019 (and earlier) to see what relevance they might have in practice as limits on the powers of the Council.

First, the prohibition of aggression. It is inconceivable, perhaps logically impossible, that the Council would impose an obligation on states that would contravene the prohibition of aggression. The use of force authorized by the Council is in principle lawful and, provided that the use of force remains within the bounds of what the Council has authorized, cannot amount to aggression.

[29] A/74/10, 10 December 2019, p. 208.
[30] A/CN.4/727, 31 January 2019, paras. 122–36.
[31] Paragraph 4 of the commentary to draft conclusion 16 (A/74/10, 10 December 2019, p. 189), which has a footnote recording the differing views of states on this matter. See Costelloe (2021).

It likewise seems inconceivable that the Security Council would act, or require states to act, in contravention of the norms of *jus cogens* prohibiting slavery, racial discrimination and apartheid, torture, or crimes against humanity, or basic rules of international humanitarian law, such as the prohibition of grave breaches of the Geneva Conventions.

It also seems inconceivable that the Council would impose an obligation on states to contravene the prohibition of genocide. However, in his Separate Opinion in the *Genocide* case, Judge *ad hoc* Lauterpacht concluded, tentatively (and rather unconvincingly), that the Security Council resolution imposing an arms embargo on the whole of the former Yugoslavia, including Bosnia, could 'be seen as having in effect called on Members of the United Nations ... to become in some degree supporters of the genocidal activities of the Serbs and in this manner and to that extent to act contrary to a rule of *jus cogens*'.[32] Judge *ad hoc* Lauterpacht would have been prepared to indicate a provisional measure that 'the continuing validity of the embargo in its bearing on the Applicant has become a matter of doubt requiring further consideration by the Security Council'.[33]

On the facts alone, it would have been difficult to substantiate a charge that either the Council or members of the UN were in breach of any prohibition amounting to a norm of *jus cogens*. But it is interesting to note the terms in which Judge *ad hoc* Lauterpacht would have been prepared to indicate a provisional measure, which seem to recognize that the decision was indeed, at least in the first place, for the Council. It would have been a highly unusual provisional measure, indirectly addressed to an international organ not party to the proceedings.

A similar scenario could be imagined where the Council's actions in a certain situation would be viewed by some as breaching a people's right to self-determination. For example, despite many years of dealing with these issues on its agenda, the Council – much like the international community and the states and entities concerned – has not been able to find a solution to the situations in Western Sahara and Palestine, or to secure their peoples' right of self-determination. Yet these are far from being situations where the Council has violated the right of self-determination, a very unlikely

[32] *Genocide* case, Separate Opinion of Judge *ad hoc* Lauterpacht at p. 441, para. 102.
[33] Ibid., at p. 442, para. 107.

scenario; moreover, the Council's role is not to ensure the exercise of self-determination but to maintain international peace and security. The Council may have failed in these situations in the pursuit of the latter aim thus far, a political failure rather than a legal one, but it is not more legally liable than any member state or other organization for the failure to achieve the fulfilment of the right of self-determination of all peoples.

It has sometimes been suggested that all non-derogable human rights are norms of *jus cogens* since otherwise they would not be non-derogable. But that is too wide a proposition.[34] None of the lists suggested recently by the ILC, those of 2001, 2006, and 2019, includes among the norms *of jus cogens* any general category of 'human rights' or 'fundamental human rights' or 'non-derogable human rights', as opposed to certain specific human rights obligations, in particular the prohibitions of torture and slavery.

There are various reasons why a right may be non-derogable under one or more human rights treaties. These might include the strength of feeling in the region (for example, prohibition of the death penalty, which is non-derogable under Protocols to the European Convention), or the fact that no one could think of circumstances in which derogation would be necessary (for example, the right not to be imprisoned for debt, which is non-derogable under the Covenant).[35] What is non-derogable varies as between the different human rights treaties.

The Security Council is most often accused of infringing the right to property, the right to a fair trial, and the right to a remedy in respect of these two rights. But these are not accepted and recognized by the international community of states as a whole as *jus cogens* norms. The right to property, though included in the Universal Declaration on Human Rights, does not appear in the International Covenants; it is in a Protocol to the ECHR. The right to a fair trial is derogable, and not a norm of *jus cogens.* Finally, the right to a remedy in respect of a right that is not itself a norm of *jus cogens* is not a *jus cogens* right.[36]

[34] Human Rights Committee, General Comment No. 29, UN Doc. CCPR/C/21/Rev.1/Add.11, 31 August 2001, para. 11.

[35] Ibid.

[36] See the Decision of the Swiss Federal Court at issue in *Al-Dulimi* v. *Switzerland*, as well as the Dissenting Opinion of Judge Sajó and the Dissenting Opinion of Judge Lorenzen, joined by Judges Raimondi and Jočienė, in the 26 November 2013 ECtHR judgment.

4.5 Checks and Balances on the Council

Perhaps the most important question for lawyers is whether and, if so, to what extent the Council is subject to controls. The Council has extensive powers; these are nevertheless subject to certain legal limits, but the Council is not clearly subject to any effective procedures by which the legality of its acts can be tested. Some see in this a grave flaw. For others, it is an important element in an effective collective security system.

Even if the legal limits on the Council are few, both in theory and in practice, and the opportunities for them to be tested are sporadic and uncertain, that does not mean that the Council acts in an untrammelled and wilful manner. There are checks and balances within the system, though these are not as widely understood as they should be, and are sometimes perhaps deliberately overlooked.

Even before a proposal is put to Council members, there is (usually) a degree of self-restraint. It must frequently happen that those in capitals, assisted by their New York missions, conclude that it would not be sensible to propose a particular course of action to the Council. The reasons are many: that the action would not secure the requisite majority, or would be vetoed; that the action, even though it might pass, would set an unfortunate precedent; that it would trigger retaliation in the form of other Council action against the interest of its proponent in another unrelated situation; that it might weaken the legitimacy of the Council, or not be effective, and/or tend to undermine the Council's authority due to expected lack of implementation by member states; or that the proposed action would be, or would be widely seen to be, outside the scope of the Council's powers.

A principal check, day-to-day *the* principal check, is the Council's decision-making procedure. This, too, is not always appreciated outside the Council. *First*, procedural votes require nine out of the fifteen Council members to vote in the affirmative though they are not subject to vetoes. Thus, while any nine Council members can initiate consideration of an issue in a Council meeting, any seven members can block issues from even being considered or placed on the Council's agenda.[37]

[37] Sievers and Daws (2014) 296, 318–20.

Second, even if they were agreed among themselves, the permanent members would need a minimum of nine out of the fifteen votes for a decision, which means that any seven members can block a Council resolution. Even if they are agreed among themselves, the permanent members need the support of at least four of the ten non-permanent members. In any event, most Council resolutions are adopted unanimously, or with very high majorities,[38] and presidential statements, in practice, require unanimous support.[39]

A *third* aspect of decision-making is, of course, the veto of each of the five permanent members. There have been considerably fewer vetoes cast since the end of the Cold War than in previous decades, though the numbers rose again in the last decade.[40] But the 'hidden' veto – the threat to veto – is often deployed behind the scenes, though even there it may be unspoken or only hinted at. The veto is no doubt most often deployed for reasons of immediate national interest, but it may also be used for reasons of principle, including a permanent member's view of the proper role of the Council.

A possible legal constraint on the Council is that, as a UN organ, its actions may involve the international (or domestic) responsibility of the UN or, under certain circumstances, possibly even the responsibility of individual members of the UN (including, but not limited to, the members of the Security Council).

This last issue has been addressed in the ILC's 2011 Draft Articles on the responsibility of international organizations. The ILC reached the conclusion that participation in the activities of an organization and its decision making, in accordance with the organization's rules, does not entail the responsibility of its member states as such.[41] At the same time, the Draft Articles do not exclude the possibility that states may aid or assist, direct or control, coerce, or try to circumvent their obligations by acting through an international organization.[42] In the

[38] For recent statistics, see Security Council Report, Security Council Statistics, www.securitycouncilreport.org/security-council-statistics/.

[39] There have been a few incidents of a Council member disassociating itself from a presidential statement. See Sievers and Daws (2014) 398–400.

[40] Security Council Report (2015); Sievers and Daws (2014) 300–10. For an up-to-date list of vetoes cast, see www.securitycouncilreport.org/atf/cf/%7B65BFCF9B-6D27-4E9C-8CD3-CF6E4FF96FF9%7D/working_methods_veto.pdf.

[41] ILC (2011), Arts. 58, 59, 62; see also the fourth report of the Special Rapporteur, A/CN.4/564 and Add. 1–2, para. 62.

[42] Ibid., Arts. 58–61.

context of the Security Council, it is important to note that member states have given the Council in the Charter the power to override their own obligations, impose binding obligations, and authorize the use of force, powers that go beyond those of the member states themselves.

In any event, as the Council became more active, the occasions on which the international responsibility of the UN may be incurred increased. What is, of course, generally lacking is any procedure to ensure the implementation of that responsibility – the same is still largely true of state responsibility.

There have been a number of attempts to challenge, directly or indirectly, decisions of the Security Council in international and domestic courts.[43] The question of a possible 'judicial review' of Security Council resolutions by the ICJ has, as we have already seen, occasioned much debate. As Sir Elihu Lauterpacht pointed out as early as 1965: '[Municipal law analogies are] more misleading than enlightening in the context of a Court that which cannot make the Council a party to a binding judgment, whose judgments are binding only as to the States parties to a contentious case and which can only be enforced by the very party it would be criticising (namely the Security Council).'[44]

It seems to be widely accepted that the ICJ has no power of direct judicial review such as is found in many national legal systems, but it may have some power of indirect review, where the legality of the Council's actions arises incidentally in the course of deciding the case or giving the opinion before it. That remains controversial.

In both the *Expenses* and the *Namibia* Advisory Opinions, the ICJ was invited to consider the lawfulness of acts of the political organs of the UN. But it was only following the Provisional Measures phase of the *Lockerbie* cases that academic writings on the subject proliferated. The Court declined to exercise a power of review over a Security Council resolution, but some read its Order as suggesting that the possibility of review was not excluded. The issue was not decided before the proceedings were discontinued. There were nevertheless some interesting things said. For example, Judge *ad*

[43] For a recent summary of these challenges, see Cockayne et al. (2018), particularly Annex I.

[44] Lauterpacht (1965) 88.

hoc Sir Robert Jennings, in his Dissenting Opinion at the Jurisdiction and Admissibility stage, said:

When, therefore, as in the present case, the Security Council, exercising the discretionary competence given to it by Article 39 of the Charter, has decided that there exists a 'threat to the peace', it is not for the principal judicial organ of the United Nations to question that decision, much less to substitute a decision of its own, but to state the plain meaning and intention of Article 39, and to *protect* the Security Council's exercise of that body's power and duty conferred upon it by the law; and to protect the exercise of the discretion of the Security Council to 'decide what measures not involving the use of armed force are to be employed to give effect to its decisions'.[45]

The question arose also in the *Genocide* case brought by Bosnia against Serbia. Again, the Court was not called upon to decide the issue. However, Judge *ad hoc* Lauterpacht took the opportunity to say

that the Court's power of judicial review is limited. That the Court has some power of this kind can hardly be doubted, though there can be no less doubt that it does not embrace any right of the Court to substitute its own discretion for that of the Security Council in determining a threat to the peace, a breach of the peace or an act of aggression, or the political steps to be taken following such a determination.[46]

While the question has not arisen in other proceedings before the ICJ, it has before other international tribunals. In *Tadić*, the first case before the ICTY, the Trial Chamber (not unreasonably) found that it did not have jurisdiction to determine the lawfulness of the resolution by which it was established, while nevertheless saying that it clearly was lawful (thus adopting an approach similar to that of the Nuremberg Tribunal).[47] The Appeals Chamber took a different line, claiming that it was empowered to determine the lawfulness of its founding resolution.[48] The Court of First Instance of the European Communities in the *Kadi* line of cases also seemed to think that it had the power to determine, for the purpose of the case before it, the lawfulness of a Security Council resolution, though only as regards its conformity with *jus cogens* norms.[49] The CJEU's subsequent judgment, striking down the implementation measures

[45] *Lockerbie*, Preliminary Objections *(Libya* v. *UK)*, at p. 110.
[46] *Genocide* case, Separate Opinion of Judge *ad hoc* Lauterpacht at p. 439, para. 99.
[47] *Prosecutor* v. *Tadić* (1995), para. 13. [48] Ibid., paras. 14–22.
[49] *Kadi* v. *Council* (2005), paras. 219–26.

of the EU, did not review the Security Council's resolutions themselves, but had the practical effect of making them inapplicable in the national legal systems of the EU members (unless they chose to ignore the CJEU).[50]

There have been a number of attempts to challenge Council acts in domestic courts. In one example, the challenge by Milošević in the Dutch courts in 2001 to the legality of the establishment of the ICTY received short shrift. Nevertheless, the District Court in The Hague, unnecessarily it has been suggested, examined briefly whether the Tribunal had been lawfully established by the Security Council, and whether it was an impartial tribunal within the meaning of Article 6 of the ECHR.[51]

Successful direct judicial review of Security Council actions in domestic courts (including among 'domestic courts', for this purpose, the courts in Luxembourg) seems unlikely in practice. What has taken place is the review of national measures implementing resolutions such as before the CJEU and the ECtHR. The possibility of judicial review by domestic courts raises an important issue of principle. If the system of collective security is to be effective, it cannot be for individual states (or entities like the EU) to determine for themselves whether a resolution of the Council is valid or not, as a matter of course. And that is true for their courts, just as much as for the executive and the legislature.

The ultimate check on the Council would be if states simply refused to carry out its decisions, either because they (or their courts) considered them to be illegal and so not binding, or for other reasons (because the Council is acting 'illegitimately', for example). Some commentators seem to encourage such a course.[52] Fortunately, examples have been rare in practice, but the issue involved is crucial. In particular, do members of the UN (including their courts) have the right to make their own assessment of the legality of decisions of the Council and, if they (or their courts) conclude that they are not lawful, ignore them? If they do have that right, where would that leave the collective security system established by the Charter? Our response would

[50] *Kadi* v. *Council* (2008).

[51] Milošević v The Netherlands (2001). Application no. 77631/01 (2002) before the ECtHR challenging this decision was declared inadmissible.

[52] E.g., Tzanakopoulos (2011).

be that states do not have the right to do this, and would be acting unlawfully if they purported to exercise such a right. But they do, of course, have the ultimate option, as a matter of policy, of simply disregarding binding obligations imposed by the Council, with all the consequences, political and legal, that might flow from such a course. That is why the Council needs to exercise self-restraint and use its undoubted powers responsibly and only where it really is necessary to do so in order to ensure prompt and effective action to maintain international peace and security. That is the most effective check on the Council's power.

5

The Security Council and Measures Not Involving the Use of Force

This chapter considers certain legal issues that arise under some of the main provisions of Chapter VII of the Charter relating to measures not involving the use of force. In this regard, the words of warning expressed by Leland Goodrich and Anne Simons are at least as relevant today as they were in 1969:

> In the use of the documentary records of the United Nations to explain how the Charter has been interpreted and applied, we have encountered the difficulty of relating particular decisions and discussions to particular articles. Sometimes the relation to a particular article is clear, but more often there is no reference in a resolution adopted or statement made to the particular article of the Charter upon which it is based. Often in the course of discussions various reasons are advanced and different articles are cited with no clear indication in the end as to which considerations have been decisive in the final decision. The tendency in the United Nations to politicize issues and to seek accommodations makes the task of using United Nations practice for the purpose of showing how specific articles have been interpreted and to what extent these interpretations have been accepted an extremely difficult one. Very often one has to rely on what seems to be reasonable inferences.[1]

The difficulty has been exacerbated by the move, since the late 1980s, to conduct much of the Council's business in informal consultations, without official documentation.

Article 39 provides that the Security Council 'shall make recommendations, or decide what measures shall be taken in accordance with Articles 41 and 42, to maintain international peace and

[1] Goodrich and Simons (1969) x.

security'. Before doing so, and '[i]n order to prevent an aggravation of the situation', under Article 40 the Council may also 'call upon the parties concerned to comply with' provisional measures.

The present chapter first considers provisional measures under Article 40, and then turns to measures not involving the use of armed force under Article 41.

5.1 Article 40: Provisional Measures

The Security Council may adopt what might be termed 'provisional measures'[2] in various contexts and under various provisions of the Charter, including Chapter VI. Here, we are concerned with the one provision that expressly uses the term 'provisional measures', Article 40, which reads:

> In order to prevent an aggravation of the situation, the Security Council may, before making the recommendations or deciding upon the measures provided for in Article 39, call upon the parties concerned to comply with such provisional measures as it deems necessary or desirable. Such provisional measures shall be without prejudice to the rights, claims, or position of the parties concerned. The Security Council shall duly take account of failure to comply with such provisional measures.[3]

The ordinary meaning of Article 40 raises several questions concerning the powers of the Council contained in it and the Article's relationship with the powers of the Council to adopt binding measures under Articles 41 and 42.

5.1.1 Are Provisional Measures under Article 40 Binding?

Article 40 provides that the Council may 'call upon' – a term normally used in a non-binding context in Council outcome documents – parties to a situation to adhere to certain temporary measures, before resorting to binding measures or recommendations under Articles 41 and 42. The preceding Article 39 speaks of the Council resorting to measures and recommendations under Articles 41 and 42 in cases of a threat to the peace, breach of the peace, or act of aggression, but does not refer to Article 40. This may

[2] Not to be confused with 'provisional measures' adopted by international courts and tribunals, which serve a quite specific and different purpose.

[3] See Goodrich et al. (1969); Krisch, 'Article 40' (2012); Nasu (2009).

suggest that provisional measures under Article 40 are not binding decisions of the Council, as opposed to the explicit authority to take such decisions to be found in Articles 41 and 42.[4]

On the other hand, this is not the only possible reading of the text of Article 40. As indicated by the ICJ, the term 'calls upon' may be used to issue a binding decision by the Council in some contexts.[5] The Council itself has even used the term to authorize the use of force.[6] And, from the very beginning, writers have interpreted the term 'calls upon' in Article 40 and provisional measures as potentially binding if so decided by the Council (much like the use of the term in Article 41).[7] Writers have also suggested that Article 40 is redundant if it does not allow for binding provisional action by the Council as the Council can make similar recommendations under Chapter VI.[8]

The Security Council's practice from its early years shows that the Council has issued binding decisions explicitly under Article 40 that have not met with opposing legal views by states.

In 1947, the Council adopted a resolution on the situation in Indonesia, calling upon the parties to cease hostilities forthwith and settle their dispute by arbitration or by other peaceful means.[9] Disagreement ensued thereafter about whether the resolution was adopted under Articles 39 and 40, as explicit references to the Articles in the original Australian draft[10] were removed from the resolution as adopted. The USA took the view that the resolution was adopted under Article 40 and was, therefore, binding on the parties.[11] Other Council members denied that the text was adopted under Article 40, but in so doing implicitly accepted the legally binding nature of provisional measures adopted under Article 40.[12]

[4] Provisional measures imposed by the Security Council are quite distinct from provisional measures indicated by the ICJ under Article 41 of its Statute and by other international courts and tribunals; it will be recalled that the ICJ's 2001 judgment in the *LaGrand* case found that its own provisional measures were binding.

[5] *Namibia* Advisory Opinion, at p. 53, para. 115.

[6] S/RES/221, 9 April 1966, para. 5.

[7] Goodrich and Hambro (1946) 159; Higgins et al., (2017b) 27.36; admittedly, this is not entirely without doubt as the ICTY declined to take an affirmative stance on the issue, see *Prosecutor* v. *Tadić* (1995), para. 33.

[8] Krisch, 'Article 40' (2012) MN 12.

[9] S/RES/27, 1 August 1947.

[10] S/454, 31 July 1947.

[11] S/PV.398, 11 January 1948.

[12] Ibid., statement of Belgium, p. 11.

Comments made by Council members on draft resolutions on the 'Greek frontier incidents' that failed adoption reflected similar views.[13]

In 1948, the binding nature of Article 40 was reflected in an official Council outcome. The Council 'ordered' a ceasefire in Palestine 'pursuant to Article 40', including an 'immediate and unconditional' ceasefire in Jerusalem to take effect within twenty-four hours.[14] The Council subsequently reminded the warring parties of their binding obligations under the resolution.[15] Then it imposed, 'as a further provisional measure' on the parties' an obligation to negotiate an armistice.[16]

In the midst of the Iran–Iraq war, explicitly citing Article 40, the Council demanded that the parties cease fire and withdraw to their respective territories.[17] This was viewed as imposing a legal obligation on the parties.[18]

When Iraq invaded Kuwait in 1990, the Council cited Article 40 to demand Iraq's withdrawal.[19] Council members considered this demand to be binding.[20] The Council explicitly invoked Article 40 in resolution 1696 (2006) to demand that Iran suspend its nuclear programme. This was considered a binding demand.[21] Indeed, the final preambular paragraph made this clear: '*Acting* under Article 40 of Chapter VII of the Charter of the United Nations in order to make mandatory the suspension required by the IAEA.' This was further evident when, in resolution 1737 (2006),[22] Iran was found to be in non-compliance with the requirements of resolution 1696

[13] S/PV.180, 12 August 1947, statement of Australia.

[14] S/RES/54, 15 July 1948, paras. 2, 5. [15] S/RES/59, 19 October 1948.

[16] S/RES/62, 16 November 1948, paras. 1–2.

[17] S/RES/598, 20 July 1987, preamble and para. 1.

[18] S/PV.2750, 20 July 1987, statement of the UK, p. 16, statement of the USA, p. 21, statement of Germany, p. 27, statement of Ghana, p. 41, statement of Argentina, pp. 46–7. Iraq also accepted the binding character of the resolution, see S/19045, 14 August 1987; see also Krisch, 'Article 40' (2012) MN 13, fn. 41, noting that Iran's refusal to accept the resolution was based on its perceived bias according to Iran.

[19] S/RES/660, 2 August 1990.

[20] S/PV.2933, 6 August 1990, statement of France, p. 21, statement of Canada, pp. 23–5, statement of China, p. 28, statement of Zaire, pp. 34–5, statement of Ethiopia, p. 37; see also Chapter 1.

[21] S/RES/1696, 31 July 2006, para. 2; S/PV.5500, 31 July 2006, statement of the USA, p. 3, statement of the UK, p. 4, statement of China, p. 4; Joyner (2017); see also Chapter 2.

[22] S/RES/1737, 23 December 2006, sixth preambular para.

(2006) and was later 'released' from its 'obligations' under resolution 1696 (2006) by resolution 2231 (2015).[23]

Though Council practice seems clear, it is important to bear in mind that, even if provisional measures under Article 40 were not binding, the Security Council could decide on such measures under Article 41.

In addition, that the Council can 'take account' of non-compliance with its provisional measures is legally redundant due to its other Chapter VII powers, though it does provide a political justification for actions against states which may have otherwise not been considered antagonists by the Council before their non-compliance.[24]

Finally, while measures under Article 40 are to be 'without prejudice to the rights, claims, or position of the parties concerned', it became evident early on that practically any provisional measure adopted by the Council can arguably prejudice one of the parties to a conflict.[25]

5.1.2 *Is a Determination under Article 39 a Necessary Prerequisite for Provisional Measures under Article 40?*

While a determination of a threat to the peace, breach of the peace, or act of aggression under Article 39 is a prerequisite for enforcement action under Articles 41 and 42, the Charter is silent with respect to provisional measures under Article 40. This raises the question as to the relationship between Articles 39 and 40. It has been suggested that the practice of the Council provides no firm answer.[26]

The drafters of the Charter intended that a determination under Article 39 should be made prior to any provisional measures being called for, as with measures under Articles 41 and 42.[27] At San Francisco, the Drafting Committee opined that the structure of Articles 39–42 was such that provisional measures would be adopted as responses to threats to the peace, and that resort to further

[23] S/RES/2231, 20 July 2015, para. 7(a). These examples also demonstrate that a Council 'demand' may be binding, see Chapter 2.

[24] Krisch, 'Article 40' (2012) MN 12.

[25] S/PV.381, 16 November 1948, statement of Syria; Krisch, 'Article 40' (2012) MN 10–12.

[26] Goodrich et al. (1969) 303.

[27] Goodrich and Hambro (1946) 158.

measures under Articles 41 and 42 would be necessary in the case of an actual breach of the peace or act of aggression.[28]

This particular course of action was not followed in practice, yet it explains the structure of the Charter, in which Article 40 is placed after Article 39 and before Articles 41 and 42. It suggests that Article 40 was meant to follow a determination under Article 39. The views of member states reflect this contextual interpretation.

When the Council's Sub-Committee on the Spanish Question reported to the Council in 1946, it noted that 'the activities of the Franco regime do not at present constitute an existing threat to the peace within the meaning of Article 39 of the Charter and therefore the Security Council has no jurisdiction to direct or to authorize enforcement measures under Article 40 or 42'.[29] When the Indonesian question was discussed in 1947, Belgium took the view that 'the Council would not, under the Charter, be justified in applying Article 40 without first having determined the existence of a threat to the peace, a breach of the peace or an act of aggression, according to the actual terms of Article 39'.[30] Indeed, Council practice, on the whole, has been to make a determination under Article 39 before proceeding to adopt provisional measures under Article 40, albeit most often without explicitly referring to either article.[31] Writers also support the necessity of following these steps.[32] There have, however, been a few possible exceptions to this practice.

During the Indo–Pakistani War of 1965, the Council, without making a determination under Article 39, demanded that a ceasefire take place and that troops withdraw to their original positions.[33] Two years later, during the Six Day War, the Council demanded a ceasefire between Israel and its neighbours, again

[28] Ibid. [29] S/75, 1 June 1946, p. 10.

[30] S/PV.172, 1 August 1948, p. 1654; see also Greece's request for the Council to make a determination under Article 39 in order to proceed with adopting provisional measures, S/451, 31 July 1947.

[31] See, for example, S/RES/1199, 23 September 1998, referring to a threat to the peace and making demands for a ceasefire and other measures; Krisch, 'Article 40' (2012) MN 5.

[32] E.g., Higgins (1963) 236; Krisch, 'Article 40' (2012) MN 3–4; Higgins et al., (2017b) 27.36.

[33] S/RES/211, 20 September 1965; see also S/RES/214, 27 September 1965 and S/RES/215, 5 November 1965.

without using any of the terms in Article 39 but rather describing the conflict as a 'menacing situation'.[34]

In resolution 1696 (2006) on the Iranian nuclear programme, the Council explicitly invoked Article 40 without invoking Article 39 or its language, but rather stated that it was '*[c]oncerned* by the proliferation risks presented by the Iranian nuclear programme, *mindful* of its primary responsibility under the Charter of the United Nations for the maintenance of international peace and security, and ... *determined* to prevent an aggravation of the situation'.[35] The Council used similar language when it proceeded to adopt binding measures under Article 41 after Iran failed to comply with its earlier decisions, still without an explicit determination under Article 39.[36]

It is possible to argue that a determination under Article 39 was implicit in all these situations, or that at least the first two examples in fact involved measures not under Article 40 but under Chapter VI.[37] In any event, these examples notwithstanding, the Council can and should resort to measures under any provisions of Chapter VII, including under Article 40, only after making a determination under Article 39 of a threat to the peace, a breach of the peace, or an act of aggression.

5.1.3 *The Temporary Nature of Measures under Article 40*

Article 40 contains an implicit requirement that the measures are temporary in nature, aimed at preventing further aggravation of a situation rather than resolving it and restoring peace and security, without prejudicing the positions of the parties concerned. The measures that the Council has adopted under Article 40 in practice reflect this.

Most common are demands for the end of hostilities, a ceasefire, and/or the withdrawal of troops to their original positions.[38] Some argue that arms embargoes may be a form of provisional measure, the argument being that such action is a temporary stopgap prior to finding a solution to a situation.[39] While this view is not entirely unreasonable, it would render almost all measures decided by the Council, such as sanctions, arguably provisional. Article 41,

[34] S/RES/234, 7 June 1967. [35] S/RES/1696, 31 July 2006.
[36] S/RES/1737, 27 December 2006. [37] Krisch, 'Article 40' (2012) MN 6.
[38] Ibid., MN 8. [39] Nasu (2009) 104.

however, makes clear that disruptions of economic relations, that is, sanctions and embargoes, are measures under Article 41. It would thus seem that the provisional measures envisioned in Article 40 are narrower in space and time, and relate more to immediate and quick steps that can be taken as the Council deliberates its response. This is reflected in the jurisprudence of the ICTY which viewed measures under Article 40 as a 'holding operation', producing a 'stand-still' or 'cooling-off effect'.[40]

The temporal element inherent in measures under Article 40 also stands in contrast with measures under Article 41, which the Charter does not indicate must be provisional in nature. Thus, while some have argued that Chapter VII measures taken by the Council cannot include permanent solutions to disputes, there is nothing in the Charter to support this assertion, except in respect of measures under Article 40.

Some – including former Secretary-General Boutros Boutros-Ghali – have taken the view that peacekeeping is a provisional measure under Article 40.[41] This is debatable, as classic peacekeeping operations operate with the consent of the host state and do not require the exercise of any specific Chapter VII powers, and are best considered recommendations under Chapter VI.[42] Furthermore, as with sanctions, peacekeeping operations, which may be deployed for years or even decades, go beyond the temporal scope envisaged in Article 40.

A more difficult question is the basis for Chapter VII authorizations for peacekeepers to use force – which are common for today's peacekeeping operations[43] – and whether they fall under Article 40 or under Article 42. The better view is that, apart from the right of peacekeepers to use force in self-defence, any further authorizations to use force are made under Article 42, the only article in the

[40] *Prosecutor* v. *Tadić* (1995), para. 33.

[41] An Agenda for Peace, S/24111, 17 June 1992, para. 44; White (1996) 52–3; Nasu (2009).

[42] E.g., S/RES/1312, 31 July 2000; Higgins (1970) 25.

[43] Many missions include authorizations to use force to implement parts of the mandate, such as protection of civilians, e.g., S/RES/2502, 19 December 2019, para. 27. At times, peacekeeping operations are given an 'enforcement' mandate, to actively engage with armed groups, see the mandate of the UN Organization Stabilization Mission in the DRC (MONUSCO) through its Force Intervention Brigade in S/RES/2463, 29 March 2019, para. 29(d).

Charter which grants the Council the authority to decide on the use of force.[44]

5.1.4 The Timing of Measures under Article 40

The Charter envisaged the Council resorting to provisional measures as an initial response, a 'holding pattern', as it contemplated further action necessary under Articles 41 and 42. Article 40 would thus cease to be relevant once the Council had taken action under the latter articles.

In practice, however, measures under Articles 40, 41, and 42 may come at the same time or without any particular sequence.[45] For example, the Council may establish or renew the mandate of a peacekeeping operation with authorizations under Article 42, while also making demands to the parties to end hostilities under Article 40 in the same text.[46] Or it can demand under Article 40 that the parties lay down their arms while imposing sanctions under Article 41.[47]

5.2 Article 41: Sanctions and Other Measures Not Involving the Use of Armed Force

5.2.1 The Legal Framework

Article 41 of the Charter reads as follows:

The Security Council may decide what measures not involving the use of armed force are to be employed to give effect to its decisions, and it may call upon the Members of the United Nations to apply such measures. These may include complete or partial interruption of economic relations and of rail, sea, air, postal, telegraphic, radio, and other means of communication, and the severance of diplomatic relations.[48]

44 Higgins et al., (2017b) 27.38; for an opposing view, see An Agenda for Peace, S/24111, 17 June 1992, para. 43.

45 Goodrich et al. (1969) 303 recall that the inclusion of Article 40 at San Francisco 'was approved on the understanding that the Council was not required to follow any fixed order and could, if necessary, call for the immediate application of enforcement measures'.

46 E.g., S/RES/2502, 19 December 2019.

47 E.g., S/RES/2360, 21 June 2017.

48 For recent writings, see Johnstone (2016); Eckert (2016); Cockayne et al. (2018).

As opposed to the Council of the League of Nations, which did not possess the ability to impose binding enforcement measures,[49] when the Council determines 'the existence of any threat to the peace, breach of the peace, or act of aggression' under Article 39, it may impose 'measures not involving the use of armed force' under Article 41.

Article 41 contains an open-ended list of potential measures and thus does not contain any built-in limitation as to the measures that the Council can adopt.[50] The Council's resort to such measures was rare during the Cold War, but it has since utilized its power under Article 41 regularly in a variety of ways responding to different situations.[51]

As discussed in Chapter 1,[52] classifying Security Council action under rubrics such as 'legislative', 'executive', 'judicial', or 'quasi-judicial', terminology analogous to the branches of domestic legal systems and thus familiar to all lawyers, does not help one ascertain whether Security Council measures exceed the scope of its mandate.

This should be borne in mind when assessing the scope and legality of Council measures under Article 41. When the Security Council identifies a threat to the peace, breach of the peace, or act of aggression, it may decide upon 'measures not involving the use of armed force' to be carried out by, and binding on, the member states, to 'remedy a conflict or an imminent threat to international peace and security'.[53] This the Council can legally do as long as it does not violate the limits of its authority found in the UN Charter or, according to a widely held view, *jus cogens.*

In any event, the Security Council enjoys a wide discretion as to the measures not involving the use of force that it chooses to adopt and when. As stated by the Appeals Chamber of the ICTY,

> the Security Council has a broad discretion in deciding on the course of action and evaluating the appropriateness of the measures to be taken. The language of Article 39 is quite clear as to the channelling of the very broad and exceptional powers of the Security Council under Chapter VII through Articles 41 and 42. These two Articles leave to the Security Council such a wide choice ... Article 39 leaves the choice of means and

49 The Covenant of the League of Nations, Art. 16.
50 *Prosecutor* v. *Tadić* (1995), para. 35; *Prosecutor* v. *Kanyabashi,* para. 27.
51 Malone (2007); Eckert (2016) 413–27. 52 See Chapter 1.2.2.
53 *Prosecutor* v. *Kanyabashi,* para. 27.

their evaluation to the Security Council, which enjoys wide discretionary powers in this regard; and it could not have been otherwise, as such a choice involves political evaluation of highly complex and dynamic situations.[54]

The International Criminal Tribunal for Rwanda (ICTR) went further, declaring the Council's discretion on when to act and how as non-justiciable:

> By their very nature, however, such discretionary assessments are not justiciable since they involve the consideration of a number of social, political and circumstantial factors which cannot be weighed and balanced objectively by this Trial Chamber . . . [T]he question of whether or not the Security Council was justified in taking actions under Chapter VII when it did, is a matter to be determined by the Security Council itself.[55]

This is how Security Council measures under Article 41 are to be assessed. Their nature as 'legislative', 'judicial', or 'executive' is immaterial for that purpose.

The same can be said about classifying Security Council enforcement measures as temporary or permanent. As some of the examples that follow will demonstrate, the Council has imposed long-term, indefinite, and even seemingly permanent measures under Article 41, without challenge to their nature as such. With such minimal constraints, the Security Council has shown innovation and versatility in the measures short of use of force that it has adopted to date. The examples surveyed in this chapter demonstrate this very point.

5.2.2 Measures Not Involving the Use of Armed Force Adopted by the Council

The measures most frequently adopted by the Council under Article 41 are what are commonly termed 'sanctions'.[56] The Council nowadays applies 'targeted' sanctions (as opposed to the more sweeping or general ones that it applied in the early 1990s, which resulted in dire effects on entire populations)[57] such as an

54 *Prosecutor* v. *Tadić* (1995), paras. 31, 39; see also Chapter 3.

55 *Prosecutor* v. *Kanyabashi*, paras. 21–6; see also Schabas (2014) 178–9.

56 As of January 2022, there were fourteen Security Council imposed sanctions regimes. See www.un.org/securitycouncil/.

57 For a survey of the effects of 'general sanctions', see Reisman and Stevick (1998).

assets freeze and a travel ban on individuals and entities for a variety of reasons.[58] These may include human rights and international humanitarian law violations,[59] undermining peace and stability in a state,[60] and illicit trade in natural resources.[61]

Another measure often applied is an arms embargo, whether on a geographical region,[62] the territory of one state,[63] or against non-state actors within a state or region.[64] The embargo may be on all arms or just some, such as heavy weaponry.[65]

That the Council may impose sanctions as a measure short of the use of force is undisputed. But in one of the first cases after the Cold War, when the Council imposed an arms embargo on the whole territory of the former Yugoslavia during the war in the Balkans,[66] the Organization of the Islamic Conference (now the Organisation of Islamic Cooperation (OIC)) took the view that the arms embargo on 'Bosnia-Herzegovina is unjust, illegal and a major factor impeding the use of the right of self-defence' under Article 51.[67] Its member states, therefore, declared themselves unbound by the embargo and called upon other states to assist Bosnia and Herzegovina by supplying arms in violation of it.[68]

Interestingly, while calling the enforcement measure of the Council under Article 41 illegal as a violation of Article 51, the OIC also stated that if the Council did, in fact, intend to impose an arms embargo on Bosnia and Herzegovina, it could do so by passing another binding resolution for that purpose,[69] presumably

58 E.g., S/RES/2399, 30 January 2018, on the CAR; S/RES/2293, 23 June 2016, on the DRC.
59 E.g., S/RES/2399, 31 January 2018, on the CAR, para. 21(b)–(d), (f)–(g); S/RES/2293, 23 June 2016, on the DRC, para. 7(d)–(f), (i).
60 E.g., S/RES/2293, 23 June 2016, on the DRC, para. 7.
61 E.g., S/RES/2399, 30 January 2018, on the CAR, para. 21(e); S/RES/2293, 23 June 2016, on the DRC, para. 7(g).
62 E.g., S/RES/1556, 30 July 2004, on Darfur, paras. 7–8.
63 E.g., S/RES/2498, 15 November 2019, on Somalia, para. 6.
64 E.g., S/RES/2293, 23 June 2016, on the DRC, para. 2.
65 E.g., S/RES/2507, 31 January 2020, on the CAR, para. 1; S/RES/1718, 14 October 2006, on the DPRK, para. 8(a)(i)–(ii).
66 S/RES/713, 25 September 1991, para. 6.
67 Res No 6/22-P, 10–12 December 1994, preamble; Tzanakopoulos (2011) 126.
68 OIC, Res. No. 7/21-P, 25–29 April 1993, para. 12; Res. No. 6/22-P, 10–12 December 1994, para. 7; Tzanakopoulos (2011) 126. See also Security Council Report (2011) 6–7.
69 Res. No. 6/22-P, 10–12 December 1994, para. 7.

accepting that the Council's enforcement measures apply notwithstanding Article 51.

This last statement in itself puts in doubt the position that the Council's powers to adopt enforcement measures are subject to the inherent right of self-defence recognized by Article 51. It is also debatable whether the arms embargo infringed on the right of self-defence of Bosnia and Herzegovina as a matter of fact. More importantly, Article 51 itself makes clear that the exercise of the right of self-defence by a member state exists 'until the Security Council has taken measures necessary to maintain international peace and security'[70] and, in any event, does not limit the Council's actions under Chapter VII.[71]

The Security Council may ban trade in particular commodities that fuel a particular conflict or fund activities of certain actors such as blood diamonds,[72] timber,[73] or coal.[74] It may also sanction trade in commodities that are unrelated to the conflict but dear to leaders, such as luxury goods, in order to incentivize them to alter their behaviour.[75]

The most active sanctions regime has been that imposed by resolution 1267.[76] Once a regime sanctioning individuals and entities related to the Taliban and then also to al-Qaida, today it lists those with ties to al-Qaida and the Islamic State of Iraq and the Levant (ISIL).[77] There have been legal challenges to sanctions measures under this regime, discussed in Chapter 4, based on due process considerations.[78] The consequent political pressure resulted in the Council establishing a Focal Point, where sanctioned individuals and entities may file their requests for delisting to the Council,[79] and ultimately the Office of the Ombudsperson for the

[70] Charter, Art. 51.

[71] See also Randelzhofer and Nolte, 'Article 51' (2012) MN 65.

[72] E.g., S/RES/1306, 5 July 2000, on Sierra Leone, para. 1; S/RES/1385, 19 December 2001, on Sierra Leone, para. 3.

[73] E.g., S/RES/1478, 6 May 2003, on Liberia, para. 17.

[74] E.g., S/RES/2498, 15 November 2019, on Somalia, para. 23.

[75] E.g., S/RES/1718, 14 October 2006, on the DPRK, para. 8(a)(iii); for a thorough list of various targeted sanctions, see table 20.1 in Eckert (2016) 416–18.

[76] See the sanctions list available at www.un.org/securitycouncil/sanctions/1267/aq_sanctions_list.

[77] The Taliban is now covered by the Afghanistan sanctions regime, see S/RES/1988, 17 June 2011.

[78] Chapter 1. [79] S/RES/1730, 19 December 2006.

1267 sanctions regime.[80] These challenges have been expanded to other sanctions regimes in recent years.[81]

Aside from sanctions, the Council has acted and adopted a variety of coercive measures in different situations. Going beyond the recommendations it can make to states on settling their disputes peacefully under Chapter VI, the Security Council has adopted coercive measures to induce states to settle their disputes. For instance, in the last few days of the 1973 war between Israel, and Egypt and Syria, the Security Council imposed an obligation on the parties to immediately commence negotiations towards a peace agreement.[82] And in an attempt to push Eritrea to engage with Djibouti to resolve their boundary dispute, the Council imposed sanctions on Eritrean individuals hampering this effort.[83]

The Security Council has gone further than incentivizing, too. In the case of Bosnia and Herzegovina, the Council condemned the Bosnian Serbs for not accepting a proposed territorial settlement accepted by the other Bosnian parties and imposed sanctions on them 'as a means towards the end of producing a negotiated settlement to the conflict'.[84] In the case of Kosovo in 1999, it decided to make obligatory 'principles on the political solution to the Kosovo crisis' adopted by the Group of Eight (G8) foreign ministers, containing content similar to that of the Rambouillet Agreement, which the Federal Republic of Yugoslavia (FRY) had refused to sign.[85] In this case and others, the Security Council also took it upon itself to administer the sovereign territory of a state temporarily, and to carry out the different functions of sovereign governments.[86]

In 2014, a draft resolution containing binding 'parameters' for the final settlement of the Israel–Palestine issue was put to a vote.[87] The resolution failed as it received only eight affirmative votes. It is

[80] S/RES/1904, 17 December 2009; S/RES/1989, 17 June 2011; S/RES/2368, 27 June 2018.
[81] See Cockayne et al. (2018), particularly Annex I.
[82] S/RES/338, 22 October 1973, para. 2.
[83] S/RES/1907, 23 December 2009, para. 15(c), with S/RES/1862, 14 January 2009.
[84] S/RES/943, 23 September 1994; Krisch, 'Introduction to Chapter VII: The General Framework' (2012) MN 29.
[85] S/RES/1244, 10 June 1999, para. 1, Annexes 1–2.
[86] S/RES/1244, 10 June 1999, on Kosovo; S/RES/1272, 25 October 1999, on East Timor.
[87] S/2014/916, 30 December 2014, para. 2.

important to note, however, that none of the fifteen Council members publicly expressed doubt as to the ability of the Council to dictate to the parties a binding framework for a permanent peace agreement.[88]

In other contexts, the Council adopted measures to settle the underlying dispute between states with finality. Some of these disputes went to issues at the core of state sovereignty such as exercising jurisdiction or boundary disputes. For instance, the Security Council utilized its enforcement powers to settle a dispute between member states in 1992, after two Libyan officials were identified as suspects in the downing of Pan Am flight 103 over Lockerbie, United Kingdom, which resulted in the death of all 243 passengers and 16 crew members, as well as 11 civilians on the ground. Libya refused to adhere to requests from the United Kingdom and the United States demanding extradition of the accused, relying on its obligations under the Montreal Convention of 23 September 1971 for the Suppression of Unlawful Acts against the Safety of Civil Aviation.[89] The Security Council then adopted a binding resolution, asserting its authority under Article 41, deciding that Libya must extradite the individuals.[90] The resolution also imposed a set of sanctions on Libya, including a flight ban, unless a flight was approved on humanitarian grounds by the Security Council, an arms embargo, and an assets freeze.[91]

Libya refused, however, to extradite the two individuals. After a few years of pushback against the sanctions from African and Arab states, due in part to the grave humanitarian situation in Libya, the Organisation of African Unity (OAU, the predecessor of the AU) issued an ultimatum to the Council, when it decided in June 1998 that if the United Kingdom and the United States refused to allow the suspects to be tried in a third country – to which Libya was willing to agree – its members would cease to comply with the sanctions regime.[92] It also decided 'on moral and religious grounds' that, with immediate effect, it would not comply with the sanctions imposed 'related to religious obligations, providing humanitarian emergencies or fulfilling OAU statutory obligations'.[93] In the end, the two permanent members agreed to the trial of the

[88] S/PV.7354, 30 December 2014.
[89] See, generally, *Lockerbie* Preliminary Objections.
[90] S/RES/748, 31 March 1992, para. 1.
[91] Ibid., paras. 4–5; S/RES/883, 11 November 1993, para. 3.
[92] AHG/Dec.127 (XXXIV), 8–10 June 1998, para. 2.
[93] Ibid., para. 3.

suspects before a Scottish court in The Netherlands, and the sanctions were lifted when the suspects were produced by Libya.[94]

The Security Council settled certain disputes with finality in the aftermath of the Gulf War in 1990–1991, after the establishment by the Secretary-General of a commission to demarcate the land and maritime boundary between Iraq and Kuwait, in accordance with resolution 687.[95] Initially, Iraq refused to accept the conclusions of the Commission, stating that 'the Security Council has imposed a specific position with regard to the Iraqi–Kuwaiti boundary, whereas the custom in law is that boundary questions are left to an agreement between States, because this is the sole basis that can guarantee the principle of stability in boundaries'.[96] In response, the Security Council affirmed that the decisions of the Commission were final,[97] demanded that both parties respect the boundary as demarcated by the Commission,[98] and conveyed its intention to ensure the inviolability of the boundary,[99] presumably by taking further enforcement action if needed. Ultimately, that proved unnecessary as Iraq accepted the boundary as determined by the Commission, and did so in expressing its desire 'for respect for the Charter of the United Nations and international law, in keeping with its commitment to comply fully with all relevant resolutions of the United Nations Security Council'.[100] According to some authors, determining the permanent boundary was *ultra vires* as a violation of the sovereign equality of states.[101] Some support for this may be found in the disclaimer made by the Council itself at the time, that, by enforcing the conclusions of the Commission, it was not reallocating territorial rights but rather carrying out a 'technical exercise' of marking the boundary, in accordance with Agreed Minutes from 1963, determining the boundary.[102] Nevertheless, this explanation seems quite strained considering that Iraq had not accepted the 1963 Agreed Minutes as binding.[103]

Also in resolution 687, the Security Council determined that Iraq was 'liable under international law for any direct loss, damage – including environmental damage and the depletion of natural resources – or

[94] S/RES/1192, 27 August 1998, para. 8. [95] S/RES/687, 3 April 1991, para 3.
[96] S/22558, 2 May 1991, p. 5. [97] S/RES/833, 27 May 1993, para 4.
[98] Ibid., para. 5. [99] Ibid., para. 6.
[100] S/1994/1288, 14 November 1994, p. 2. [101] De Wet (2004) 362–66.
[102] S/RES/83, 27 May 1993, preamble; de Wet (2004) 365.
[103] See the Report of the Commission in S/25811, 23 May 1991; de Wet (2004) 364; Johnstone (2016) 778; Mendelson and Hulton (1993) 144–50, 178–85, 192–3.

injury to foreign Governments, nationals and corporations as a result of its unlawful invasion and occupation of Kuwait'.[104] It then decided to establish a compensation fund and a compensation commission for that purpose.[105] Funded by proceeds of Iraqi oil sales,[106] the Commission has paid a total of about USD 52.4 billion to individuals and corporations for death, injury, loss of or damage to property, commercial claims, and claims for environmental damage.[107]

The Security Council has also utilized its enforcement powers to bypass the requirement of state consent to be bound (or unbound) by treaties, another fundamental principle underpinning international law.[108]

Despite the DPRK's express will to renounce and not be bound by the NPT, the Security Council demanded that it retract its announcement of withdrawal and implement the NPT and the International Atomic Energy Agency (IAEA) safeguards agreement.[109]

After the assassination of former Lebanese Prime Minister Rafik Hariri along with twenty-two other casualties, the Security Council requested that the Secretary-General negotiate an agreement to establish a tribunal to adjudicate this and related events.[110] The agreement was signed by the Secretary-General and the Lebanese government, but four months later, Lebanese Prime Minister Fouad Siniora informed the Secretary-General that while the agreement enjoyed majority support in the parliament, due to internal political processes Lebanon would not be able to ratify the agreement.[111] He then asked that the Security Council establish the tribunal through a binding decision.[112] Recognizing that terrorist acts constitute a threat to international peace and security, the Council then adopted resolution 1757 (2007), deciding that the provisions of the document annexed to the resolution (the agreement on the establishment of the Special Tribunal for Lebanon) would enter into force eleven days later.[113]

Thus, the Council saw fit to intervene in the domestic affairs of Lebanon and bring into force the provisions of a treaty, circumventing the requirement of Lebanese consent to be bound by ratification of

[104] S/RES/687, 3 April 1991, para. 16. [105] Ibid., para. 18.
[106] S/RES/1483, para. 21; see also the United Nations Compensation Commission (UNCC) website, available at https://uncc.ch/home.
[107] UNCC, https://uncc.ch/home. [108] Wood (2011).
[109] S/RES/1718, 14 October 2006; S/RES/1874, 12 June 2009.
[110] S/RES/1664, 29 March 2006. [111] S/2007/281, 15 May 2007. [112] Ibid.
[113] S/RES/1757, 30 May 2007, para. 1; see Wood (2011) 250; Sthoeger (2016) 513–14.

the Treaty. This is a prime example of how measures the Council adopts under Chapter VII in order to maintain international peace and security may override any considerations of non-intervention, as foreseen under Article 2(7) of the UN Charter.

More generally, the Council has taken several enforcement measures relating to international criminal law. It has established commissions of inquiry to assess individual responsibility for violations of international criminal law.[114] It established the ICTY as well as the ICTR, both of which operated for more than two decades, and handed down long prison sentences.[115] The ICTY Appeals Chamber explained that, in doing so, the Council was exercising 'its own principal function of maintenance of peace and security'.[116] When the ICTY and the ICTR were established, one or two Council members questioned the Council's authority to establish a criminal tribunal, but ultimately they voted to establish the tribunals, and member states have not challenged the legality of the measures since.[117]

The Security Council established the Residual Mechanism for the ICTY and the ICTR to deal with outstanding issues like prosecuting remaining fugitives and other issues that may arise as the convicted serve their sentences.[118] While not necessarily a permanent institution, the Residual Mechanism will presumably function for many years. The territorial administrations established by the Council in Timor-Leste and Kosovo established judicial bodies to try perpetrators of war crimes as well.[119]

The Council has twice referred situations to the ICC, acting in accordance with a provision in the Rome Statute and granting the Court jurisdiction in situations in which it would otherwise not be able to exercise it.[120] On these occasions, and in other resolutions,

114 E.g., S/RES/1564, 18 September 2004, on Sudan, para. 12; S/RES/2235, 7 August 2015, para. 5 with S/RES/2118, 27 September 2013, on Syria; S/RES/2127, 5 December 2013, on the CAR, para. 24; the Security Council may also establish such commissions under Article 34 of the UN Charter.

115 S/RES/827, 25 May 1993 establishing the ICTY; S/RES/955, 8 November 1994, establishing the ICTR.

116 *Prosecutor* v. *Tadić* (1995), para. 38.

117 S/PV.3217, 25 May 1993, in which resolution 827 was adopted unanimously, see statement of China, p. 33; S/25540, 6 April 1993 from Brazil on the formation of the *ad hoc* tribunals; see also Sthoeger (2016) 507.

118 S/RES/1966, 22 December 2010; Sthoeger (2016) 512.

119 Schabas (2014) 186.

120 S/RES/1593, 31 March 2005, on Sudan; S/RES/1970, 26 February 2011, on Libya.

the Council adopted a clause excluding personnel from a state not party to the Rome Statute, acting under authorization of the Council, from the jurisdiction of the ICC.[121] These clauses arguably contradict the language of the Rome Statute, by discriminating between parties to the same conflict.[122]

The Security Council has also adopted measures imposing legal obligations on states with respect to non-state actors in the field of terrorism and proliferation of weapons of mass destruction. A few days after the events of 11 September 2001, the Security Council adopted resolution 1373, obliging states to refrain from supporting terrorist acts, to criminalize participation in and financing of terrorist acts, and to freeze assets relating to terrorist activities, among other things.[123] The regime imposes strict reporting requirements on states, and a highly active subsidiary body, the Counterterrorism Committee, was established in order to monitor compliance with the regime and assist states in building up their capacities.

Over the years, the Council has added to these obligations by adopting additional measures, for example relating to incitement to commit terrorist acts.[124] The Council has also adopted measures imposing obligations on states with respect to 'foreign terrorist fighters', that is, individuals travelling to foreign countries to participate in terrorist activities.[125] States are now obliged to deny and criminalize such travel through their territory or assistance to it within their domestic systems.[126] The Council added to this regime, obligating states to take measures against foreign terrorist fighters returning to their country of origin and their families.[127]

5.2.3 What Are the Limits of Article 41?

There are several conclusions that can be drawn as to the nature of Council measures short of the use of force and their legal boundaries.

121 Resolution 1593, 31 March 2005; Resolution 1970, 26 February 2011; S/RES/1422, 12 July 2002; S/RES/1483, 22 May 2003.

122 Sthoeger (2016) 517–18, 522. For more on the binding nature of these measures, see Chapter 2.

123 S/RES/1373, 28 September 2001.

124 S/RES/1624, 14 September 2005.

125 S/RES/2178, 24 September 2014.

126 Ibid.

127 S/RES/2396, 21 December 2017.

First, Council decisions that have been qualified as 'legislative', generally applicable and not related to any specific situation, while indefinite in time, have led to much discussion by writers about the Council's prerogatives. As has already been explained,[128] such decisions may be needed to address peace and security challenges the world is facing today and there is nothing in the Charter that imposes a limited case-by-case approach to meet these challenges.[129] When and in what context the Council may act in this way depends on whether the matter in question has been determined to be a threat to the peace, breach of the peace, or act of aggression, and it is not unreasonable for the Council to identify terrorism, for example, as a constant threat to the peace, global in nature and unrelated to one specific country or region.[130]

In fact, and although some have at times expressed the general view that it is not for the Council to act as a 'world legislator',[131] states have not challenged the legality of the Council's 'legislative' resolutions and the requirements therein, though they have often complained about the burdens they impose.[132] For example, during the negotiations over resolution 2396 (2017) on returning foreign terrorist fighters, the disagreements that arose revolved around the technological requirements and the consequent financial burden that deploying sophisticated border controls imposed on developing countries in order to meet their obligations under the resolution, as well as the exact terms for criminalizing certain forms of assistance to foreign terrorist fighters.[133] Whether or not the Council can legally impose such obligations was not raised but, rather, assumed.

Such 'regulatory' measures are still rare due to the political limits imposed by the member states. For example, just as in the case of anti-terrorism 'legislation' by the Council, the controversy surrounding Council action on environmental issues such as climate

[128] See Chapter 1. [129] See also Johnstone (2016) 777. [130] Ibid.

[131] Eg., S/PV.5059, 19 October 2004, statement of Brazil, p. 11; S/PV.5059 (Resumption 1), 19 October 2004, statement of Costa Rica, p. 20; Conforti and Focarelli (2016) 263–4.

[132] See, for example, S/PV.8018, 3 August 2018, statement of Tayé-Brook Zerihoun, Assistant Secretary-General for Political Affairs, p. 3; statement of the UK, p. 4.

[133] See What's in Blue, Foreign Terrorist Fighters: Resolution, 20 December 2017, available at www.whatsinblue.org/2017/12/foreign-terrorist-fighters-resolution.php.

change (and assuming a link between climate change and peace and security can be established) concerns what the Council *can* or *should* do as a matter of policy, not whether it *can legally act.*

Second, the Council's authority to settle disputes can be based on its powers under Chapter VII and does not need to be based on its peaceful settlement of disputes functions under Chapter VI. When the Council determines that a dispute is a threat to the peace, breach of the peace, or act of aggression, it can take measures to settle that dispute under Article 41 and is not limited to its recommendatory powers under Chapter VI.

States have not challenged the Council's authority to settle disputes without state consent, whether by making legal determinations or by adopting measures under Chapter VII. Quite the opposite, the establishment of the ICTY and the ICTR is an example of the Council exercising its functions by establishing a criminal court, a subsidiary organ conclusively determining criminal liability. As the ICTY has said, its establishment

> does not signify . . . that the Security Council has delegated to it some of its own functions or the exercise of some of its own powers. Nor does it mean, in reverse, that the Security Council was usurping for itself part of a judicial function which does not belong to it but to other organs of the United Nations according to the Charter.[134]

The ICTY then noted that the Council opted to create a 'judicial organ in the form of an international criminal tribunal as an instrument for the exercise of its own principal function of maintenance of peace and security'.[135] This, in essence, is reflective of the unique position of the Council in the international system: measures such as establishing a criminal tribunal are within the powers of the Security Council under Article 41 to address situations that trigger Chapter VII action, and are entirely independent of whether the Council is a judicial body and enjoys adjudicative functions.[136]

[134] *Prosecutor* v. *Tadić* (1995), para. 38; see also *Effect of Awards* Advisory Opinion, at pp. 61–2.

[135] *Prosecutor* v. *Tadić* (1995), para. 38.

[136] *Prosecutor* v. *Kanyabashi*, para. 27. In *Kanyabashi*, the Tribunal also pointed out that, similarly, the Council may take enforcement measures to address human rights violations, even though it is not the UN organ entrusted with competence with respect to human rights as such, see paras. 28–9.

That is also why, in theory, the Security Council could utilize its powers under Article 41 to obligate two states to settle a dispute that threatens international peace and security before the ICJ, even though it can only recommend such action under Chapter VI. The Council could do so not because it has a judicial function but because it is a measure to maintain international peace and security under Chapter VII.[137]

The Council is not bound to respect the statutes of other courts and tribunals, as its relationship with the ICC demonstrates. While the ICC Statute lays down the confines of referrals and deferrals, if the Council steps outside of these boundaries in a binding resolution acting under Article 41, as it arguably has when it referred the situations in Darfur and Libya to the Court by excluding certain nationals from the Court's jurisdiction, as UN members, states party to the Rome Statute are still legally obligated to comply with the Council's decision, notwithstanding their obligations under the Statute.[138]

Third, several of the decisions discussed here demonstrate that the Security Council has, in practice, imposed long-term measures and legally binding solutions, and has made permanent determinations to settle disputes. There is nothing in the UN Charter that negates this practice. Only Article 40 speaks of 'provisional measures'. Article 41 does not contain a temporal element, and, whether it was envisaged by the drafters or not, it allows the Council to take measures to maintain international peace and security, temporary or permanent if need be.

It is important to stress in this regard that while some would equate Council powers with 'police powers',[139] responding to unfolding events and putting out fires as it were, that is not what the UN Charter says. What the Charter does grant the Council are extensive powers, but confined to the cases identified in Article 39.

Some have challenged the ability of the Council to adopt permanent measures. In his dissenting opinion in the *Namibia* Advisory Opinion, Judge Fitzmaurice opined: '*Even when acting under Chapter VII of the Charter itself*, the Security Council has no power to abrogate or alter territorial rights, whether of sovereignty or administration.'[140]

[137] See Chapter 8. [138] See Chapter 2.
[139] See, for example, Krisch, 'Introduction to Chapter VII' (2012).
[140] *Namibia* Advisory Opinion, p. 294, para. 115.

Accordingly, he concluded that the Security Council did not have the power to revoke South Africa's Mandate.[141] However, the majority reached the opposite conclusion, accepting the Council's ability to make binding decisions of a permanent nature over the legality of the administration of a territory.

In the case of the Iraq–Kuwait boundary dispute, it seems that the Council's decisions and Iraq's acceptance of them confirm that very conclusion with respect to sovereignty over territory itself. Ultimately, neither Iraq nor any other country challenged the legality of the Security Council's decision. The Council's attempt to present its actions as a 'technical exercise' in the preamble to its decision speaks to the political sensitivities over such actions, but does not change their legal nature.[142]

The Security Council failed to adopt a resolution on parameters for the final peace agreement between Israel and Palestine. Here, at most some Council members expressed their view as to the futility of such action for bringing about peace, not that such a resolution would have been *ultra vires.*[143]

Fourth, some writers find that there can be legal justification for states deciding not to comply with binding measures, such as sanctions regimes.[144] Certainly in the case of the arms embargo on the former Yugoslavia, some states made legal arguments to that effect.[145] With respect to the 1267 sanctions regime, courts appear to have come close to reaching the same conclusion.[146]

The Security Council itself has expressed 'the need to ensure that sanctions are carefully targeted in support of clear objectives and designed carefully so as to minimize possible adverse consequences',[147] as well as its commitment 'to ensuring that fair and clear procedures exist for placing individuals and entities on sanctions lists and for

141 Ibid., p. 295, para. 117.

142 De Wet has argued that the Council's decision provided for a provisional boundary that was made permanent based on the agreement of the parties; thus they would be free to alter the boundary if they so choose, see de Wet (2004) 367. However, that is true of any boundary and, presumably, at the very least implicit with respect to a boundary determined by the Security Council itself.

143 S/PV.7354, 30 December 2014, statement of the USA, p. 3, statement of Australia, p. 7.

144 Tzanakopoulos (2011). 145 See Chapter 4, Section 4.4.

146 *Kadi* v. *Council* (2008).

147 S/PRST/2012/1, 19 January 2012; S/PRST/2011/10, 29 June 2011; S/RES/1325, 31 October 2000, para. 16.

removing them'.[148] These and similar statements have been said to acknowledge the legal confines of the Council's measures.[149] Nevertheless, these are not expressions of conditions for the legality of a particular measure; put differently, states cannot quote the absence of such guarantees, in their view, as a legal justification under international law for not complying with binding Security Council measures.

Accordingly, there are no *legal* justifications for non-compliance with binding Security Council measures under Article 41 in those cases, as the analysis of the limits imposed on Security Council actions, including under Article 41, demonstrates.[150] Rather, the Security Council's adaptation of its binding measures in order to meet the demands of states threatening non-compliance concerns policy, legitimacy, and effectiveness.

When the Security Council shifted from wide-ranging sanctions to targeted sanctions in the mid-1990s, it did so because of the realization that such measures were causing significant hardships – and not necessarily for the decision-makers that were in a position to adjust their policies to alleviate these hardships, thus proving to be of little benefit in terms of effectiveness.[151] The permanent members made that evident when they published a policy paper reflective of this view.[152]

But this policy shift was not a legal imperative any more than are other measures that the Council has taken over time to ease the humanitarian impact of sanctions. These are rather reflective of policy decisions in an attempt to avoid certain consequences that caused harm and contributed little to the effective execution of the Council's mandate. When the Security Council lifted sanctions over Libya after two of its permanent members accepted the Libyan proposal on trying the two individuals suspected of being responsible for the Lockerbie incident, it did so because of political pressure and its dependency on member states to enforce its decisions.[153]

[148] S/PRST/2012/1, 19 January 2012; S/RES/1730, 19 December 2006.

[149] Krisch, 'Introduction to Chapter VII' (2012) MN 43; Krisch, 'Article 41' (2012) MN 19–23.

[150] See Chapter 4 and earlier in this chapter.

[151] On this point, see, for example, S/PV.8018, 3 August 2018, statement of Ethiopia, p. 7, statement of Kazakhstan, p. 5, statement of France, p. 12.

[152] See S/1995/300, 13 April 1995; see also Reisman and Stevick (1998) 126–7.

[153] While some states argued before the Security Council that Libya had abided by its international commitments, they refrained from explicitly calling the measures imposed by the Council illegal. See S/PV.3864, 20 March 1998.

The same goes for the establishment of the Office of the Ombudsperson for the 1267 sanctions regime in response to pressure from member states facing domestic and regional challenges over compliance with due process requirements. The legal obligation of member states under international law was that of compliance with measures imposed by the Council, regardless of domestic or other international obligations, under Article 103 of the UN Charter.[154] Indeed, even the CJEU in the *Kadi* case did not dispute the existence of such an obligation imposed on members outside of European law, choosing instead to focus exclusively on the position under EU law.[155] It acted like a court in a dualist legal system where cases may be decided based on domestic law, notwithstanding existing international obligations and without prejudice to them.[156] And while the jurisprudence of the ECtHR – or the Canadian courts in *Abdelrazik*[157] – has stretched this basic legal understanding to its limit by way of interpretation of the relevant resolutions, it has not challenged the basic structure of the UN system.[158]

Member states' legal views, including those advocating for expanding due process rights afforded to individuals sanctioned by the Council, reflect this understanding. The Non-Aligned Movement (NAM) has regularly criticized the Council's practice in terms of when and how it imposes sanctions, but has not denied their binding nature.[159] The members of 'the Group of Like-Minded States on Targeted Sanctions'[160] remain 'strongly committed' to the sanctions measures imposed by the Council, while pushing for expanding the Office of the Ombudsperson in order to further procedural guarantees.[161] They argue that effective implementation will be hindered, for 'as long as national and regional courts consider that

[154] See Chapter 1; see also Johnstone (2016) 777.

[155] '[A]ny judgment given by the Community judicature deciding that a Community measure intended to give effect to such a resolution is contrary to a higher rule of law in the Community legal order would not entail any challenge to the primacy of that resolution in international law', see *Kadi* v. *Council* (2008), para. 288; Lenaerts (2014) 711.

[156] See, for example, *Medellín* v. *Texas*, opinion of Justice Roberts.

[157] *Abdelrazik* v. *Canada*.

[158] See Chapter 1.

[159] See, for example, the Final Document of the 17th Summit of Heads of State and Government of the Non-Aligned Movement, 17–18 September 2016, para. 98.5.

[160] Austria, Belgium, Chile, Costa Rica, Denmark, Finland, Germany, Liechtenstein, the Netherlands, Norway, Sweden, and Switzerland.

[161] S/2018/1094, 11 December 2018, pp. 1, 3.

United Nations sanctions imposed on individuals fall short of minimum standards of due process, national authorities may find themselves legally unable to implement those sanctions fully at the national level'.[162] While the argument here refers to legal challenges on the *domestic* level, there is no challenge to the binding nature of Council measures under international law.

Implementing more due process considerations in the 1267 sanctions regime was a result of a political process achieved 'through a pattern of defiance, threats, and ultimately negotiation between the Security Council and States, pushed on by their courts, primarily, and also by public opinion or relevant engaged interest groups'.[163] These cases demonstrate the most important check or limit on the powers of the Security Council, including measures under Article 41, which is the Council's dependency on member states to carry out its decisions. As stated in the Council by the United Kingdom, '[f]or such measures to be truly effective, it is absolutely essential that all States implement them fully. It is not good enough just for the majority of countries to do so. A chain is only as strong as its weakest link'.[164] Aware of this reality, the Council's most (politically) controversial measures have been taken in light of extreme security and political realities. But when Council practice is without perceived legitimacy, member states will not carry out the measures, notwithstanding their legal obligations. Without compliance, the Security Council will be ineffective. This, practice has shown, is an effective restraint on the powers of the Security Council.[165]

[162] Ibid.; see also S/2017/534, 23 June 2017, containing the report of the assessment of the High-Level Review of United Nations Sanctions initiated by Australia.
[163] Tzanakopoulos (2016) 6; Cockayne et al. (2018).
[164] S/PV.8018, 3 August 2018, statement of the UK, p. 4.
[165] See also Chapter 4.

6

The Security Council and the Use of Force

In Chapter 9 we consider, in general terms, the contribution of the Security Council to the development of international law. Here we focus specifically on the Council's contribution to the international law on the use of force (the *jus ad bellum*),[1] an area of international law that is central to the Security Council's role in the maintenance of international peace and security and the collective security system of the UN.[2]

The chapter addresses, first, the general state of the rules of international law on the use of force. It then outlines the rules themselves. This is followed by sections relating directly to the Security Council: the prohibition of the use of force; use of force by or authorized by the Council; the Council and the right of self-defence; and the Council and 'humanitarian intervention' and 'responsibility to protect'. The chapter does not address the use of force during peacekeeping operations, which is a quite different matter.[3]

6.1 The Current State of International Law on the Use of Force

We begin with a few words on the general state of the law on the use of force. As throughout this book, we try to confine ourselves to law

[1] For recent writings in the field, see Wood (2013); Corten (2014); Weller (2015); Dinstein (2017); Wood (2017a); Gray (2018); Ruys et al. (2018); Henderson (2018); ILA (2018); Wood (2020).

[2] Higgins (1963) 167–239; Franck (2002); Matheson (2006) 131–66; Lowe et al. (2008); Zacklin (2010); Higgins (2016) 13–16; Wood (2019).

[3] Sheeran (2015).

and not stray into policy or discuss such nebulous matters as 'legitimacy', still less notions derived from international relations theory or medieval theology. Nor is there any need to consider whether the rules of international law on the use of force are dead;[4] or whether there is some fundamental gulf between Americans, Europeans, or others on this branch of international law. The answer is 'no' to both of these questions.

But the fact that such questions are asked doubtless reflects concerns about the many serious breaches of the *jus ad bellum* both during and after the Cold War. It also reflects growing concern at failures to respond adequately to modern security threats (such as terrorism and weapons of mass destruction) and man-made humanitarian catastrophes (such as Rwanda, Darfur, Syria, and Yemen). Such concerns have led some to push the boundaries of the law, with notions such as implied or *ex post facto* authorization by the Security Council and preemptive (or preventive) use of force. In part this reflects a degree of frustration with existing rules and the Charter framework for collective security, with the Security Council at its heart. Such frustration may sometimes be based on lack of understanding. A better grasp of existing rules, and the potential of the Security Council, could help avoid unilateralism or a worldview which sees the rules of international law on the use of force as obsolete.

Recourse to armed force by the United Kingdom over the years illustrates some key issues. The Security Council was engaged in all these cases. Kosovo in 1999 raised a major issue of principle,[5] as did Syria from 2013 onwards:[6] Is there a right of humanitarian intervention (or, as the British government put it more narrowly, an exceptional right to use force to avert an overwhelming humanitarian catastrophe)? The intervention in Afghanistan in 2001[7] also raised an important issue, the right of self-defence against attacks

[4] Franck (1970). [5] Franchini and Tzanakopoulos (2018).

[6] Lagerwall (2018); UK Prime Minister's Office, 'Chemical Weapon Use by Syrian Regime: UK Government Legal Position', policy paper (29 August 2013), 84 *BYIL* (2013) 806–7 'Syria Action – UK Government Legal Position', policy paper (14 April 2018), available at www.gov.uk/government/publications/syria-action-uk-government-legal-position/syria-action-uk-government-legal-position. The UK and Russian statements in the Council on 14 April 2018 are revealing (S/PV.8233, 14 April 2018).

[7] Byers (2018).

by non-state actors. Iraq in 2003, on the other hand, while politically and indeed among lawyers the most controversial, properly understood raised no great issue of principle: the legality of the use of force in March 2003 turned solely on whether or not it had been authorized by the Security Council.[8] No one disputes that the Council can authorize the use of force; the question was whether it had done so. That turned on the interpretation of a series of Security Council resolutions.[9] The majority view was that the Council had not done so.[10]

It has sometimes been asked whether the existing rules of international law on the use of force are adequate to meet current threats, especially from terrorist groups and weapons of mass destruction. The General Assembly, meeting at the level of heads of state and government, answered this question in the 2005 World Summit Outcome. The heads of state and government reaffirmed 'that the relevant provisions of the Charter are sufficient to address the full range of threats to international peace and security. We further reaffirm the authority of the Security Council to mandate coercive action to maintain and restore international peace and security. We stress the importance of acting in accordance with the purposes and principles of the Charter.'[11] In this, they were following similar statements by the UN Secretary-General in his report *In Larger Freedom*[12] and the High-Level Panel in its report *A More Secure World.*[13] Of course, in a sense they did not have much choice; it would have been unrealistic to think of

[8] Other arguments hinted at occasionally, such as self-defence or an 'unreasonable veto', had no merit.

[9] Weller (2018).

[10] This is also the position that one of the authors took while still legal adviser to the UK Foreign and Commonwealth Office (FCO), as is clear from his evidence to the Chilcot Inquiry: *The Report of the Iraq Inquiry*, 6 July 2016 (Volumes I–XII), available at www.gov.uk/government/publications/the-report-of-the-iraq-inquiry; Chilcot Inquiry, Statement of Sir Michael Wood, para. 15, available at https://webarchive.nationalarchives.gov.uk/20171123122659tf_/http://www.iraqinquiry.org.uk/the-evidence/witness-statements/. See also Wood (2015) 657–8; Wood (2016a). For a detailed account that reaches the same conclusion, see Murphy (2004).

[11] UN General Assembly resolution 60/1, 16 September 2005 (World Summit Outcome), para. 79.

[12] Report of the Secretary-General, *In Larger Freedom: Towards Development, Security and Human Rights for All*, A/59/2005, 21 March 2005.

[13] The Secretary-General's High-Level Panel Report on Threats, Challenges and Change, *A More Secure World: Our Shared Responsibility*, A/59/565, 2 December 2004, in particular at para. 198.

amending the relevant provisions of the Charter. But they were fully justified in what they said then as they are today. Properly interpreted and applied, the rules on the use of force in the Charter and in customary international law are flexible enough to meet the new challenges, given the political will. And they are in any event better than proposals for new rules that would excessively relax existing constraints and increase the risk of international anarchy.

It is important to ensure that the rules of international law on the use of force, and the potential of the Council, are properly understood. This is no easy task when there remain important differences of views, as is evident from the General Assembly debate on the report *In Larger Freedom* in April 2005,[14] the ICJ's pronouncements in the *Wall* and the *Democratic Republic of the Congo* v. *Uganda* cases, and much of the current writing in the field.

Whatever one may think of particular uses of force, or of certain policy documents or statements, states generally remain alert to the importance of upholding the rules of international law on the use of force. And there remains a broad consensus among states on what the rules are (except on certain specific points such as the right of anticipatory self-defence, and self-defence against non-state actors[15]). The 2018 International Law Association (ILA) *Final Report on Aggression and the Use of Force* shows that much common ground can be reached among individual experts in the field.[16]

The overall conclusion is that the contemporary rules of international law on the use of force, and in particular those on self-defence and Security Council authorization, properly understood, are adequate to address current threats. Efforts to radically change these rules are neither desirable nor likely to succeed. The rules in this field develop case-by-case, including through the practice of the Security Council. Whatever else may have changed on 11 September 2001, international law did not.

6.2 The Rules of International Law on the Use of Force

The rules of international law on the use of force are relatively easy to state; their application to particular situations is another matter.

14 A/59/2005, 21 March 2005, paras. 122–3.
15 For a range of views, see O'Connell et al. (2018).
16 ILA (2018); Lubell and Wood (2019).

The rules are to be found in the Charter of the UN and customary international law. The Charter contains, among the Principles of the UN, a general prohibition on the threat or use of force (Article 2, paragraph 4). The Charter refers to two not unrelated circumstances in which the prohibition does not apply: *first*, when forcible measures are taken or authorized by the Security Council, acting under Chapter VII of the Charter; and *second*, when force is used in self-defence, recognized by Article 51 of the Charter. A possible, but controversial third justification, not mentioned in the Charter and presumably to be found, if at all, in customary international law, could be an exceptional right (perhaps akin to necessity in domestic law) to use force to avert an overwhelming humanitarian catastrophe. The use of force in retaliation (as punishment, revenge, or reprisal) is not legal; such terms are best avoided, even in political rhetoric. Intervention with the consent of the territorial state (sometimes called 'intervention by invitation' or 'military assistance on request') is not a true exception to the prohibition, being based upon consent. In practice, it may nevertheless give rise to difficult legal questions.[17]

It is not helpful when some commentators seek to merge the exceptions. One author refers to Article 51½ and appears to suggest that self-defence 'authorized' by the Security Council is wider than Article 51 self-defence.[18] Likewise, advancing the Charter's Purposes, or taking account of or even 'enforcing' Security Council resolutions which do not themselves authorize the use of force cannot be a basis for a unilateral right to use force. 'Implicit' authorization is unlikely to carry weight: to suggest that the Security Council 'can and has implicitly recognized the propriety of using force', quite apart from being a highly subjective conclusion, has no support in practice. Some have suggested that this was the case over Kosovo because the Council failed to adopt a Russian draft resolution condemning the NATO action as unlawful.[19]

6.3 The Security Council and the Use of Force

Before turning to the Security Council's contribution to the law and practice on the use of force, there is one methodological

[17] These are currently under study by an ILA Use of Force Committee established in 2019. See also de Wet (2020).

[18] Stahn (2003). [19] Henkin (1999) 827; Franck (2002) 135–73.

point to be made. It is essentially the point made by Rosalyn Higgins when she said that 'the fact that voting patterns to some extent conform to political pressures rather than to legal beliefs must be recognized'.[20] The same is true of what the Council and states say and do, and perhaps especially what they do not say and do not do. It may sometimes even be questionable whether a positive decision of the Council, for example to condemn some action, means that the action is contrary to international law. All circumstances need to be taken into consideration. Certainly, the fact that the Council does not condemn a use of force cannot normally be taken as evidence that the Council or states consider it lawful. Yet this is how one author seemed to read the Council in his Lauterpacht lectures on *Recourse to Force*.[21] As a consequence, he tended to reach overly generous conclusions about the permissible use of force.[22]

6.3.1 Prohibition of the Use of Force

Article 2, paragraph 4 of the Charter provides that:

> All Members shall refrain in their international relations from the threat or use of force against the territorial integrity or political independence of any state, or in any other manner inconsistent with the Purposes of the United Nations.

It has in the past been argued that this is not a general prohibition of the use of force, being limited by the words 'against the territorial integrity or political independence of any state'. That argument has not been accepted by the Council or more widely. It is clear from the negotiating history that these words were inserted with the aim of strengthening the Principle, not creating a loophole.[23] The heads of state and government did not include these words when reiterating in the 2005 World Summit Outcome 'the obligation of all Member States to refrain in their international relations from the threat or use of force in any manner inconsistent with the Charter'.[24]

[20] Higgins (1963) 6. [21] Franck (2002). [22] Byers (2003); Wood (2019).
[23] Goodrich and Hambro (1946) 68–9.
[24] UN General Assembly resolution 60/1, 16 September 2005 (World Summit Outcome), para. 77. See also para. 5.

6.3.2 Use of Force by or Authorized by the Council

By way of a preliminary point, we are here referring only to the use of force by or authorized by the Council. The General Assembly has no power to authorize a use of force that would otherwise be contrary to international law. This is unaffected by the Uniting for Peace resolution.[25]

It was occasionally argued that, in the absence of the arrangements laid down in Articles 43 to 47 of the Charter, the Council is not empowered to take measures involving the use of armed force. That argument was based largely on a reading of the *travaux préparatoires* of the Charter, but never had much merit. Article 42 itself makes no such linkage. As the ICJ held as long ago as 1962 in the *Expenses* case, '[i]t cannot be said that the Charter has left the Security Council impotent in the face of an emergency situation when agreements under Article 43 have not been concluded'.[26] The established practice of the Council on the matter is conclusive.

Acting under Chapter VII (Article 42), the Security Council has now authorized states (and states acting through international organizations) to use force on many occasions.[27] Such authorizations have become so much a part of the international landscape that we forget how relatively recent they are, and how hesitant the Council was in the early days, indeed until the end of the Cold War. Since then, the Council has authorized the use of force by coalitions led by the United States and others (Iraq in 1990–1, Somalia, and Haiti); by France (Operation Turquoise in Rwanda); by Italy (Operation Alba in Albania); by Australia (East Timor); by 'Member States that have notified the Secretary-General, acting nationally or through regional organizations or arrangements' (Libya);[28] by France in Mali; and by France in the CAR. It authorized the first-ever use of force by NATO (Bosnia in the mid-1990s); and it has authorized the use of force by EU forces in the CAR and the DRC.

The Council's readiness to find threats to the peace in situations of civil war or internal conflict is a relatively recent development. In

25 Zaum (2008); Johnson (2014).

26 *Certain Expenses* Advisory Opinion, at p. 167.

27 'Authorization' is the correct legal framework, not 'delegation' of powers: see Berman (2004) 162 n. 1.

28 S/RES/1973, 17 March 2011.

1995 in its *Tadić* judgment, the ICTY Appeals Chamber noted that 'the practice of the Security Council is rich with cases of civil war or internal strife which it classified as a 'threat to the peace' and dealt with under Chapter VII'.[29] This is a very important element in the practice of the Council, which has been well documented elsewhere.[30]

The principal legal significance of the 2005 World Summit Outcome passage on 'responsibility to protect' is that the heads of state and government clearly acknowledged the Security Council's right to act under Chapter VII should national authorities manifestly fail to protect their populations from genocide, war crimes, ethnic cleansing, or crimes against humanity. There was here no reference to a need to find some international element, to find some 'anomalous fiction'.

The Security Council has by now an extensive practice of determining that acts of terrorism are threats to international peace and security, justifying action under Chapter VII of the Charter. If its action in this field has thus far been confined to the adoption of measures not involving the use of force, there is no reason why, in appropriate circumstances, the Council should not authorize the use of force to avert terrorist threats.[31] This could be done both in circumstances where the victim state might exercise the right of self-defence and where such right is not (yet) available because the terrorist threat, though real, cannot be said to be imminent.

The precise terms in which the Security Council authorizes the use of force vary. Since 1990, the formula 'all necessary means' has been frequently used and is generally understood to include the use of force.[32] Sometimes there are references to 'implied' or 'implicit' Council authorizations to use force.[33] But these are misleading. Either the use of force has been authorized or it has not, and that depends upon the interpretation of the resolution or resolutions in question. So-called implied or implicit authorizations are not a separate category or mode of authorization by the Council for the use of force.

It is occasionally suggested that the Security Council, by assisting to bring a conflict to an end, or by assisting at the post-conflict stage,

[29] *Prosecutor* v. *Tadić* (1995), para. 30.
[30] Krisch, 'Article 39' (2012); de Wet and Wood (2022). [31] Wood (2020).
[32] Hajjami (2013). [33] Hakimi (2018).

has retrospectively endorsed the original use of force as lawful. For example, it was argued that by adopting, on 10 June 1999, resolution 1244 (1999), following the Kosovo conflict, the Council somehow accepted the lawfulness of the NATO intervention.[34] There was no basis for this in the terms of the resolution, or in the Council's discussions. Similarly, following the military action in Iraq in 2003, there was concern that the Council's co-operation with the occupying Powers might be interpreted as endorsing the original intervention.[35] Such concerns were without foundation. It should be clear that the Council cannot be taken to have implicitly rendered lawful *ex post facto* a use of force merely because it assists with the follow-up. Any other view would make it harder to secure the support of the Council when it is most needed.

Possible *ex post facto* Council authorization of the use of force has been raised in particular in connection with the actions of regional organizations.[36] The starting point is that, whatever the political importance of acting collectively, states acting collectively within a regional, subregional, or other organization have no greater legal right to use force than they have as individual states. It was not, for example, claimed that NATO, when it intervened over Kosovo in 1999, had any right to use force over and above that of its members.

This basic legal position is reflected in Article 53 of the Charter, which provides that the Council may utilize regional organizations for enforcement action under its authority, but which goes on to provide that 'no enforcement action shall be taken under regional arrangements or by regional agencies without the authorization of the Security Council'. There have been a few cases where a regional or subregional organization has taken enforcement action without the prior authorization of the Council, and then it has been argued that authorization after the event would be sufficient;[37] there have even been cases where the Council has subsequently indicated its support.[38] This practice has led some to suggest that, to comply with Article 53 of the Charter, it is sufficient if the Council's authorization for enforcement action by a regional organization is sought and received after the event. The Secretary-General's High-Level

[34] Henkin (1999) 826–7. [35] Kirgis (2003).
[36] Walter, 'Article 53' (2012) 1501; Chinkin (2000).
[37] By the United States in the 1962 Cuban missile crisis.
[38] S/RES/788, 19 November 1992, para. 1.

Panel, after correctly stating that '[a]uthorization from the Security Council should in all cases be sought', goes on to suggest 'that in some urgent cases that authorization may be sought after such operations have commenced'.[39] This was not repeated by the Secretary-General in his report *In Larger Freedom* or in the 2005 World Summit Outcome.

Any notion of *ex post facto* authorization would pose risks for the UN collective security system. If adopted as a regular feature, it could effectively release states acting collectively within a regional organization from the central requirement of the Charter, to refrain from the use of force except in self-defence or with the authorization of the Security Council. It is difficult to see how it would work in practice, or indeed how it could provide a satisfactory basis for states wanting to take action. Can the lawfulness of a use of force really depend upon what happens subsequently? To act in the expectation that the Council will subsequently authorize the action taken preempts the Council, takes it for granted as it were – or suggests that those acting do not really mind whether their actions are eventually seen as lawful or not.

It is difficult to square the notion of *ex post facto* authorization with the text of the Charter. The Council has discretion whether to authorize, or not to authorize, the intervention. So it cannot be said that the action is lawful before the authorization has been given.

What applies to one regional or subregional organization presumably applies to all of them. Moreover, it is difficult to see why the same should not then apply to *ad hoc* groups of states ('coalitions of the willing') or even to individual states.

It needs to be stated clearly that the fact that a decision adopted under Chapter VII imposes legal obligations, such as sanctions, does not mean that states are entitled to use force to enforce the resolution, any more than the fact that a state is in breach of a treaty means that force can be used against it. Only if they otherwise have a legal basis to use force for that purpose, such as Council authorization or self-defence, may states do so. It was not, for example, suggested at the time of the invasion of Iraq in 2003; while Iraq was in non-compliance with Security Council resolutions, this in itself

[39] A/59/565, 2 December 2004, para. 272.

did not mean that force could be used. Any authorization for the use of force had to be found elsewhere.

6.3.3 Self-Defence

There has sometimes been a degree of uncertainty, at least among writers, as to whether in particular cases the Security Council is itself authorizing a use of force under Chapter VII of the Charter or recognizing the exercise of the inherent right of self-defence, including the right of collective self-defence.[40] Security Council resolutions 83 (1950) and 84 (1950) essentially recommended that states join in the collective self-defence of the Republic of Korea, whereas resolution 678 (1990) clearly authorized the use of force. The distinction is important, not least because a Security Council authorization may well cover a wider use of force.[41]

The right of self-defence is recognized in Article 51 of the Charter, not established thereby. Article 51 provides that:

> Nothing in the present Charter shall impair the inherent right of individual or collective self-defence if an armed attack occurs against a Member of the United Nations . . ..

The Article recognizes the right of self-defence under customary international law. At the same time, the right of self-defence is now embedded in the collective security system established by the Charter. Article 51 itself contains three relevant requirements.

First, the right of self-defence applies only 'until the Security Council has taken measures necessary to maintain international peace and security'. Under the Charter, self-defence is a residual, unilateral right that is needed only to the extent that the Council has not taken the measures necessary to prevent or reverse an armed attack.

It has occasionally been suggested that once the Security Council has taken *any* measures, sanctions for example, the right to take measures in self-defence ceases. Acceptance of such an argument would be a serious impediment to the adoption by the Council of non-forcible measures. It overlooks the fact that Article 51 speaks of 'measures *necessary* to maintain international peace and security', not just any measures. The Council itself has sometimes recalled the

[40] See Berman (2004); Wood (2015). [41] Bowett (1994) 425–40.

continuing right of self-defence in its resolutions; though this is not legally required, it may sometimes be a useful clarification.

Second, members of the UN are required to report immediately to the Security Council measures taken by them in exercise of the right of self-defence.[42] This usually takes the form of a letter to the Council President setting out, briefly, the circumstances giving rise to the right of self-defence and the fact that action in self-defence is being undertaken. Such a report should be made promptly upon the commencement of the action concerned. The ICJ has attached evidential importance to whether a state has, or has not, informed the Council that it is acting in self-defence.[43] It does not seem to be the practice to send follow-up letters. Indeed, keeping the Council informed about the specific measures being taken in self-defence does not seem to be a requirement either under the terms of Article 51 or in the practice of the Council. However, the purpose of notification under Article 51 – to ensure that the Council is informed so that it can perform its functions and, perhaps, exercise some degree of oversight – might suggest that this should be done.

There has been a good deal of notification practice, not least in connection with action against ISIL in Syria and Iraq.[44] But notifications do not always mention Article 51, and it is not always clear whether a state is notifying the Council of action taken in self-defence under Article 51 or informing the Council of other action involving the use of force.[45] The Secretariat does not publish a comprehensive list of Article 51 notifications, which are not routinely, or indeed often, discussed in the Council. This is not regarded as entirely satisfactory, and initiatives have recently been taken to draw attention to these matters.[46]

Third, Article 51 provides that measures taken in exercise of the right of self-defence 'shall not in any way affect the authority and

42 Charter, Art. 51.

43 *Military and Paramilitary Activities* (1986), at pp. 121–2, para. 235.

44 Green (2015); Wood (2017a); see further Sievers and Daws (2014), updates available at www.scprocedure.org/chapter-7-section-12-changes; Lewis et al. (2019) with an extensive annex of 'communications to the Security Council of measures taken by United Nations Member States in purported exercise of the right of self-defense: October 24, 1945 through December 31, 2018'.

45 See, for example, Israel's letter to the Council President dated 12 May 2021 (S/2021/463).

46 Mexican proposal in the Charter Committee, A/AC.182/L.154; Arria-formula meeting on Article 51, 24 February 2021 (letter dated 8 March 2021 from the Permanent Representative of Mexico to the President of the Security Council).

responsibility of the Security Council under the present Charter to take at any time such action as it deems necessary in order to maintain or restore international peace and security'. This emphasizes the priority of measures taken by the Council.

It is often asked whether the right of self-defence includes the rescue of nationals abroad where the territorial state is unable or unwilling to take the necessary action.[47] Where such rescue involves the use of armed force without the consent of the territorial state, it would contravene Article 2(4) of the UN Charter unless authorized by the Security Council or falling within the scope of self-defence. It is most often viewed as action in self-defence, especially where those concerned are being targeted because of their nationality, as was the case with the Entebbe raid in 1976.[48]

We now turn to the scope of the right of self-defence to see what the practice of the Council tells us about three main questions: Is there a right of anticipatory self-defence? Does the right of self-defence apply in response to attacks by non-state actors, in particular terrorist groups? And, if so, how does the requirement of imminence apply in this context?[49] As we will see, these issues are interrelated.

Whether Article 51 of the Charter recognizes a right of anticipatory self-defence remains controversial, among writers as among states. During the Cold War, the Soviet Union and its allies took the position that self-defence was available only if an armed attack had actually been launched. The United States, the United Kingdom, and some other Western countries, following the *Caroline* approach,[50] took the position that self-defence was permitted in the face of an imminent attack.

The end of the Cold War and the new threats have not yet led to general agreement among states on this question. In some respects, new differences may have arisen (not least as a result of references to preventive action in the US *National Security Strategy* of 2002). Yet states are perhaps now somewhat closer in their views on the law than during the Cold War or indeed before 9/11. Practice – and hence the discussion – has shifted from anticipatory attacks by one state against another to anticipatory attacks against threats posed by terrorist groups. But

[47] Forteau (2015); ILA (2018) 17–18. [48] Kreß and Nußberger (2018).

[49] For attempts to answer these and other questions, see Wilmshurst (2006); the Leiden Policy Recommendations on Counter-Terrorism and International Law in van den Herik and Schrijver (2010); the Bethlehem Principles (see Bethlehem (2012)); Wilmshurst and Wood (2013).

[50] Wood (2018).

while they often seem to agree on the legality of specific actions, the reaction of many states to the categorical affirmation of a right of anticipatory self-defence in the High-Level Panel's report and in the Secretary-General's report *In Larger Freedom* shows the difficulties with abstract debate, as opposed to a case-by-case approach.

The next question is whether the right of self-defence is available in response to attacks by non-state actors, such as terrorist groups. The day after 9/11, on 12 September 2001, the Council adopted resolution 1368 (2001) in which it recognized 'the inherent right of individual and collective self-defence in accordance with the Charter'. Some two weeks later it adopted resolution 1373 (2001), reaffirming 'the inherent right of individual and collective self-defence as recognized by the Charter of the United Nations'.[51] While some commentators have tried to argue the contrary, it is difficult to read this language, in context, as doing anything other than recognizing the right of self-defence in response to attacks by non-state actors. In any event, state practice, including the practice of the Security Council, NATO, the Organization of American States (OAS), and other states, strongly supports such a right, notwithstanding the Court's pronouncement in the *Wall* opinion.[52]

The adoption of resolution 2249 (2015) concerning the use of force against ISIL in Syria led to much instant discussion, with some describing it as ambiguous, a hybrid, confusing, etc. It was suggested that it 'might also portend a new blurring of the long-standing bright line between Chapter VII resolutions that authorize force and those that do not'.[53] As has been explained elsewhere, it was none of these. Rather, it provides further evidence of the recognition of the right of self-defence against non-state actors as was the case with the previous resolutions mentioned.[54]

Assuming that there is a right of self-defence against non-state actors, as well as the right to resort to an anticipatory act of self-defence against such actors, perhaps the most difficult issue is to understand what constitutes an imminent attack in the context of terrorism. There would seem to be broad agreement, among states and writers, that, to quote the UK Attorney General in the House of Lords in April 2004,

[51] S/RES/1373, 28 September 2001.
[52] *Wall* Advisory Opinion, at p. 194, para. 138.
[53] Deeks (2015).
[54] Wood (2017a).

> [t]he concept of what constitutes an "imminent" armed attack will develop to meet new circumstances and new threats .... It must be right that States are able to act in self-defence in circumstances where there is evidence of further imminent attacks by terrorist groups, even if there is no specific evidence of where such an attack will take place or of the precise nature of the attack.[55]

It seems doubtful whether it would be useful to try to adopt more specific tests for imminence, as opposed to assessing practice on a case-by-case basis. It is important in this connection to have in mind the principle of good faith.

More recently, the US, UK, and Australian governments have set out their positions on the law of self-defence. The United States' position on the two questions, whether anticipatory self-defence is permitted and, if so, how the criterion of imminence is to be applied in the case of self-defence against non-state armed groups, was set out by the Obama administration in December 2016 in the following terms:

> Under the *jus ad bellum*, a State may use force in the exercise of its inherent right of self-defense not only in response to armed attacks that have already occurred, but also in response to imminent attacks before they occur. When considering whether an armed attack is imminent under the *jus ad bellum* for purposes of the initial use of force against another State or on its territory, the United States analyzes a variety of factors. ... Finally, as is now increasingly recognized by the international community, the traditional conception of what constitutes an "imminent" attack must be understood in light of the modern-day capabilities, techniques, and technological innovations of terrorist organizations.[56]

The UK government explained its position on imminence in January 2017,[57] as did the Australian government in April 2017.[58]

[55] Lord Goldsmith, Lords Sitting of 21 April 2004, Hansard, Vol. 660, Cols. 370–1.

[56] The passage quotes from Principle 8 of the Bethlehem Principles, see Bethlehem (2012). For earlier collective attempts to set out principles, see Wilmshurst (2006); van den Herik and Schrijver (2010).

[57] On 11 January 2017, the British Attorney General, the Rt. Hon. Jeremy Wright QC MP, delivered a speech entitled 'The Modern Law of Self-Defence', available at www.gov.uk/government/uploads/system/uploads/attachment_data/file/583171/170111_Imminence_Speech_.pdf. Among other things, the Attorney General endorsed the factors included in Principle 8 of the Bethlehem Principles, see Wood (2017a); Wood (2017b).

[58] On 11 April 2017, the Australian Attorney General, the Hon. George Brandis QC, delivered a speech entitled 'The Right of Self-Defence against Imminent Armed Attack in International Law', available at https://law.uq.edu.au/files/25365/2017%2004%2011%20-%20Attorney-General%20-%20Speech%20-%

A word may be needed about expressions such as 'war on terrorism', 'war on terror', and 'global war on terror'. They are generally used in a non-legal sense. Politicians use the rhetoric of war in all kinds of context, far removed from armed conflict. When asked in Parliament whether the use of the term 'war against terrorism' meant that the United Kingdom was legally at war, a government minister responded that 'the term "the war against terrorism" has been used to describe the whole campaign against terrorism, including military, political, financial, legislative and law-enforcement measures'.[59] The United States has gone on record in somewhat similar terms. In a speech at the London School of Economics on 31 October 2006, the then State Department legal adviser John B. Bellinger III explained that '[w]e do not believe we are in a legal state of war with every terrorist everywhere in the world. Rather, the United States uses the term "global war on terrorism" to mean that all countries must strongly oppose, and must fight against, terrorism in all its forms, everywhere around the globe.'[60]

6.3.4 *'Humanitarian Intervention' / 'Responsibility to Protect'*

The practice of the Security Council has had considerable influence on the development of the notion of 'responsibility to protect'.[61] The current debate took off following the NATO action over Kosovo in 1999, but the Council itself had become involved in situations where humanitarian concerns were central long before that. The Council's early actions over Southern Rhodesia and South Africa were to some degree manifestations of concern for human rights abuses. In many cases, the Council demanded that the parties to conflicts comply with humanitarian law. In other contexts, too, the Council called for full respect for humanitarian law. (Sometimes it really meant human rights law, but, because of sensitivities, the Council tended to avoid that term.) The Council

20The%20Right%20of%20Self-Defence%20Against%20Imminent%20Armed%20Attack%20in%20International%20Law%20-%20for%20publication.pdf.

59 Hansard, 22 November 2001, Col. WA153.

60 Legal Adviser Bellinger speech, 'Legal Issues in the War on Terrorism' (31 October 2006), available at https://2009-2017.state.gov/s/l/2006/98861.htm.

61 Butchard (2020).

established the two *ad hoc* international criminal tribunals, for the former Yugoslavia[62] and for Rwanda;[63] it helped to set up the Special Courts for Sierra Leone[64] and Lebanon;[65] and it referred the situations in Darfur and Libya to the ICC.[66]

The British government has been a leading proponent of an exceptional right of states to use force to avert an overwhelming humanitarian catastrophe. This is not, it should be noted, expressed as a broad right of humanitarian intervention, and may be viewed as somewhat similar to an exceptional defence or justification of necessity such as is found in some domestic legal systems. The United Kingdom relied on this legal basis to justify the safe havens in northern Iraq in 1991, and the northern and southern no-fly zones;[67] on a much larger scale, the Kosovo intervention; and the operations against Syria over chemical weapons in 2018. The United States, on the other hand, appears not to have asserted any such right, justifying its actions to protect the Kurds in the north and the Shia in the south, and the interventions over Kosovo and Syria, on political grounds. Other states, too, have been reluctant to accept such a right.

A former State Department legal adviser has explained the American position in the following terms: '[T]he assertion by states or regional organizations of a *legal right* to carry out such "benign" uses of force on their own authority could create precedents for future interventions by others that might be destabilizing and dangerous. This is one of the main reasons the United States has never asserted the doctrine.'[68] He goes on to say that, in any event, 'there is a much stronger legal and political basis for forcible humanitarian intervention under Chapter VII or VIII'.[69]

It was, in fact, along these lines that the United Kingdom and others have been working since shortly after the Kosovo conflict. The United Kingdom sought to promote criteria for the circumstances in which the Security Council should be ready to authorize the use of force in the face of an overwhelming humanitarian crisis. This was an attempt to develop the underlying policy for Council

62 S/RES/827, 5 May 1993. 63 S/RES/955, 8 November 1994.
64 S/RES/1315, 14 August 2000. 65 S/RES/1757, 30 May 2007.
66 S/RES/1593, 31 March 2005, on Sudan; S/RES/1970, 26 February 2011, on Libya.
67 Wood (2010). 68 Matheson (2006) 139. 69 Ibid.

action, not to develop the law as such. The British initiative did not lead to concrete results. As we have already suggested, the law and practice often develop best case-by-case, not through abstract debate. Few states wish to commit themselves, especially in the Security Council, to abstract propositions on matters such as the use of force.

Various other initiatives followed, stimulated by concern at the unilateralism inherent in the Kosovo campaign: the Dutch and the Danish foreign ministries produced studies;[70] and the Canadian government set up the International Commission on Intervention and State Sovereignty, which produced an influential report.[71] So the Secretary-General's High-Level Panel on Threats, Challenges and Change had plenty to go on. The Panel endorsed 'the emerging norm that there is a collective international responsibility to protect, exercisable by the Security Council authorizing military action as a last resort, in the event of genocide and other large-scale killings, ethnic cleansing or serious violations of international humanitarian law which sovereign Governments have proved powerless or unwilling to prevent'.[72] It did not explain what it meant by that notoriously obscure word 'norm' or indeed by an 'emerging' norm, but it does not appear to have been suggesting that it was propounding existing international law. The Panel went on to propose that the Council adopt guidelines (as the British government had already suggested, without success) as to when it should act, expressly to ensure the legitimacy of its actions, not their legality. *In Larger Freedom* was in similar terms.[73]

The General Assembly was not prepared to go so far. In the 2005 World Summit Outcome, the heads of state and government noted that '[e]ach individual State has the responsibility to protect its populations from genocide, war crimes, ethnic cleansing and

70 Fijnaut and Larik (2021); Kendal (2013).

71 International Commission on Intervention and State Sovereignty, *Responsibility to Protect* (2001).

72 The Secretary-General's High-Level Panel Report on Threats, Challenges and Change, *A More Secure World: Our Shared Responsibility*, A/59/565, 2 December 2004, para. 203. Many authors have since addressed 'responsibility to protect', though few have done so from a legal angle. See, for some relatively recent contributions, Bellamy and Dunne (2016).

73 Report of the Secretary-General, *In Larger Freedom: Towards Development, Security and Human Rights for All*, A/59/2005, 21 March 2005, para. 126.

crimes against humanity'.[74] They went on to say that '[t]he international community, through the United Nations' also has the responsibility to use appropriate peaceful means, in accordance with Chapters VI and VII of the Charter, to help protect populations. The key sentence then follows:

> In this context, we are prepared to take collective action, in a timely and decisive manner, through the Security Council, in accordance with the Charter, including Chapter VII, on a case-by-case basis and in cooperation with relevant regional organizations as appropriate, should peaceful means be inadequate and national authorities are manifestly failing to protect their populations from genocide, war crimes, ethnic cleansing and crimes against humanity.[75]

This sentence merits careful study, as much for what it does not say as for what it includes. The first question, based on its use of the word 'responsibility', is whether the Assembly was asserting that 'each individual State' has an obligation under international law to protect populations from genocide, war crimes, ethnic cleansing, and crimes against humanity, or whether it was stating that the obligation is exclusively that of 'the international community, through the United Nations'. Clearly, individual states have positive obligations under human rights law that would be encompassed in the concept of 'responsibility to protect'. But it does not follow that 'responsibility to protect' amounts to a new international legal obligation. So to claim might even impede genuine acceptance of the principle at a political level. States (particularly those that would bear the burden of action) may be reluctant to agree to any legal obligation to act to achieve objectives that could require huge resources or where success may be uncertain.

As a political commitment, the passage on 'responsibility to protect' in the World Summit Outcome is potentially significant, and has received a good deal of support, at least verbal, from states and others; it showed how far states had come by 2005, though it was cautiously drafted. The heads of state and government said that they were 'prepared to take collective action'. This action was to be taken 'through the Security Council' and 'in accordance with the Charter'. Such action would be taken 'on a case-by-case basis'. So whether action would be taken and, if so, in what way, was for the

[74] A/RES/60/1, 16 September 2005, para. 138. [75] Ibid., para. 139.

members of the Council to decide in a given situation. In express terms, the commitment applied only in cases of protection against 'genocide, war crimes, ethnic cleansing and crimes against humanity', but that did not preclude Council action in the event of grave violations not falling within these four categories, especially if they were comparable, given the Council's wide discretion on what it considers 'necessary'.

It must, however, be recognized that the high hopes for 'responsibility to protect' have hardly been realized. One example of Council action that some see as an implementation of the 'responsibility to protect' was resolution 1973 (2011), which authorized the use of force 'to protect civilians and civilian populated areas under threat of attack' in Libya and to enforce a 'no-fly zone' to serve that purpose.[76] But political controversy over the resolution and its implementation – which assisted in toppling the Ghaddafi regime – may have tempered the attractiveness of the concept as a call to action.[77]

What was important, legally as well as politically, was that the 2005 World Summit Outcome confirmed that enforcement action to protect populations from genocide, war crimes, ethnic cleansing, and crimes against humanity was within the remit of the Security Council under Chapter VII, though seemingly illegal without its authorization. And the General Assembly, that is to say, the membership of the UN as a whole, clearly said that it expected the Council to take such action in appropriate cases, although this did not mean that the Council would do so.

[76] S/RES/1973, 17 March 2011, paras. 4, 6–7.
[77] See, for example, Keeler (2011).

7

The Security Council, International Organizations, and the Use of Force

This chapter considers the interaction of the Security Council with other international organizations in relation to the use of force and the role that international organizations may play in implementing Council authorizations to use force. This is an area where the Security Council, the international organizations concerned, and member states have shown great flexibility, with the provisions of the UN Charter (both Chapter VII and Chapter VIII) and the constituent instruments of the regional and other organizations being developed through extensive practice.[1]

7.1 Legal Framework

As with other issues, the starting point is the UN Charter and its provisions, which govern these relationships. Chapter VII, Article 48, paragraph 2 addresses member state action through UN agencies and international organizations other than the UN, while Chapter VIII specifically addresses Council interaction with 'Regional Arrangements', with regard to which Articles 52 and 53 are relevant for our purposes.

Article 48 provides:

1. The action required to carry out the decisions of the Security Council for the maintenance of international peace and security shall be taken by all the Members of the United Nations or by some of them, as the Security Council may determine.

[1] Higgins (1998); Helal (2018); de Wet (2015); Walter (2012).

2. Such decisions shall be carried out by the Members of the United Nations directly and through their action in the appropriate international agencies of which they are members.

The premise of Article 48, paragraph 2 is that the obligation to carry out Council decisions lies with the UN member states and they can fulfil this obligation through 'appropriate international agencies of which they are members', a term understood to include international organizations separate from the UN itself. Doing so does not create an obligation for the other organizations themselves.[2]

Chapter VIII, entitled 'Regional Arrangements', contains the only UN Charter articles pertaining to regional bodies' interaction with the UN, and does so in the context of international peace and security specifically.[3] Article 52, paragraph 1 states:

Nothing in the present Charter precludes the existence of regional arrangements or agencies for dealing with such matters relating to the maintenance of international peace and security as are appropriate for regional action, provided that such arrangements or agencies and their activities are consistent with the Purposes and Principles of the United Nations.

The drafting history of the Charter shows that it was not possible to agree on a definition of 'regional arrangements or agencies'.[4] The terms used in the article recognize that member states may choose to politically organize themselves loosely via an arrangement without creating any institutions, on the one hand, or by creating an international organization with various organs and capacities, on the other.[5]

Some equate the 'regional' requirement with arrangements with a territorial link that are internally focused, that is, their functions and capacity are aimed at solving disputes within the relevant region. Common examples are the OAS and the AU.[6]

[2] Reinisch and Novak (2012) MN 9; de Wet (2015) 317; see also Chapter 2.

[3] Co-operation with regional arrangements on economic and social matters was considered, but not included in the UN Charter, see Goodrich and Hambro (1946) 184.

[4] Ibid., 183–4. [5] Walter, 'Article 52' (2012) MN 19–20.

[6] Ibid., MN 6–16; de Wet (2015) 315; although, even when these organizations were given observer status, the General Assembly avoided referring to Article 52 in view of the uncertainty.

This definition excludes arrangements based on 'collective self-defence', that is, a pact designed for members to come to the aid of a pact member attacked by an outside element.[7] An example would be an organization such as NATO, as initially established,[8] or the defence pact of the EU inherited from the now disbanded Western European Union (WEU). It would also exclude organizations based on a linkage other than geography, such as religion, ethnicity, or other common ties.

An Egyptian proposal to define regional arrangements in the UN Charter as geographically linked countries 'which, by reason of their proximity, community of interests or cultural, linguistic, historical or spiritual affinities, make themselves jointly responsible for peaceful settlement of any disputes which arise between them and for the maintenance of peace and security in their region' was rejected as overly narrow.[9]

In contrast, in his 1992 'Agenda for Peace', Secretary-General Boutros Boutros-Ghali gave a broad and all-inclusive definition of regional arrangements and agencies, avoiding any such distinctions:

> The Charter deliberately provides no precise definition of regional arrangements and agencies, thus allowing useful flexibility for undertakings by a group of States to deal with a matter appropriate for regional action which also could contribute to the maintenance of international peace and security. Such associations or entities could include treaty-based organizations, whether created before or after the founding of the United Nations, regional organizations for mutual security and defence, organizations for general regional development or for cooperation on a particular economic topic or function, and groups created to deal with a specific political, economic or social issue of current concern.[10]

Council practice tends to support this broader view, as resolutions regarding NATO and WEU operations during the crisis in the

[7] Walter, 'Article 52' (2012) MN 13; de Wet (2015) 316–19.

[8] On NATO, see Beckett (1950); Higgins (1998); Marauhn (2016). NATO has expanded its operations beyond action based on collective self-defence, but it still is not considered a 'regional arrangement' within the meaning of Chapter VIII according to de Wet (2015) 315–17.

[9] UNCIO, Interim Report to Committee III/4 by Subcommittee III/4/A on the Amalgamation of Amendments, Doc. 533, III/4/A/9, 23 May 1945, p. 3; Goodrich and Hambro (1946) 183–4.

[10] A/47/277, 17 June 1992, para. 61.

former Yugoslavia indicate.[11] This interpretation is also better aligned with the language of Article 53, which speaks of the Council utilizing 'regional arrangements or agencies for enforcement action under its authority'.[12]

In any event, in practical terms the difference is of no significance: States can carry out Council measures through any international organization its members wish when mandated by the Council, be it under Article 48, Article 52, or Article 53.[13] The critical question is not whether the organization in question is a 'regional arrangement or agency' but rather the legality of the action involved.[14]

7.2 Chapter VIII in Practice

We have already seen the reality of the Council having to rely on member states to implement its decisions, as opposed to the arrangements envisaged by the Charter.[15] Indeed, the Council has recognized the increasingly essential role of other international entities in the maintenance of peace and security. For example,

> [w]hile reaffirming its primary responsibility under the Charter of the United Nations for the maintenance of international peace and security, [the Security Council] underlines the increasingly important role of regional arrangements and agencies, and of coalitions of Member States in the conduct of activity in this field. The Council reaffirms that all such activity taken under regional arrangements or by regional agencies, including enforcement action, shall be carried out in accordance with Articles 52, 53 and 54 of Chapter VIII of the Charter of the United Nations.[16]

The Council has authorized member states to act through international organizations of which they are members as well as unilaterally to implement Council resolutions authorizing the use of force. For example, as the conflict in Bosnia worsened, the Council acted to ensure compliance with the flight ban over Bosnia, authorizing 'Member States . . . acting nationally or through

[11] See, for example, S/RES/781, 9 October 1992; Walter, 'Article 53' (2012) 58.
[12] Goodrich and Hambro (1946) 184. [13] See also de Wet (2015) 317.
[14] Akehurst (1967) 180, 184; Simma (1999) 10; Johnstone (2015) 229–30; Gray (2018) 387–453.
[15] Chapter 6. [16] S/PRST/1998/35, 30 November 1998.

regional organizations or arrangements, to take, under the authority of the Security Council and subject to close coordination with the Secretary-General and UNPROFOR, all necessary measures in the airspace of the Republic of Bosnia and Herzegovina, in the event of further violations to ensure compliance with the ban on flights'.[17] This allowed for NATO enforcement of the flight ban. Later the Council used similar wording to authorize NATO's use of air power to protect the so-called safe areas established in Bosnia.[18]

Similarly, when the Council decided to authorize the use of force in Libya, it authorized 'Member States that have notified the Secretary-General, acting nationally or through regional organizations or arrangements, and acting in cooperation with the Secretary-General, to take all necessary measures ... to protect civilians and civilian populated areas under threat of attack in the Libyan Arab Jamahiriya'.[19] This served as authorization for the NATO operation in Libya. The Security Council authorization was, at least partially, in response to a request from the League of Arab States.[20]

In the case of Afghanistan, in accordance with the agreement reached at the conclusion of the UN Talks on Afghanistan in December 2001 at Bonn, the Security Council established the International Security Assistance Force (ISAF).[21] Though neither the resolution nor the Bonn Agreement references NATO, ISAF was composed of NATO states (acting as part of a NATO operation) and other states. NATO eventually took command of ISAF on 11 August 2003 and the Council later recognized NATO's contribution to the force.[22]

As the language of these resolutions itself indicates, the legal framework of these authorizations to use force remains identical: the Council authorizes collective security measures, and this authorized use of force can be carried out by member states individually or through an international organization.[23] In any event, it is the

[17] S/RES/816, 31 March 1993. [18] S/RES/836, 4 June 1993.
[19] S/RES/1973, 17 March 2011. [20] S/2011/137, 15 March 2011.
[21] S/RES/1386, 20 December 2001.
[22] S/RES/1707, 12 December 2006, preamble.
[23] One may argue that member states may choose to implement a Council authorization to use force through an international organization even if that option is not explicitly mentioned by the Council. However, as the international organization will often have its own international legal personality, it is questionable

Council that defines the scope of the mandate to use force and the actors authorized to exercise collective security measures, as will be explained in Section 7.3.

Another form of authorization of use of force is Council mandated peacekeeping operations under Chapter VII. These may relate to international or regional organizations in various ways, as Council practice demonstrates.

The Council may authorize a peacekeeping operation under Chapter VII to be carried out by an international organization as opposed to creating a UN peacekeeping operation. Thus, for example, the Council authorized the deployment of the AU MISCA to carry out peacekeeping operations in the CAR.[24]

In a different context, the Council authorized a peacekeeping operation to implement what was agreed in the Dayton Peace Accords that brought an end to the conflict in Bosnia. In this case, the Council authorized a force consisting of NATO forces and other states under single command. Perhaps for political reasons, resolution 1031 (1995) did not refer to NATO by name; it referenced to it solely as the organization mentioned in the Accords: '14. *Authorizes* the Member States acting through or in cooperation with the organization referred to in Annex 1-A of the Peace Agreement to establish a multinational implementation force (IFOR) under unified command and control in order to fulfil the role specified in Annex 1-A and Annex 2 of the Peace Agreement.'[25] Annex 1-A of the Peace Agreement itself referred to the role of the Council in its implementation:

> The United Nations Security Council is invited to adopt a resolution by which it will authorize Member States or regional organizations and arrangements to establish a multinational military Implementation Force (hereinafter "IFOR"). The Parties understand and agree that this

whether it itself may use force without explicit Council authorization. The fact that Council resolutions specifically refer to member states acting through other organizations tends to support this. Yet, the language of Article 48 of the UN Charter, which states that 'decisions shall be carried out by the Members of the United Nations directly and through their action in the appropriate international agencies of which they are members', suggests that the option to act through an international organization to fulfil Council resolutions is generally available. Such was the practice in the case of the EU deployment of Operation ARTEMIS (EUFOR DRC) despite the fact that resolution 1484 (2003) did not specifically mention action through international organizations.

24 S/RES/2127, 19 December 2013. 25 S/RES/1031, 15 December 1995.

Implementation Force may be composed of ground, air and maritime units from NATO and non-NATO nations . . . It is understood and agreed that NATO may establish such a force, which will operate under the authority and subject to the direction and political control of the North Atlantic Council ("NAC") through the NATO chain of command . . . It is understood and agreed that other States may assist in implementing the military aspects of this Annex. The Parties understand and agree that the modalities of those States' participation will be the subject of agreement between such participating States and NATO.

This paved the way for Russian participation in IFOR alongside NATO forces and under the latter's command, an essential element in reaching agreement at Dayton.

The Council may authorize a peacekeeping operation to be carried out by another organization but with some UN participation and assistance. This was done in the case of AMISOM. The Council initially authorized the deployment of the AU operation in February 2007.[26] Later, under pressure from the AU for financial support for AMISOM, the Council authorized logistical support to AMISOM through the provision of certain equipment and services by the UN, normally performed for UN peacekeeping operations.[27] Thus, the AU mission became partially funded by UN assessed contributions.

The Council may create a peacekeeping force under Chapter VII that takes over from an existing mission of another organization already in place.[28] For example, going back to the CAR, about four months after it authorized MISCA, the Council created the Multidimensional Integrated Stabilization Mission in the Central African Republic (MINUSCA) in April 2014,[29] to replace the AU force. The resolution decided that the transfer of authority from MISCA to MINUSCA would take place in September of that year.

Rather than a peacekeeping operation carried out by an international organization, an international organization may serve as just one contingent or element in such an operation, as initially with

[26] S/RES/1744, 21 February 2007.

[27] S/RES/1863, 16 January 2009; see also the Secretary-General's detailed plans for support in S/2008/804, 19 December 2008. The necessary budget was later approved by the General Assembly.

[28] This is sometimes referred to as 're-hatting' as the contingents of the existing force then become contingents of a UN peacekeeping operation, wearing 'blue helmets'.

[29] S/RES/2149, 10 April 2014.

NATO in Afghanistan, or be authorized to assist a UN peacekeeping mission. When the security situation in the town of Bunia in the DRC province of Ituri rapidly deteriorated in 2003, the Council authorized an 'Interim Emergency Multinational Force' to be deployed to the area.[30] It was pursuant to this authorization that the EU launched operation ARTEMIS, its first operation outside Europe, and sent an EU force to assist the UN Organization Mission in the Democratic Republic of the Congo (MONUC, the forerunner of MONUSCO) in Bunia.[31]

In the case of the CAR, the EU Council first agreed on sending a military force to assist MISCA. The EU High Representative for Foreign Affairs and Security Policy then sent a letter to the President of the Security Council seeking Council authorization of the EU deployment, stating: 'A mandate by the Security Council is necessary to allow for the adoption of a decision to establish an operation by the Council of the European Union and therefore the deployment of the European Union force.'[32] The Security Council then proceeded to authorize the EU 'to deploy an operation in the Central African Republic as referenced in the letter' and to take 'all necessary measures' for this purpose.[33]

The Council may also choose to create a 'hybrid mission', a joint peacekeeping operation together with another international organization. The only example of this practice to date is the UN–AU Mission in Darfur (UNAMID). Here, instead of replacing or 're-hatting' the existing AU Mission in Sudan (AMIS), the two organizations created a hybrid peacekeeping operation, authorized by both the Security Council[34] and the AU PSC.[35] The head of the mission and its force commander were appointed jointly, and reported to both Councils, each of which renewed the mandate annually in a resolution.

7.3 The Need for Prior Security Council Authorization for Use of Force

While the options just discussed depart from the classic format of a UN peacekeeping operation, they do not change the legal

[30] S/RES/1484, 30 May 2003.
[31] EU Council Joint Action 2003/423/CFSP, 5 June 2003.
[32] S/2014/45, 26 February 2014. [33] S/RES/2134, 28 January 2014.
[34] S/RES/1769, 31 July 2007. [35] PSC/PR/Comm(LXXIX), 22 June 2007.

framework for the authorization of the use of force through peacekeeping. Whether the Council creates a UN peacekeeping operation, authorizes another international organization to create a peacekeeping operation, or takes over an existing peacekeeping operation, the Council is always the body authorizing the use of force, which can be carried out by various actors and in changing sequences.

This basic and important principle, which governs the relationship between the Council and other international arrangements, is made explicit in Article 53, paragraph 1:

> The Security Council shall, where appropriate, utilize such regional arrangements or agencies for enforcement action under its authority. But no enforcement action shall be taken under regional arrangements or by regional agencies without the authorization of the Security Council, ...

The Council thus remains the body vested by member states with the power to authorize 'enforcement action', correctly understood to mean the use of force,[36] in situations where the use of force would otherwise be illegal.

The case of the ECOWAS intervention in The Gambia in 2017 exemplifies both the legal contours of Article 53(1) and, at the same time, the political nature of the Security Council. Here, after Gambian President Yahya Jammeh refused to accept his defeat by Adama Barrow in the 1 December 2016 elections, ECOWAS decided on 17 December to ensure a transition of power, including by taking 'all necessary measures' to enforce the election results.[37] The Security Council then welcomed this decision in a presidential statement.[38]

After failed mediation efforts, on 19 January 2017, Barrow was sworn in as President in The Gambia's Embassy in Senegal. ECOWAS troops then advanced into The Gambia's territory later that day. The same day, with the military intervention unfolding, or at the very least imminent, the Security Council adopted resolution 2337 (2017). The resolution again welcomed the

[36] Walter, 'Article 53' (2012) MN 7–25; Goodrich and Hambro (1946) 184.

[37] Final Communique of Fiftieth Ordinary Session of the Authority of Heads of State and Government of the Economic Community of West African States (17 December 2016), para. 38, available at www.ecowas.int/wp-content/uploads/2016/12/Communiqué-Final_50th-Summit_Abuja_Dec-16_Eng.pdf.

[38] S/PRST/2016/19, 21 December 2016.

17 December 2016 decision of ECOWAS and endorsed the decisions of ECOWAS and the AU to recognize Barrow as President of The Gambia. Despite an earlier attempt by Senegal to include an authorization for ECOWAS to take 'all necessary measures' to oust Jammeh, such language was not included in the resolution.[39]

In their explanation of vote, several Council members stressed that the Council was not authorizing the ECOWAS intervention, as required under international law.[40] Uruguay specifically stated, 'pursuant to Article 53 of the Charter of the United Nations, that no enforcement action shall be taken under regional arrangements or by regional agencies without the authorization of the Security Council. Such authorization must be express, affirmative and prior. Uruguay underscores that nothing in resolution 2337 (2017) can be interpreted as express authorization of the use of force.'[41] Egypt similarly stated that 'today's resolution does not endorse any mandatory automatic enforcement, as such processes require the Security Council's clear and unquestioned authorization, in accordance with Chapter VIII of the Charter of the United Nations'.[42] These statements correctly reflect the need for Council authorization under Article 53(1) and an accurate reading of the text of resolution 2337 (2017).[43]

Nevertheless, no Council member, including those stressing the need for Council authorization for the ECOWAS intervention, condemned or explicitly addressed the operation that commenced earlier that day. And while Senegal, Russia, and the United Kingdom implicitly justified the operation on the basis of an invitation from the newly inaugurated Barrow,[44] the legal basis for such a justification has been questioned.[45]

39 What's in Blue, Resolution on the Gambia (19 January 2017), available at www.whatsinblue.org/2017/01/resolution-on-the-gambia.php.
40 S/PV.7866, 19 January 2017, statement of Uruguay, p. 3, statement of Bolivia, p. 3, statement of Egypt, p. 6.
41 Ibid., 19 January 2017, statement of Uruguay, p. 3.
42 Ibid., 19 January 2017, statement of Egypt, p. 6.
43 Helal (2018) 926–7; Kreß and Nußberger (2017) 242–4.
44 S/PV.7866, 19 January 2017, statement of Senegal, p. 2; Edith M. Lederer, 'UN Adopts Resolution Backing Gambia's New President Barrow' (AP News, 19 January 2017), available at https://apnews.com/44fe8d11a7134ad084794fb450c95556/un-adopts-resolution-backing-gambias-newpresident-barrow.
45 On the illegality of the operation, see Helal (2018); but see Kreß and Nußberger (2017), who consider the operation as possibly justified as an 'intervention by invitation'.

7.4 Consent by Prior Treaty to Use of Force by Regional Organizations

That a state may consent to another state's or international organization's use of force within its territory at a time of need or invite such an intervention is not controversial and does not, in principle, raise issues of conformity with the UN Charter.[46]

A difficult question, however, arises where member states grant regional organizations the authority to carry out such interventions without the target state's consent to the specific action and without Council authorization.

One example of such a treaty could be Article 8 of the Inter-American Treaty of Reciprocal Assistance, which allows the Organ of Consultation to agree on the use of force in the case of a conflict between members;[47] and, it has been argued, Article 8 of the Treaty Establishing the Organization of Eastern Caribbean States, which recognizes the responsibility of the Organization's Defence and Security Committee for 'coordinating the efforts of member States for collective defence and the preservation of peace and security against external aggression ... in the exercise of the inherent right of individual or collective self-defence recognised by Article 51 of the Charter of the United Nations',[48] though the Article seems to be concerned with external aggression exclusively.[49]

Decisions of these organizations served as the claimed basis for the naval blockade that the USA imposed on Cuba in 1962 during the Cuban missile crisis, and the US intervention in Grenada in 1983, respectively.[50]

An ECOWAS Protocol also allows for military action in the following circumstances, without the consensus of its members:

[46] See, among recent writings, ILA (2018); de Wet (2020).

[47] Inter-American Treaty of Reciprocal Assistance (Rio Treaty), signed 2 September 1947, entered into force 3 December 1948, 21 UNTS 77.

[48] Treaty Establishing the Organization of Eastern Caribbean States, 18 June 1981, 1338 UNTS 97; see S/PV.2491, 27 October 1983, statement of Jamaica, para. 141, statement of the USA, paras. 71–5.

[49] S/PV.2491, 27 October 1983, statement of Afghanistan, para. 262, statement of Mongolia, para. 338.

[50] For more on these situations, see Hajjami (2018); Harrell (2008); Hakimi (2007).

In case of internal conflict:

that threatens to trigger a humanitarian disaster, or that poses a serious threat to peace and security in the sub-region;

In event of serious and massive violation of human rights and the rule of law.

In the event of an overthrow or attempted overthrow of a democratically elected government.[51]

Interestingly, this Article was not cited by ECOWAS states as a legal justification for its operation in The Gambia discussed earlier, though the practice of ECOWAS can be said to be reflective of its spirit.

Nowadays, much discussion on this issue has concentrated on Article 4(h) of the Constitutive Act of the AU. It reads:

The Union shall function in accordance with the following principles:

...

(h) the right of the Union to intervene in a Member State pursuant to a decision of the Assembly in respect of grave circumstances, namely: war crimes, genocide and crimes against humanity; ....

An amended version of the Article, which adds to Article 4(h) that intervention is also possible when there is 'a serious threat to legitimate order', has yet to come into force.[52]

The Protocol Relating to the Establishment of the Peace and Security Council of the AU further elaborates as to the modalities of action under Article 4(h). First, it states that the PSC shall be guided by certain principles, including 'the right of the Union to intervene in a Member State pursuant to a decision of the Assembly in respect of grave circumstances, namely war crimes, genocide and crimes against humanity, in accordance with Article 4(h) of the Constitutive Act'.[53] Further, one of the PSC's functions is to 'support operations and intervention, pursuant to Article 4(h)'.[54]

[51] Protocol Relating to the Mechanism for Conflict Prevention, Management, Resolution, Peace-Keeping and Security, ECOWAS Doc. A/P10/12/99 (1999), Article 25.

[52] Protocol on Amendments to the Constitutive Act of the African Union, adopted 11 July 2003, will come into force when two-thirds of the AU membership ratifies it. Currently, thirty of fifty-five members have ratified the Protocol.

[53] Protocol Relating to the Establishment of the Peace and Security Council of the African Union, Art. 4(j).

[54] Ibid., Art. 6(d).

The procedure to be followed in such a scenario is set out in Article 7(e) of the Protocol, which says that the PSC, in conjunction with the chairperson of the AU Commission, is to 'recommend to the Assembly, pursuant to Article 4(h) of the Constitutive Act, intervention, on behalf of the Union, in a Member State in respect of grave circumstances, namely war crimes, genocide and crimes against humanity, as defined in relevant international conventions and instruments'. The Assembly can then take a decision on intervention under Article 4(h) by a two-thirds majority.[55]

Article 4(h) was invoked by the AU PSC on 17 December 2015, after political turmoil and violence broke out in Burundi, following President Pierre Nkurunziza's announcement that he would run for a highly controversial third term in April 2016, which many believed was unconstitutional. Recalling its duty to anticipate and prevent 'policies that may lead to crimes against humanity', the PSC decided to authorize the deployment of a 5,000-strong African Prevention and Protection Mission in Burundi (MAPROBU), mandated to protect civilians and contribute to the creation of the necessary conditions for the successful holding of dialogue, among other tasks.[56]

Burundi was given a ninety-six-hour ultimatum to accept the deployment of MAPROBU. The PSC decided, however, that

> in the event of non-acceptance of the deployment of MAPROBU, to recommend to the Assembly of the Union, in accordance with the powers which are conferred to Council, jointly with the Chairperson of the Commission, under article 7(e) of the Protocol Relating to the Establishment of the Peace and Security Council, the implementation of article 4 (h) of the Constitutive Act relating to intervention in a Member State in certain serious circumstances.[57]

The PSC did not seek Security Council authorization, though it did request 'the UN Security Council, in view of its primary responsibility for the maintenance of international peace and security, to support the deployment of MAPROBU and authorize the urgent establishment, in its favor, of a logistical support package funded by assessed contributions to the UN budget'.[58] Burundi refused to accept the force and threatened to attack its troops if deployed.

[55] Constitutive Act, Art. 7(1). [56] PSC/PR/COMM.(DLXV). [57] Ibid.
[58] Ibid.

The AU PSC ultimately decided not to pursue deployment but to continue mediation efforts.[59] Thus, the full extent of Article 4(h) remains untested, but it raises important questions on the legality of a potential AU intervention force in such a scenario.

A first question concerns the relationship between the AU Constitutive Act and the UN Charter, particularly Article 53, paragraph 1. Does the AU Constitutive Act allow for intervention without Security Council authorization, or is intervention dependent on Council authorization? This is essentially a matter of interpretation of the Constitutive Act and the Protocol Relating to the Establishment of the Peace and Security Council of the AU.

This may be academic for the time being. At present, the AU is unlikely to be in a position to deploy an intervention or peacekeeping force without UN financial assistance.[60] From a practical point of view, the Security Council will presumably need to decide whether to authorize the force in order to assist it. The Burundi example demonstrates this point. While not asking for Council authorization, the PSC did request the Security Council's assistance, thus asking the Council, albeit indirectly, to approve of the intended action in order to make MAPROBU operational.

That said, the question remains of legal significance for possible scenarios in the future. The AU Constitutive Act contains little on co-operation with the UN.[61] Article 17 of the Protocol Relating to the Establishment of the Peace and Security Council of the AU, however, states the following on the co-operation of the AU PSC with the UN Security Council:

1. In the fulfillment of its mandate in the promotion and maintenance of peace, security and stability in Africa, the Peace and Security Council shall cooperate and work closely with the United Nations Security Council, which has the primary responsibility for the maintenance of international peace and security . . .
2. Where necessary, recourse will be made to the United Nations to provide the necessary financial, logistical and military support for the African Unions' [*sic*] activities in the promotion and maintenance of peace, security and stability in Africa, in keeping with the provisions of

[59] PSC/AHG/COMM.3(DLXXI), 29 January 2016. [60] De Wet (2015) 321, 327.
[61] Art. 3(e).

Chapter VIII of the UN Charter on the role of Regional Organizations in the maintenance of international peace and security.

Three points can be extracted from the Article:

- Article 17 recognizes the primacy of the Security Council for the maintenance of international peace and security.
- Article 17 recognizes that the relationship between the AU and the UN is governed by Chapter VIII of the UN Charter.
- The AU PSC will ask for 'necessary financial, logistical and military support' from the UN. However, authorization per se is not mentioned in the Article, and recourse to support will be only 'where necessary'.

Article 17 can be said to recognize, in principle at least, the AU's obligations as a regional arrangement under the UN Charter and the primacy of the UN Security Council over its own organs on issues of international peace and security. Nevertheless, the issue of Council authorization is strikingly absent from the text and implies that the AU Assembly, upon the recommendation of the AU PSC, can authorize the use of force independently of the Council. Nothing in Article 17 specifically addresses intervention under Article 4(h) or indicates any limits to the contrary on the AU organs. And, when discussing subregional arrangements in Africa, the Protocol states that the AU has 'the primary responsibility for promoting peace, security and stability in Africa'.[62]

Other AU documents may shed light on the matter. The Common African Position on the Proposed Reform of the United Nations (also called the Ezulwini Consensus) was adopted at an Extraordinary Session of the Executive Council of the AU on 8 March 2005.[63] In it, '[t]he African Union agrees with the Panel [the High-Level Panel on Threats, Challenges and Change] that the intervention of Regional Organisations should be with the approval of the Security Council; although in certain situations, such approval could be granted "after the fact" in circumstances requiring urgent action'. Putting aside the issue of retroactive authorization discussed in Chapter 6, this statement seems rather

[62] Protocol Relating to the Establishment of the Peace and Security Council of the African Union, Art. 16.1.

[63] Ext/EX.CL/2 (VII).

straightforward. However, on the issue of legality, the document continues:

> With regard to the use of force, it is important to comply scrupulously with the provisions of Article 51 of the UN Charter, which authorise the use of force only in cases of legitimate self-defence. In addition, the Constitutive Act of the African Union, in its Article 4 (h), authorises intervention in grave circumstances such as genocide, war crimes and crimes against humanity.

Just like the Protocol Relating to the Establishment of the Peace and Security Council of the AU, the 'Common Position' does not explain the relation between the principled position recognizing the primacy of the Security Council and Article 4(h), which seems to stand as an independent ground for the use of force. It should also be noted that, according to the 'Common Position', intervention 'should' be with Security Council authorization, rather than 'shall'.

In addition, on 25 March 2005, an expert-level meeting of AU member states adopted a Roadmap for the Operationalization of the African Standby Force, in which they agreed that, '[a]t the strategic level, and in terms of the provisions of the Protocol establishing the PSC, the AU constitutes a legitimate mandating authority under Chapter VIII of the UN Charter. In this regard, the AU will seek UN Security Council authorisation of its enforcements [*sic*] actions.'[64] As opposed to the 'Common Position', however, this is a document adopted by lower-level military officials, focused on strategy rather than legality.

Nevertheless, given the obligations of AU member states under the UN Charter, the recognition by the Protocol of the primacy of the Security Council in the maintenance of international peace and security, the acceptance of the applicability of UN Charter Chapter VIII to the AU, the Roadmap for the Operationalization of the African Standby Force, and the rule of treaty interpretation that aims at interpreting potentially contradictory treaties in a harmonious way, it is not unreasonable to argue that the correct interpretation of the AU Constitutive Act is that intervention under Article 4(h) is subject to the Council's authorization.[65]

[64] EXP/AU-RECs/ASF/4(I), para. 10. [65] Corten and Koutroulis (2021).

On the other hand, some authors view Article 4(h) as giving the AU the right to intervene, even without the Security Council's blessing.[66] While the texts discussed here may indicate that prior authorization by the Council is preferable, it is not a necessity. The text of the Constitutive Act and the Protocol Relating to the Establishment of the Peace and Security Council of the AU support this conclusion; any language that may indicate otherwise in the relevant texts is ambivalent and general.[67] The same can be said of the AU 'Common Position' document. In addition, the context in which the Constitutive Act was adopted, after the passiveness of the Security Council in preventing a genocide in Rwanda, may suggest that independent AU action was on the AU member states' minds at the time.[68]

But perhaps more important than the correct interpretation of the clause is the broader issue, which is the legality of AU intervention under Article 4(h) without Security Council authorization. Using Article 4(h) as a case study, the following analysis generally applies to interventions under any similar provisions authorizing the use of force in other treaties.

One possible argument is that Article 4(h) stands in the forefront of the responsibility to protect doctrine and part of the wider argument that humanitarian intervention is a legal form of the use of force in the event of atrocities.[69] Yet this argument does not have any sound legal basis. In line with the conclusion that humanitarian intervention without Council authorization is illegal, is there any other way to justify AU intervention in such circumstances?

Given the primacy of the UN Charter over other treaties, not to mention the prohibition of the use of force as a possible *jus cogens* norm, the AU members are not able to allow for intervention within their region by agreement (or by a 'regional custom' for that matter), in derogation from their obligations under the UN Charter.

Perhaps the strongest argument for the legality of Article 4(h) is that it does not contradict Article 53, paragraph 1 or the primacy of the Security Council since Article 4(h) is consent-based, and thus

[66] De Wet (2015) 320; Kioko (2003); Kuwali (2009); Amvane (2015); Kindiki (2003).
[67] De Wet (2015) 320. [68] De Wet (2015) 320; Kuwali (2009) 44–5.
[69] Kuwali (2008) 64–5; Kioko (2003).

the question of use of force does not come into play: 'By ratifying the AU Constitutive Act, AU Member States must be understood to have agreed that the AU can intervene in their domestic affairs in the face of war crimes, genocide and crimes against humanity.'[70] Further, 'by endorsing Art 4(h), AU Member States waived their right to be free from intervention. They empowered the AU as a multilateral organ, to intervene in AU Member States in question, which does not affect the rights of non-AU Members.'[71]

Thus, in the case of Burundi, for example, when Burundi ratified the Constitutive Act, it arguably consented to any future decision of the AU to intervene in its territory – including by use of force – under Article 4(h), despite its later protests. Moreover, the consent-based argument entails that the *jus cogens* status of the prohibition on the use of force in Article 2(4) of the Charter becomes irrelevant in this context, since the norm itself is not violated once consent for the use of force is present.[72] However, the irrelevance of *jus cogens* or Article 2(4) of the UN Charter, when the state has made it clear that it has rescinded its invitation and no longer consents, assumes that the consent would remain valid.[73]

Indeed, this argument cannot be entirely dismissed as a valid portrayal of the consequences of ratification of the AU Constitutive Act. Nevertheless, the idea that intervention under Article 4(h) without Security Council authorization, based on a presumption of consent given at the time of ratification of the AU Constitutive Act, rather than in relation to the specific situation, should be rejected for several reasons.

Upon closer scrutiny, this argument is bound to fail. *Firstly*, Article 53(1) states that 'no enforcement action shall be taken under regional arrangements or by regional agencies without the authorization of the Security Council'. It does not allow for exceptions for another collective system of a regional organization, even one that is purportedly consent-based. The ordinary meaning thus negates this possibility. And while one could argue that consent-based action is not 'enforcement' by definition, it is clear that the AU, ECOWAS, and other organizations understand their relationship with the Security Council as governed by Article 53(1) and their military measures against their respective members as

70 Kuwali (2014) 36; Kindiki (2003) 287. 71 Kuwali (2014) 31.
72 Harrell (2008). 73 Reisman (1980) 151–2.

enforcement. In addition, the possibility of intervention by consent/invitation is explicitly contemplated in Article 4(j) of the AU Constitutive Act.[74] Thus, intervention under Article 4(h) is to be read as enforcement action, not as based on prior agreement.

Secondly, viewing Article 4(h) as a carte-blanche for an 'intervention by invitation' is highly problematic as it subjects the application of Article 4(h) to the confines of that doctrine. Questions might, for example, be asked as to whether the invitation would be valid if the country were in the midst of a civil war? What if the government that ratified the AU Constitutive Act no longer had effective control over its territory? Or if the ratifying government were not legitimately representative of its people? If the action were intended against the inviting leader? These questions and others would have to be evaluated on a case-by-case basis if Article 4(h) were premised on 'intervention by invitation'. And perhaps most problematic is that such an intervention is likely to be carried out against the contemporaneous will of the state, which has the right to retract its invitation to intervene at any time, as the ICJ has recognized.[75]

Some have argued that if the consent is treaty-based, it can be revoked only in accordance with the law governing that treaty, and thus more often than not a state will remain bound by its consent, despite its change of heart.[76] But since obligations under the UN Charter enjoy primacy over other treaties, as well as the status of the prohibition of aggression, if not the use of force more generally, as *jus cogens*, once a state no longer consents to an intervention, its previous treaty obligation becomes contrary to these higher sources of law.

Thus, even if one accepts the notion that an invitation to intervene can be given in advance, one cannot ignore the fact that when intervention becomes a reality, the same state may decide to withdraw its invitation, as was the case with Burundi. While this may constitute a violation of Burundi's obligations under the AU Constitutive Act, it creates at the same time a situation where a state does not consent to an intervention. Given the possible violations of *jus cogens* rules, as well as the primacy of the UN Charter under Article 103, AU member states would be prohibited

74 See also de Wet (2015) 318.

75 *Democratic Republic of the Congo* v. *Uganda*, at p. 197, paras. 46–7; Kreß and Nußberger (2017) 246–7.

76 Harrell (2008) 430–1.

from conducting a forceful intervention, even if the AU Constitutive Act were to obligate them so to do. In effect, a treaty-based consent to intervention is unenforceable if later retracted, the treaty obligation notwithstanding. Moreover, in a given situation when the scope of the prohibition on the use of force is at stake, a better interpretation is that it curtails the exception to the *jus cogens* rule potentially implicated, rather than expands it. This is all the more the case when prohibition on the use of force is involved. The prohibition is at the centre of maintaining international peace and security, the first Purpose of the UN Charter.

Thirdly and finally, this position also stands in opposition to the structure of the UN Charter collective security system, thus defying its object and purpose. The logic of the 'consent' argument can be applied to the Security Council as well. In the consent-based international legal order, by joining the UN, states have given their consent in advance for intervention in their territory when the Security Council so decides.

That the UN collective security system is consent-based is, of course, true. But the fact that UN member states agreed to the system does not mean that coercive measures under Chapter VII – including military action under Article 42 – are not in fact enforcement. This is not how we understand the UN Charter, the prohibition on the use of force, and its exceptions.

It is understood and accepted that collective security measures under Article 42 are an exception to the prohibition on the use of force, not intervention by invitation. That Article 42 is an exception to the prohibition on the use of force is further evident from the fact that Article 41 concerns measures short of the use of force, thus Article 42 inherently concerns the use of force. Indeed, by ratifying the UN Charter, states consented to the role of the Security Council, although this consent was given to the UN system and is a general one; it is not consent to military intervention decades later in a particular situation. Enforcement measures adopted by the Council do not just implement existing obligations; they also create new legal obligations for the member states. The latter are bound by these decisions under Article 25.[77]

[77] In addition, if one were to frame collective security measures under Chapter VII within an 'intervention by invitation' paradigm, that could allow a member state to withdraw that invitation when enforcement measures were adopted against it

The same logic necessarily applies to the AU Constitutive Act. By ratifying the Constitutive Act, a distinction must be made between 'buying in' to an elaborate international organization and its mechanisms and consent for the use of military force in a specific scenario facing a state.

Furthermore, if regional bodies such as the AU adopt this approach within their region, it de facto strips the Security Council of its primacy in the maintenance of international peace and security, and leaves regions with an independent collective security mechanism that is detached from that envisaged in the UN Charter, particularly under Chapters VII and VIII. In such a scenario, the use of force in international law will no longer be limited to self-defence and that authorized by the Security Council; it will also become a matter for the decision-making processes of regional organizations. For these reasons, it cannot be said that Article 4(h) of the AU Constitutive Act, or similar provisions, allow for the use of force without Security Council authorization.

***

In the UN Charter era, military enforcement action by international organizations which is not in collective self-defense or pursuant to a Security Council authorization is illegal under international law. Nevertheless, there have been a few instances where international organizations have used force without Council authorization, seemingly basing themselves on regional treaties, such as the US embargo on Cuba in 1962 and the US operation in Grenada in 1983; NATO in Kosovo in 1999; and the ECOWAS interventions in Liberia in 1990 and The Gambia in 2017, although NATO and ECOWAS did not justify their actions on the treaty-based consent argument. These were met with various levels of acceptance, condonation, or condemnation by the Security Council and the international community.[78] The AU PSC decided to, but ultimately did not, intervene in Burundi in 2015. All this has led some to argue the existence of a new rule of customary international law allowing for regional humanitarian intervention[79] or

by the Security Council, thus stripping the measures of their stated object and purpose.

78 For thorough reviews of these situations, see Harrell (2008); Hakimi (2007); Helal (2018).

79 Suyash (2010); more generally on the legality of humanitarian intervention, see Henkin (1999); Reisman (1994); Greenwood (1999).

pro-democratic intervention,[80] though these views are generally rejected.[81]

Others, while not claiming that such actions are legal, refer to 'acceptable breaches'[82] or the existence of an 'operational system' that works alongside the UN Charter, where regional organizations can intervene when legitimate or appropriate, despite the inconsistency with the Charter,[83] or justifications based on 'legitimacy' as opposed to 'legality'.[84] These notions attempt to address the unavoidable gap that sometimes exists between decisions based on policy, by states as well as the Security Council, and those based on international law.

80 On this see Kreß and Nußberger (2017); Wippman (2015).
81 See Chapter 6. 82 Wippman (2015) 815. 83 Hakimi (2007).
84 Franck (2006).

8

The Security Council and the International Court of Justice

Within the framework of the peaceful settlement of disputes, and more broadly, the Charter provides for several points of interaction between the Security Council and the ICJ.[1] The UN Charter envisaged a symbiotic relationship between the Security Council and the ICJ, the principal judicial organ of the UN. One of the tools available to the Council to settle peacefully disputes that may affect international peace and security is to seek to engage the ICJ's contentious jurisdiction or to ask it to provide advisory opinions on legal questions that arise in the Council's work. In addition, the Charter gives the Council responsibility for addressing instances of non-compliance by states with the Court's judgments that are brought before the Council. However, the Council has rarely taken advantage of this potential relationship or played a role in addressing non-compliance with judgments. For the most part, the role of the ICJ has been neglected by Council members, by disputing states, and by the Secretariat.

According to Article 36(3) of the Charter, the Council should take into consideration that legal disputes 'should as a general rule' be referred by the parties to the ICJ; under Article 96 of the Charter, the Council *may* request the Court to provide an advisory opinion on any question of law; under Article 94(2) of the Charter, the Council *may, if it deems necessary*, make recommendations or decide upon measures to be taken to give effect to an ICJ judgment. The

[1] Sievers and Daws (2014) 597–606. For other recent writings, see Oellers-Frahm (2012, 2019); Security Council Report (2016); Sthoeger (2016); Giegerich (2012).

language used by the drafters of the Charter undoubtedly reflects the wide discretion the Council has been given in performing its responsibilities.

At the same time, these articles empower the Council to have recourse to and interact with the ICJ and with states that are unwilling to abide by a judgment in their case. The Council has thus been provided with significant tools by the Charter; what is in question is the political will to make use of them in the exercise of its functions when it might prove beneficial.

This point was made by the President of the Court, Judge Rosalyn Higgins, in an open debate in the Council on the rule of law on 22 June 2006, with reference to Article 36(3) of the UN Charter. President Higgins said: 'I am obliged to say that the Security Council has failed to make use of this provision for many years. This tool needs to be brought to life and made a central policy of the Security Council.'[2] This has not happened.

This chapter examines the history and nature of the Security Council's relationship with the ICJ and the role that this relationship may play in the exercise of the Council's functions. It briefly recalls the drafting history pertaining to the Court, including its relationship to the Council, the Charter provisions governing the relationship between the two principal organs, and the relationship between them – both potentially and in practice.

8.1 Drafting History

The ICJ was preceded by the Permanent Court of International Justice (PCIJ), provided for by Article 14 of the 1920 Covenant of the League of Nations. The PCIJ held its inaugural sitting in 1922 and its last public sitting on 4 December 1939, following several years of diminished activity in the 1930s and after the onset of World War II.[3] The Permanent Court was formally dissolved by a League of Nations resolution in 1946.

With a view to establishing a successor to the Permanent Court, the United Kingdom constituted in 1943 the Informal Inter-Allied Committee of Experts, which met in London and was attended by jurists from eleven countries. The Inter-Allied Committee issued its report on 10 February 1944, recommending, inter alia, that the

[2] S/PV.5474, 22 June 2006, p. 8. [3] Spiermann (2019).

statute of a future international court should be based on that of the Permanent Court; that it should retain advisory jurisdiction; that acceptance of the jurisdiction of the Court should not be compulsory; and that it should have no jurisdiction to deal with essentially political matters.[4]

The United States, the Soviet Union, the United Kingdom, and China, as the powers attending the 1944 Dumbarton Oaks Conference (the Washington Conversations on a new International Peace and Security Organization), agreed that a Committee of Jurists would prepare a draft statute for what was to become the ICJ, for submission to the 1945 San Francisco Conference, where the UN Charter would be drawn up. The Committee of Jurists, comprising representatives from forty-four states, was chaired by US State Department legal adviser Green Hackworth.

Within the Committee, the issue of compulsory jurisdiction once again emerged as a major source of contention (as it had done in 1920), with opposition from the United States and the Soviet Union in particular. As an alternative to compulsory jurisdiction for the Court over UN members, another suggestion was put forward: that willing countries enter into a treaty accepting as binding Security Council and General Assembly recommendations to adjudicate specific classes of cases before the Court. The position of the United States and the Soviet Union ultimately prevailed at the 1945 San Francisco Conference, in which fifty states participated. The conference decided against compulsory jurisdiction (just as the League of Nations had done in the 1920s) but in favour of the creation of a new court that would be a principal organ of the UN. It was also decided that the ICJ Statute would be annexed to the UN Charter. The United States and the Soviet Union were more amenable on the issue of advisory jurisdiction and eventually agreed to empower the General Assembly and the Security Council to request advisory opinions and to empower the General Assembly to authorize other organs of the UN and specialized agencies to request such opinions. However, proposals to allow states to request advisory opinions were not adopted, most likely as these would allow individual states to use advisory procedures as a guise for contentious cases against other states.

[4] Informal Inter-Allied Committee Report (1945).

The election of the first members of the ICJ took place on 6 February 1946 at the inaugural session of the General Assembly and the ninth meeting of the Security Council.[5] In April 1946, the ICJ met for the first time and elected Judge José Gustavo Guerrero (El Salvador), the last President of the Permanent Court, as its President. The ICJ held an inaugural public sitting on 18 April 1946, with the first case submitted in May 1947, concerning incidents in the Corfu Channel brought by the UK against Albania.[6]

8.2 The Security Council and the ICJ: Practice and Potential

8.2.1 Council Referral to the ICJ

Under Article 36(1) of the UN Charter, the Council may recommend 'appropriate procedures or methods of adjustment' for situations that endanger international peace and security. Article 36(3) of the Charter provides that, in doing so, the Council 'should' take into consideration 'that legal disputes should as a general rule be referred by the parties' to the ICJ.

Despite this language, the Council has recommended that states follow the 'general rule' on only one occasion. The sole instance was in the *Corfu Channel* case – the first proceeding before the ICJ – when it recommended that Albania and the UK immediately refer their dispute to the Court. The draft resolution sponsored by the UK was adopted on 9 April 1947 with eight votes in favour and two abstentions, from Poland and the Soviet Union, while the United Kingdom, as a party to the dispute, abstained from voting in accordance with Article 27(3) of the Charter.[7]

In its statement before the vote, Albania claimed that the Council did not have sufficient evidence to refer the case to the ICJ. Australia, on the other hand, defended the complementary roles of the Court and the Council:

> [T]he International Court of Justice can do very fully the very things we were not able to do here. It can collect additional evidence, and, particularly in the oral hearings provided under Article 43 of its Statute, it can call

5 S/PV.9, 6 February 1946.
6 On the drafting history, see Security Council Report (2016) 4–5.
7 S/PV.127, 9 April 1947.

in witnesses, experts, counsel and advocates. It can obtain material witnesses for examination and cross-examination so that justice shall be done.

Almost thirty years later, the Council recalled the potential of the ICJ in resolving the dispute between Greece and Turkey over the continental shelf in the Aegean Sea, though it refrained from making a recommendation. In a 10 August 1976 letter to the Council, Greece requested that it convene an urgent meeting to discuss Turkish 'violations of its sovereignty'.[8] After convening a meeting during which the two parties to the dispute addressed the Council,[9] on 25 August 1976, the Council adopted resolution 395 (1976) inviting the two to 'take into account the contribution that appropriate judicial means, in particular the International Court of Justice, are qualified to make to the settlement of any remaining legal differences that they may identify in connection with their present dispute'.[10]

Although Article 36(3) of the UN Charter speaks only of the Council recommending states to take their dispute before the ICJ, the wide discretion of the Council on how to perform its responsibilities may provide the Council with the possibility to go beyond mere recommendations with respect to the ICJ.

As seen in Chapter 5, acting under Chapter VII, the Council has developed a wide range of measures not involving the use of force in order to maintain or restore international peace and security. Over the years, these have included the establishment of judicial bodies, such as the international criminal tribunals, with which all UN member states are obliged to co-operate.

Similarly, the Council may have the power to require two or more states to submit to the jurisdiction of the Court regarding a particular dispute, as a measure not involving the use of force under Article 41.

Though this is uncharted waters for the Council, an analogy may be drawn from previous Council practice. An example is when the Council decided to compel Kuwait and Iraq to settle their boundary dispute by a binding procedure as a matter of international peace

[8] S/12167, 10 August 1976. [9] S/PV.1949, 12 August 1976.

[10] Greece submitted the dispute to the Court; however, the Court found that it did not have jurisdiction to hear the case, as neither the General Act nor the joint communiqué Greece relied upon in its application contained Turkish consent to the proceedings. See *Aegean Sea Continental Shelf*.

and security in resolution 833 of 27 May 1993.[11] However, it remains an open question whether the Court would accept that the Council is empowered to override the fundamental principle of international law that states can be required to submit to the jurisdiction of an international court or tribunal only if they consent to do so.[12]

There seems to be no reason of principle why, in the case of disputes or situations that threaten international peace and security, the Council could not adopt a Chapter VII resolution obligating states that are parties to a dispute to refer some or all of the legal aspects of the dispute to the ICJ. The Council could also obligate the relevant states to accept the jurisdiction of the Court for this purpose if they have otherwise not done so. Under a Security Council decision, the states would be obligated to have their dispute decided by a binding judgment of the Court. This would be the case even if the states involved had agreed otherwise, due to Article 103 of the UN Charter, which gives the UN Charter overriding power over other international treaties.[13]

In her intervention in the 2006 debate, President Higgins said: 'Litigation before the Court is not a hostile act. This fact can be testified by the many friendly States that have been wise enough to know that the best way to avoid deterioration in their good relations, if that cannot be done by negotiations, is to have a dispute between them resolved by the Court.'[14]

Compelling states to submit to the Court's jurisdiction in an international legal system based on consent is not a step the Council will or should take lightly. Yet even consistent usage of the Council's power to recommend to parties to a dispute that their differences be settled before the ICJ could influence more states to do so over time.

The Council's powers and its authority to create obligations for states entail that a recommendation from the Council to states to take their dispute before the ICJ may, in certain circumstances, impact the conduct of those states. However, the Council has thus

[11] For a detailed account, see Chapter 5.

[12] See the discussion in *Arbitral Award of 3 October 1899* (*Guyana* v. *Venezuela*), *Jurisdiction*, Judgment.

[13] An interesting question is whether the ICJ could establish jurisdiction based on a Security Council resolution, even if the states in question did not proceed to submit the dispute to the Court as required by the resolution.

[14] S/PV.5474, 22 June 2006, p. 8.

far refrained from making use of this power of recommendation; the incentives for states to settle their disputes peacefully will only increase if the Council considers this option more frequently and on occasion acts upon it.

That Council consideration of disputes between states related to ICJ cases – even without making recommendations for states to go before the ICJ – may affect those states' behaviour is evident from past examples, such as the tension that arose between Thailand and Cambodia concerning their boundary near the Temple of Preah Vihear. In 1962, the Court ruled that the temple was situated on Cambodian territory, and that consequently Thailand was under an obligation to withdraw its forces from the temple and from its vicinity on Cambodian territory.[15] Thailand subsequently withdrew its forces from the temple and erected a fence, which divided the temple ruins from the rest of the promontory of Preah Vihear.

Almost fifty years later, in February 2011, there were exchanges of fire in the temple area between Thai and Cambodian soldiers, resulting in at least eight killed and thousands displaced. Following the outbreak of fighting, on 5 February both Thailand and Cambodia sent the President of the Council letters, giving their descriptions of the incidents that had taken place.[16] On 6 February, Cambodia wrote to the Council President again, documenting continued attacks on the border and citing how they violated international law.[17] The Cambodian letter also asked the Council to convene an 'urgent meeting' to stop 'Thailand's aggression'. Thailand responded with a letter the following day, reiterating its commitment to using bilateral frameworks and channels of communication to resolve the situation.[18]

The Council held consultations on the matter under 'any other business' on 7 February, after which the Council President conveyed elements to the press, calling for a ceasefire and urging the parties to resolve the situation peacefully. The Council held consultations again the following day, during which Council members were briefed by the President of the Council on her phone conversation with Marty Natalegawa, then minister of foreign affairs of

[15] *Cambodia* v. *Thailand* (1962).

[16] S/2011/56 and S/2010/57, 5 February 2011, were from Cambodia and Thailand.

[17] S/2011/58, 6 February 2011.

[18] S/2011/59, 7 February 2011.

Indonesia and chair of the Association of Southeast Asian Nations (ASEAN), who was attempting to mediate between the two states.

This was followed by a private meeting attended by the Cambodian Minister of Foreign Affairs and International Cooperation and Thailand's Minister of Foreign Affairs. In 'elements to the press' after the meeting, Council members urged the parties to establish a permanent ceasefire, to implement it fully, and to resolve the situation peacefully through effective dialogue. Clashes in the border area broke out again on 22 April, following which both states wrote to the Council President, though neither requested the Council to discuss the matter.

Eventually, Cambodia instituted further proceedings against Thailand before the ICJ, requesting the Court to interpret its 1962 judgment. After indicating provisional measures in July 2011, the Court issued its judgment on the matter on 11 November 2013, concluding that its 1962 judgment had decided that Cambodia had sovereignty over the whole territory of the promontory of Preah Vihear and that consequently Thailand was under an obligation to withdraw from that territory.[19]

The Thailand–Cambodia situation shows that Council consideration may play a role in nudging states into finding a way to settle their dispute peacefully. Under Article 36(3) of the UN Charter, the Council itself could have seized the opportunity to recommend to the states concerned that they take their dispute to the ICJ.

It is possible, though politically improbable in most cases, that the Council would recommend or even decide that member states should take their long-standing and protracted conflicts that are on the Council's agenda, some of which have been stagnant for decades, before the ICJ to resolve their legal aspects, or at least some legal issues that may later assist the states – and the Council – to resolve the greater differences.

8.2.2 Requests for Advisory Opinions from the ICJ

Pursuant to Article 96 of the Charter, the General Assembly or the Security Council may request the Court to provide an advisory opinion on any legal question.

[19] *Cambodia* v. *Thailand* (2013).

The possibility of the Council requesting an advisory opinion surfaced in its deliberations several times in the first few years of its existence. A draft resolution put forward by Belgium on 26 August 1947 for an advisory opinion on the competence of the Council to deal with the situation in Indonesia did not receive the required majority.[20] A Syrian draft resolution proposed on 27 July 1948 requesting an advisory opinion on the legal status of Palestine after the termination of the British Mandate similarly failed to receive the required majority.[21]

In fact, the Council has requested an advisory opinion on only one occasion. On 29 July 1970, it sought an advisory opinion on the 'legal consequences for States of the continued presence of South Africa in Namibia'.[22] The request came as members of the Council were growing increasingly concerned about South Africa's disregard of previous UN resolutions, including Council resolutions 264 (1969), 269 (1969), and 276 (1970), requiring it to end its presence in Namibia. By requesting the Court's opinion, the Council gave effect to a recommendation of the Ad Hoc Subcommittee of the Council, set up by resolution 276 (1970), to determine ways by which to address South Africa's refusal to withdraw from Namibia in defiance of UN resolutions.

The draft resolution, sponsored by Finland, was adopted, with Poland, the Soviet Union, and the United Kingdom abstaining, after more than five months of negotiation. One argument put forward in support of the request was the 'need to reactivate the International Court of Justice itself', which was underutilized in terms of caseload, contributing to its declining authority. Statements by other delegations drew attention to the limited scope of the question asked of the Court, which could be interpreted as a signal to the ICJ not to overstep the limited and focused scope of the opinion requested from it. Syria and Zambia stressed that the request in no way prevented the Council from considering the situation while the Court was seized of the issue. The Soviet Union voiced serious doubts about the effectiveness of requesting an advisory opinion in resolving a crisis that requires 'serious

[20] S/PV.195, 26 August 1947. [21] S/894, 27 July 1948.
[22] S/RES/284, 29 July 1970.

political action on the part of the Security Council'. So did Poland, which also warned against measures that would 'only give the appearance of genuine action'.[23]

In its advisory opinion of 21 June 1971, the Court found that the continued presence of South Africa in Namibia was illegal and that UN member states were obligated to refrain from any acts and in particular any dealings with the South African government that implied recognition of the legality of, or lent support or assistance to, such presence and administration.

In resolution 301 of 20 October 1971, the Council 'took note with appreciation' of the advisory opinion, agreed with its operative conclusions, and called upon all states to conduct themselves in accordance with the advisory opinion. France and the United Kingdom abstained on the resolution.

Advisory opinions may not suit fast-moving and evolving situations which require a timely response by the Council, or situations which are ultimately political rather than legal in the eyes of some states. However, they may prove effective in untangling particular aspects of a situation on the Council's agenda. They may also be useful in providing legal clarity and greater legitimacy to certain Council decisions that are being challenged by domestic and regional actors on legal grounds.[24]

Advisory opinions – and the right to request them – by other UN organs and agencies may also impact the Council. The General Assembly has requested several advisory opinions over the years, including on matters that relate to issues on the Council's agenda, in particular the *Wall* and *Kosovo* Advisory Opinions.

In addition, of relevance to the Council are past discussions over the ability of the Secretariat, with the Secretary-General as its head, to request advisory opinions of the ICJ on legal issues that arise within the Secretariat's work, including work related to matters of international peace and security. Several Secretaries-General have proposed that the General Assembly should use its Article 96(2) powers to authorize the Secretary-General to request advisory

[23] S/PV.1550, 29 July 1970.

[24] One such example could have been the legal and political challenges to the then al-Qaida and Taliban sanctions regime, which ultimately led the Council to establish the Office of the Ombudsperson.

opinions.[25] One member state expressed its support for such a possibility more recently:

> The involvement of the Secretary-General directly or through his envoys or special representatives is vital to early warning of conflicts and could be key in prevention efforts. Enabling the Secretary-General to request advisory opinions from the International Court of Justice could be a valuable instrument of preventive diplomacy that would strengthen the work of the Secretariat within the framework of the purposes of the Charter.[26]

The intention was that the Secretary-General would then be able to use this power to assist his or her role as mediator and provider of good offices between states. It could also help the Secretary-General overcome legal uncertainties that might arise in the context of the Secretariat's work while performing tasks given to it by the Council. This would equally apply to legal questions concerning issues that are on the Council's agenda, including instances when the Secretariat has been mandated to perform certain tasks by the Council itself. At the same time, there is a reluctance by the member states to give this power, in effect, to a single individual, as opposed to UN organs or agencies where the member states vote on such decisions.[27]

8.2.3 Enforcement of ICJ Judgments

Another potential area of interaction for the Court and the Council is in the case of non-compliance with an ICJ judgment. Article 94(2) of the Charter gives the Council the power to 'make recommendations or decide upon measures to be taken to give effect to the judgment' if a request is made by one of the parties to the dispute. In practice, however, the Council has never used its power to enforce an ICJ judgment, though it should be noted that the parties to disputes mostly comply with ICJ judgments.

One attempt to have the Council exercise its authority under Article 94(2) was when Nicaragua requested, in a letter to the President of the Council on 20 October 1986, an emergency

[25] E/1732, 26 June 1950 was on means by which the proposed Human Rights Commission might be able to obtain advisory opinions from the ICJ; A/47/277, 17 June 1992.

[26] S/PV.7858, 10 January 2017, statement of Mexico, p. 74.

[27] For more on this, see Security Council Report (2016) 12.

meeting to consider the failure of the United States to execute the ICJ's judgment of 27 June 1986 in the *Military and Paramilitary Activities in and against Nicaragua* case.[28] In its judgment, the Court found that the United States had violated the prohibition on intervention in the affairs of another state and the prohibition on the use of force by supporting the 'contras' rebels operating against the Nicaraguan government, and by conducting direct attacks in Nicaraguan territory and laying mines in Nicaraguan waters, respectively.[29] A draft resolution calling for full and immediate compliance with the ICJ judgment was vetoed by the United States on 28 October 1986.[30] In a statement before the vote, the United States rejected the jurisdiction and competence of the Court to render the 27 June judgment. France, Thailand, and the United Kingdom abstained from the vote.

While not within the purview of Article 94(2) of the Charter per se, the Council was instrumental in the implementation of the Court's judgment that determined the land boundary between Libya and Chad in 1994 in the Aouzou Strip. At that time, the Council had imposed sanctions on Libya, including a flight ban, in relation to Libyan involvement in the Lockerbie incident. After the judgment was issued, Libya and Chad signed an agreement on implementation that requested the Secretary-General to supervise Libyan withdrawal from territories determined to be Chadian under the judgment.

Upon the recommendation of the Secretary-General,[31] the Council established the United Nations Aouzou Strip Observer Group (UNASOG) by resolution 915 of 4 May 1994, and called on both parties to co-operate with the mission. Acting under Chapter VII, the Council exempted the mission from the flight ban. The Council further stressed its determination 'to assist the parties in implementing the Judgment of the International Court of Justice concerning their territorial dispute and thereby to help promote peaceful relations between them, in keeping with the principles and purposes of the Charter'. UNASOG completed its task on 30 May 1994 and the Council terminated its mandate by resolution 926 of 13 June 1994.

[28] S/18415, 17 October 1986.
[29] *Military and Paramilitary Activities* (1986).
[30] S/18428, 28 October 1986.
[31] S/1994/512, 27 April 1994.

Allegations of non-compliance with another judgment came before the Council in 2002 when Honduras claimed that El Salvador had not complied with the Court's judgment of 1992 concerning their land and maritime boundary. Though the two states agreed in 1998 to demarcate their boundary in accordance with the judgment within a year, by 2002 the process was far from completed.

On 28 November 2000, Honduras had informed the Council of border tensions and said that it had requested El Salvador to comply with the judgment and move ahead on demarcation, asserting that demarcation would help to reduce tension and promote a better climate of understanding.[32] With no significant progress in the demarcation process, on 22 January 2002 Honduras sent a letter to the President of the Council, pursuant to Article 94(2) of the Charter, requesting the Council to 'intervene and assist in securing the execution of and faithful compliance with the judgment of the International Court of Justice'.[33] El Salvador responded on 24 September 2002, denying accusations of non-compliance and adding that it did not object to the issues raised by Honduras being discussed by the Council.[34] El Salvador conveyed its intention to request the ICJ to revise its judgment. The Council took no action in response to the letter. El Salvador proceeded to make such a request to the Court, but the Court rejected its application.[35] The two sides then reached a further agreement on the demarcation of the boundary.[36]

In another case of non-compliance, Mexico sent a letter to the Council on 28 March 2014, bringing to the attention of the Council the fact that the United States had not complied with a judgment of the Court in the *Avena* case between the two countries.[37] The Court found that the United States was in violation of the Vienna Convention on Consular Relations because it had not notified the Mexican authorities of the incarceration of fifty-one Mexican nationals sentenced to death in Texas. It ordered the United States to stay the executions and to provide, by means of its own choosing, a review and reconsideration of their conviction and

[32] S/2000/1142, 28 November 2000. [33] S/2002/108, 22 January 2002.
[34] S/2002/1102, 24 September 2002.
[35] *Application for Revision of the Judgment.*
[36] See Security Council Report (2016) 6.
[37] The letter has not been made public.

sentences.[38] Mexico noted that three of the individuals had already been executed without any such review by the authorities. The Council did not consider the letter or take any action, which would have been highly improbable as it concerned a permanent member. It seems that, aware of this, Mexico refrained from asking the Council to take action, but merely brought the issue to its attention. Furthermore, there was some sympathy for the United States among some Council members since its federal government was in favour of implementing the judgment, but state authorities in Texas refused to co-operate in a matter that was deemed to be under state jurisdiction.

With respect to the Council's role in the implementation of ICJ judgments, the *Nicaragua* and *Mexico* cases concerning the United States' non-implementation of judgments show that when a question of implementation concerns a permanent member, Council action is highly unlikely. That is why, in the aftermath of the failed Council resolution, Nicaragua sought and succeeded in having the General Assembly pass a resolution urging the United States to fully and immediately comply with the Court's judgment.[39] Mexico, for its part, did not even attempt to have the Council pronounce on the United States' non-compliance with the Court's judgment.

That said, the case of implementing the ICJ's judgment on the land boundary between Libya and Chad in 1994 demonstrates that the Council may sometimes have an important role to play in implementation of judgments. In that case, the Council acknowledged that lack of implementation of judgments might threaten international peace and security. It further demonstrates that the Council can use the powers at its disposal, in that case by authorizing a Council observer mission to assist in implementing a judgment and adjust measures previously taken, such as sanctions already imposed on one of the states involved. The successful implementation of the judgment serves as a positive example of how the ICJ, the Council, and the Secretary-General co-operated to ensure that the border dispute was resolved peacefully.

Similarly, the Honduras–El Salvador dispute serves as an example of how Council oversight assisted the implementation of an ICJ judgment (which was achieved after El Salvador had sought to

[38] *Avena*, at p. 73, para. 153. [39] A/RES/41/31, 3 November 1986, para. 1.

return the matter to the Court for review). Thus, the Council has a positive role to play in implementation of ICJ judgments and could aspire to be more proactive in this respect. Moreover, if implementation of ICJ judgments is deemed to be a matter of international peace and security, the Council's wide discretion in the exercise of its responsibilities allows it to discuss occurrences of non-implementation on its own initiative, and to take action if necessary, including binding action such as sanctions on non-implementing states.

8.2.4 Election of ICJ Judges

The Security Council, along with the General Assembly, is responsible for the election of judges to the ICJ.[40] The ICJ consists of fifteen judges elected for nine-year terms by the General Assembly and the Council. Five seats come up for election every three years, normally in November.

According to Article 2 of the Statute, '[t]he Court shall be composed of a body of independent judges, elected regardless of their nationality from among persons of high moral character, who possess the qualifications required in their respective countries for appointment to the highest judicial offices, or are jurisconsults of recognized competence in international law'. Although there is no formal requirement for geographical distribution, Article 9 of the ICJ Statute requires representation of the 'main forms of civilization and of the principal legal systems of the world'. The practice of the election process takes account of geographical distribution.

According to Article 2 of the Statute, members of the Court are to be elected 'regardless of their nationality' and are to be completely independent. No two nationals from the same state can hold office at the same time, and, once elected, a judge is a delegate neither of the government of his or her own country nor of any other state. However, it is important to note that it has been the practice of the Security Council and the General Assembly to ensure that a judge from each of the permanent members is on the Court, thus reflecting the composition of the Council.[41]

[40] Higgins et al., *Oppenheim* (2017b) 1141–3.

[41] This practice was not followed when, in 2017, a UK national was not elected to serve as judge.

Candidates are nominated not by governments but by the national groups on the Permanent Court of Arbitration (PCA) (an intergovernmental organization established in 1899 to facilitate arbitration and other forms of dispute resolution between states, currently with a membership of 122 member states) or an equivalent national group. When making nominations, members of each national group are recommended to consult their highest national court, national legal faculties, and national schools of law. No group may nominate more than four persons. The names of candidates are then communicated to the Secretary-General, who prepares a list of nominations.

Article 8 of the ICJ Statute states that the General Assembly and the Security Council shall proceed independently of one another to elect the members of the Court in a secret ballot. Candidates who obtain an absolute majority of votes (i.e., a majority of all electors, whether or not they vote) in both the General Assembly and the Council are elected. A candidate therefore must (as of 2022) obtain ninety-seven votes in the former and eight votes in the latter. In the Council vote, there is no distinction between permanent and non-permanent members.

Each elector may vote for five candidates on the first ballot. If the number of candidates obtaining an absolute majority is fewer than five on the first ballot, a second ballot for the remaining positions will be held and balloting will continue until five candidates have obtained the required majority. If more than the required number of candidates obtain an absolute majority on the same ballot in either organ, a new vote on all the candidates will be held. In the event that the five candidates elected by one organ are not the same as those elected by the other, both will proceed (independently) to new balloting to fill the unresolved seats. This process will continue for three meetings when, if any positions are still not filled, the Council and the General Assembly may decide to convene a conference of six members (three from each organ) to recommend a candidate for acceptance by the General Assembly and the Council.

8.2.5 The Council and the ICJ: Competing Competences

Another point of interaction between the Council and the ICJ is found in several decisions of the ICJ. As it is a judicial institution, legal issues that touch upon international disputes with which the Council is dealing have inevitably arisen before the ICJ. When such instances occur, the intricate dynamics between the two bodies come to the fore and raise questions as to the extent of their respective authority. Indeed, one controversial issue that has been debated for years is the overlapping competence of the Council and the Court on certain matters of international peace and security. This raises two questions: The first concerns whether the Court may consider a matter that is already before the Council. The other is whether the Court can review a decision of the Council or act as a form of appellate body adjudicating the legality of Council action.

The Court answered the former question positively in the *Case Concerning Diplomatic and Consular Staff in Tehran*, when it decided to indicate provisional measures to ensure the inviolability of the premises of the United States embassy and other places in Teheran, and the immediate release of US nationals being held hostage. The Court noted that the Council had already expressed its deep concern over the issue and the potential consequences for international peace and security in its resolution 457 of 4 December 1979. However, it said that 'no provision of the Statute or Rules contemplates that the Court should decline to take cognizance of one aspect of a dispute merely because that dispute has other aspects, however important'.[42] The Court's interpretation of its competence was reinforced a few weeks later when the Council, in resolution 461 of 31 December 1979, deplored the continued holding of hostages by Iran contrary to resolution 457 (1979) and noted the order of the Court calling upon Iran to ensure the immediate release of the hostages.

In the *Military and Paramilitary Activities* case, the Court reiterated this point. It found that while the UN Charter gives the Council primary responsibility for the maintenance of international peace and security, it does not give it exclusive responsibility. It noted that the Charter assigns the Council functions of a political nature, whereas the Court exercises purely judicial functions. The Court added that it 'cannot be debarred' from adjudicating a legal dispute between States 'by the existence of a procedure for the States concerned to report to the Security Council' when acting in self-defence under Article 51 of the Charter. Therefore, both organs

[42] At p. 15, para. 24.

can perform their separate but complementary functions with respect to the same events.[43]

8.2.6 Review of Council Decisions

The ICJ made clear in the *Namibia* Advisory Opinion that it does not possess powers of judicial review or appeal in respect of the decisions of the Council.[44] Yet the Court has, in fact, reviewed decisions by the Council and the General Assembly and found them to be within the competence of those two bodies.

The Court has also hinted that it could review a Council decision if it was necessary in order to decide a legal matter arising in a contentious case between two states. In the *Lockerbie* cases, Libya claimed that the United States and the United Kingdom had violated its rights under the Montreal Convention of 23 September 1971 for the Suppression of Unlawful Acts against the Safety of Civil Aviation, by demanding the extradition of the suspects in the downing of Pan Am flight 103. According to Libya, the Convention gave it a choice between extradition and domestic prosecution of the alleged offenders. The United States and the United Kingdom contended, however, that even if the Montreal Convention did confer on Libya the rights it claimed, these were 'superseded' by the relevant decisions of the Security Council under Chapter VII of the UN Charter.[45] Libya argued that the decision of the Security Council was 'contrary to international law', and considered that the Council had 'employed its power to characterize the situation for purposes of Chapter VII simply as a pretext to avoid applying the Montreal Convention'.[46] The proceedings were eventually terminated when Libya reached an agreement with the United States and the United Kingdom on the prosecution of the two suspects, and the Court did not have to adjudicate the legality of the US and UK demands.

Although the merits of Libya's claims were never determined, the Court did find that it had jurisdiction to hear the cases.[47] Since the

[43] *Military and Paramilitary Activities* (1984), at pp. 433–6, paras. 93–8.
[44] *Namibia* Advisory Opinion, at p. 45, para. 89.
[45] *Lockerbie* Provisional Measures (*Libya* v. *US*), at p. 125, para. 35.
[46] *Lockerbie* Provisional Measures (*Libya* v. *US*), at pp. 125–6, paras. 38–9.
[47] *Lockerbie* Preliminary Objections.

resolutions in question decided that Libya must comply with the US and UK requests for co-operation and extradition,[48] under Chapter VII, such a judgment on the merits would have had to touch upon the legality of the Council's resolutions themselves.

In its judgment on jurisdiction, the Court also observed that it could consider the merits of Libya's claims based on the fact that, at the time Libya's application was submitted, resolution 748 (1992) had yet to be adopted. The preceding resolution 731 (1992) urged Libyan co-operation, which 'could not form a legal impediment to the Court's jurisdiction because it was a mere recommendation without binding effect'.[49] Thus, one can argue that the Court hinted that had Libya presented its legal claim after a binding resolution under Chapter VII had been adopted, it might not have been able to hear the case.

Libya also made a request for provisional measures in that case. While rejecting Libya's request (without passing judgment on the legality of the Security Council resolutions concerned), the Court observed:

> Members of the United Nations are obliged to accept and carry out the decisions of the Security Council in accordance with Article 25 of the Charter; whereas the Court, which is at the stage of proceedings on provisional measures, considers that *prima facie* this obligation extends to the decision contained in resolution 748; and whereas, in accordance with Article 103 of the Charter, the obligations of the Parties in that respect prevail over their obligations under any other international agreement, including the Montreal Convention.[50]

Thus, while not entering into the legal validity of the Council's decision, the ICJ did observe that a binding Council decision under Chapter VII prevails, in principle, over other legal obligations, such as those contained in the Montreal Convention.

8.2.7 Interpretation of Council Resolutions

The interaction of the Council and the Court has also manifested itself in the Court's interpretation of Council resolutions. In its

[48] S/RES/748, 31 May 1992.

[49] Ibid., p. 26, para. 44; S/RES/731, 21 January 1992 urged Libyan compliance with the requests of the United States and the United Kingdom for co-operation and extradition.

[50] *Lockerbie* Provisional Measures (*Libya* v. *US*), at p. 126, para. 42.

jurisprudence, the Court has given guidance on the interpretation of Council documents, taking into account the special nature and context of Council resolutions – as opposed to treaties – and the function of the Council within the wider UN framework.[51]

8.2.8 Provisional Measures

The Court is authorized under Article 41 of its Statute to indicate provisional measures to preserve the respective rights of the parties before it. The Article requires that the Court inform the Security Council of the measures indicated. The issue of provisional measures was discussed in the Council in 1951, when the United Kingdom initiated ICJ proceedings against Iran after the latter nationalized its oil industry, including the Anglo-Iranian Oil Company. At the request of the United Kingdom, the Court indicated provisional measures, which Iran refused to accept as it claimed that the Court lacked jurisdiction in the case.[52] In response, on 29 September 1951, the United Kingdom requested the Council to consider the issue as a matter of 'extreme urgency'.[53] Attached to the request was a draft resolution calling on Iran to act in conformity with the provisional measures.[54] The Council considered the matter several times without taking any action, with states mainly debating whether the issue was one that falls within the domestic affairs of Iran, and, on 19 October, France proposed to adjourn the discussion until the ICJ determined whether it had jurisdiction in the case.[55] Later, the Court found that it lacked jurisdiction to entertain the United Kingdom's application.[56]

The Council has referred to provisional measures indicated by the ICJ on a few occasions. In 1979, it deplored the continued detention of US nationals by Iran, contrary to its previous resolution and the provisional measures indicated by the Court.[57] In 1993, the Council made certain demands of the FRY and the Bosnian Serbs and recalled the provisional measures issued by the Court, requiring that the FRY take all measures to prevent the commission of genocide.[58] In 1996, the Council requested that the Secretary-General keep it informed on

[51] See Chapter 2. [52] *Anglo-Iranian Oil*, Order of July 5th.
[53] S/2357, 29 September 1951. [54] S/2358, 29 September 1951.
[55] S/PV.565, 19 October 1951. [56] *Anglo-Iranian Oil*, judgment.
[57] S/RES/461, 31 December 1979, para. 2. [58] S/RES/819, 16 April 1993.

the situation in the Bakassi Peninsula, 'bearing in mind the Order of the International Court of Justice on provisional measures on the matter issued on 15 March 1996'.[59] In February 2020, the Council convened informal consultations to discuss the provisional measures issued by the Court against Myanmar, to prevent any harm to the Rohingya and prevent the destruction of evidence related to allegations of genocide.[60]

Article 94(2) speaks of the Council's role in giving effect to 'judgments'. The question whether this applies to other decisions, such as provisional measures, arose early on. When the Council considered UK proposals to take action after the provisional measures issued by the ICJ to Iran, the President of the Council suggested asking the ICJ – presumably in an advisory opinion – whether the Council can act under Article 94(2) with regard to non-compliance with provisional measures.[61]

It would seem that Article 94(2) is specific to judgments, as opposed to Article 94(1) which refers to the obligations of states to comply with the 'decisions' of the Court.[62] This would include provisional measures, which are now considered binding.[63] There is also a debate on whether Council recommendations or measures regarding non-compliance with judgments fall under Chapter VI or Chapter VII, or under Article 94(2) itself.

In practical terms, as with judgments, in the case that non-compliance with provisional measures endangers international peace and security, the Council is free to make recommendations – or take binding measures if necessary – based on its powers under Chapters VI and VII. Thus, for example, when the United Kingdom brought the issue of Iranian non-compliance with provisional measures before the Council, it referred to 'the dangers inherit in this situation and . . . the threat to peace and security that may thereby be involved'.[64]

[59] S/1996/391, 29 May 1996.

[60] What's in Blue, Briefing on Myanmar following the ICJ Order Indicating Provisional Measures Tomorrow (4 February), 3 February 2020, available at www.whatsinblue.org/2020/02/briefing-on-myanmar-following-the-icj-order-indicating-provisional-measures.php.

[61] S/PV.562, 17 October 1951, para. 39.

[62] See Oellers-Frahm (2019) MN 98–101.

[63] *LaGrand*, at. p. 506, para. 109.

[64] S/2357, 29 September 1951; see also statement of Ecuador, S/PV.559, 1 October 1951, p. 2 and its statement in S/PV.562, 17 October 1951, p. 8.

8.2.9 Meetings between the Council and the Court

In recent years, the Council and the Court have taken a number of initiatives to invigorate their relationship.

A relatively new practice is the annual closed briefing of the Council by the President of the ICJ, held since 2000. The President normally updates the Council on pending cases before the Court, recent decisions, and the Court's budget.

The complementary roles that the Court and the Council play in the promotion of the rule of law and substantive links between issues considered by these bodies have also been discussed. In the rule of law open debate in the Council initiated by Denmark on 22 June 2006, then ICJ President Higgins briefed the Council.[65] A further topic of discussion has been the need to increase the number of states that accept the Court's compulsory jurisdiction. To that effect, in the 29 October 2014 briefing by the ICJ President, some Council members welcomed the development of a handbook on accepting the jurisdiction of the ICJ, co-sponsored by Botswana, Japan, Lithuania, the Netherlands, Switzerland, the UK, and Uruguay, and published in July of that year.

The Council undertook its first formal visit to the Court's seat in The Hague on 11 August 2014. Chile co-chaired the meeting that took place, which aimed to express the Security Council's support for the work of the Court. The occasion also provided Council members with the opportunity to meet with the President and other members of the Court, as well as the Registrar. The main issues discussed included the challenge of increasing acceptance by member states of the compulsory jurisdiction of the Court and the execution of its judgments.[66]

***

As has been seen, the UN Charter provides for several areas of potential interaction between the Council and the ICJ. Nevertheless, the Council has scarcely made use of the ICJ as an instrument, or 'tool', in the exercise of its responsibility for the maintenance of international peace and security.

Over the years, the Council has been reluctant to resort to other UN organs and external actors that are independent of it – actors that it does not control and whose actions it cannot necessarily

[65] S/PV.5474, 22 June 2006. [66] S/PV.7245, 19 August 2014, p. 3.

predict. Instead, the Council has opted to retain control and decision-making powers at the possible expense of effectiveness and taking full advantage of its options.

From the perspective of the permanent members, the Court's jurisprudence has, at times, been perceived as contrary to their interests. After judgments were given against them in sensitive cases, the United States and France withdrew their acceptance of the compulsory jurisdiction of the Court. China and Russia, for their part, have taken a position of principle that states should resolve their differences through bilateral negotiations, not third-party dispute settlement procedures.

Undoubtedly, it was not the intention of the drafters of the UN Charter to allow the ICJ to serve as an 'appellate court' and regularly monitor and review Council action or that of the other UN organs. Yet a more prominent role for the Court, within the confines set by the Council itself in this context, could strengthen the effectiveness and legitimacy of the Council as an institution. Under the framework set out in the UN Charter and considering the Council's wide discretion as to how it carries out its responsibilities, the Council could and may want to consider making use of the ICJ as a valuable option.

As then President Higgins observed in 2006, 'we are all partners in the same magnificent enterprise – the enterprise spelled out in the Purposes and Principles in the United Nations Charter. The International Court of Justice stands ready to work alongside the Security Council in the fulfilment of these goals.'[67]

[67] S/PV.5474, 22 June 2006, p. 8.

9

The Contribution of the Security Council to the Development of International Law

The UN Charter does not envisage a role for the Security Council in the development of international law. The political organ which, under the Charter, is expressly endowed with such a role in relation to the codification and progressive development of international law is the General Assembly, though the drafters of the Charter were careful not to endow the Assembly with legislative power. Instead, the Charter provides that '[t]he General Assembly shall *initiate studies and make recommendations* for the purpose of ... *encouraging* the progressive development of international law and its codification ...'.[1] In implementing this provision, by a resolution adopted in 1947, the General Assembly established the ILC as a subsidiary organ with, for its object, 'the *promotion* of the progressive development of international law and its codification'.[2] The ILC, like its parent body, has no legislative powers. The legal force of its output depends upon its reception by states.[3]

It was entirely appropriate that it was the Assembly which, under the Charter, was expressly given a role in connection with the development and codification of international law; the Assembly

[1] Charter, Art. 13(a) (emphasis added).

[2] GA/RES/174(III), 21 November 1947, Statute of the International Law Commission, Art 1.1 (emphasis added).

[3] As the ILC itself has explained, '[t]he weight to be given to the Commission's determinations depends ... on various factors, including the sources relied upon by the Commission, the stage reached in its work, and above all upon States' reception of its output': commentary (2) to Part Five of the *Conclusions on Identification of Customary International Law,* in A/73/10, Report of the International Law Commission on Its Seventieth Session (30 April–1 June and 2 July–10 August 2018) 143.

is the plenary organ, whose membership is now virtually universal. But that does not, of course, preclude other UN organs from playing their part in relation to international law, and the Security Council has done so.

Much has been written about the contribution of the UN to international law. First and foremost, there is Rosalyn Higgins' pioneering work from 1963, her book on the development of international law through the political organs of the UN.[4] Her writings on the matter have continued to this day.[5] Other authors, too, have specifically addressed the role of the Security Council in the development of international law.[6] The Security Council and its subsidiary organs, including the two *ad hoc* international criminal tribunals, have made significant contributions to the development of international law in various fields. These include statehood and recognition/non-recognition;[7] the law of treaties;[8] state responsibility;[9] international criminal law; the *jus ad bellum*; international humanitarian law[10] and international human rights law;[11] the law of the sea;[12] and the law relating to the international administration of territory.[13]

No attempt will be made here to give a comprehensive account across all these areas of the law; rather, the aim is to illustrate the processes, whether deliberate or not, through which the Security Council and its members contribute to the development of international law.

The chapter first looks at four distinct ways in which international law may be developed by and within the Security Council; it then

4 Higgins (1963). In the acknowledgments (at ix), Rosalyn Higgins records that the subject-matter of her doctorate was originally recommended by Elihu Lauterpacht.

5 Higgins (1965); Higgins (1970b); Higgins (2016); Higgins (2017a) 413–28.

6 Higgins (1994) 181–4; Ratner (2004); de La Sablière (2015); Johnstone (2016).

7 'The UN's practice with regard to the admission and non-admission of states and the participation of other entities in the work of the organization has influenced the international law on statehood and recognition': Higgins et al., (2017) 12.06. See, among others, Higgins (1963) 11–57; Dugard (1987); Crawford (2006) 174–95 and *passim*.

8 Higgins (1963) 241–346; Talmon (2009); Wood (2011).

9 Gaja (2009); Gowlland-Debbas (2011).

10 Fox et al. (2018) 649–731; Sassòli (2019) 99–102.

11 Higgins et al., (2017) 12.07 fn. 23, s. 2.3; Higgins (2016) 9–10; Akande (2009).

12 Neri (2020) 177–90.

13 Knoll (2008); Wilde (2008).

considers the role of the Council in relation to the main sources of international law: treaties and customary international law.

9.1 Development of International Law by the Security Council: Four Distinct Processes

9.1.1 The Council 'Lays Down the Law'

The Council may itself 'lay down the law'. It does so in part through what are sometimes referred to as its 'legislative' and 'quasi-judicial' functions, discussed in Chapter 1. The Council may opine on questions of international law both when dealing with specific cases and when engaged (as it has been increasingly in recent years) in 'thematic debates'. There are many examples, some of which have been cited in previous chapters, and it suffices to give a few further examples, set forth in Security Council resolutions and presidential statements.

In 1980, for example, the Council determined that Israel's 'basic law' annexing East Jerusalem was 'null and void'.[14] In resolution 2334 (2016) on Israeli settlements, the Council reaffirmed that the establishment of settlements had 'no legal validity and constitutes a flagrant violation under international law'.[15] It further reaffirmed 'the inadmissibility of the acquisition of territory by force' and condemned 'all measures aimed at altering the demographic composition, character and status of the Palestinian Territory occupied since 1967 ... in violation of international humanitarian law and relevant resolutions'.[16]

In resolution 1540 (2004), the Council decided that all states shall refrain from providing any form of support to non-state actors that attempt to develop, acquire, manufacture, possess, transport, transfer, or use nuclear, chemical, or biological weapons. A subsidiary body, the 1540 Committee, was established to monitor the implementation of the regime.[17]

In resolution 1483 (2003) on post-war Iraq, beyond recognizing the occupying Powers, the Council also expressed its support for and requested the Secretary-General to assist in the formation of an interim government 'until an internationally recognized, representative government is established by the people of Iraq',[18] thus

[14] S/RES/478, 20 August 1980. [15] S/RES/2334, 23 December 2016, para. 1.
[16] Ibid., preamble. [17] S/RES/1540, 28 April 2004.
[18] S/RES/1583, 22 May 2003, paras. 4, 9.

supporting a political role for the occupying Powers, which goes beyond the temporary administration of an occupied territory under the law of occupation.[19]

These are just a few of the many examples of the Council creating new legal obligations, modifying existing obligations, or determining legal facts.

9.1.2 The Council Interprets and Develops the Law of the Charter

The Security Council, through its actions, may interpret and develop the law of the Charter.[20] Examples include its interpretation through practice of the expression 'including the concurring votes of the permanent members' in Article 27(3) of the Charter,[21] the expansion of the term 'threat to the peace' in Article 39, and what may be considered to 'endanger international peace and security' and thus not be a matter 'essentially within the domestic jurisdiction of any state'.[22]

The Council has used various interpretative techniques to interpret the law of the Charter.[23] These include what one author has described as breaking down the barriers among articles and even between chapters of the Charter. A prime example of the latter is peacekeeping (sometimes referred to as 'Chapter 6 ½'). In short, as that author put it rather graphically, the members of the Council 'did not succumb to a paralytic textualism'.[24]

One of the most significant developments of the law of the Charter has been the Council's expansive interpretation of the concept of 'threat to the peace' in Article 39. A determination of a 'threat to the peace' (or, much less frequently, a 'breach of the peace' or 'act of aggression') is required before enforcement measures may be taken under Chapter VII of the Charter.[25]

9.1.3 The Council Determines Rules of International Law

The Security Council itself and states within the Council (whether Council members or not) may clarify or even develop the law

[19] See also Alvarez (2004) ch. 3.3.4.
[20] Higgins (1970b) 44–6; de La Sablière (2015). [21] Chapter 2. [22] Chapter 3.
[23] Kadelbach (2012) MN 56–66; Higgins et al., (2017) 12.10 fn. 29.
[24] Ratner (2004) 596–7; see also de La Sablière (2015).
[25] De Wet and Wood (2022); Chapter 3, Section 3.3.

through treaty interpretation and the determination of rules of customary international law or general principles of law. The Council is a forum in which states continually take positions, individually or collectively, on questions of or relevant to international law. But caution is required. In her 1963 book, Rosalyn Higgins includes some important caveats, which are sometimes overlooked. In particular, she points out that 'the fact that voting patterns to some extent conform to political pressures rather than to legal beliefs must be recognized'.[26] That is putting it quite gently.[27]

An illustrative example of how conclusions on legal positions of Council members can be drawn, but with great attention to the political context, is the Council deliberations and (attempted) action after the Israeli raid on Entebbe, Uganda in 1976, to free the remaining hostages of Air France flight 139 being held at the local airport.[28] Intense exchanges and diverging views were expressed among states over five meetings. Uganda complained of the 'act of aggression ... against the sovereignty and territorial integrity of Uganda'.[29] Israel made clear its position that the operation to save its nationals abroad was legal as part of the inherent right of self-defence.[30]

During the last meeting in the Council on this issue, the United Kingdom and the United States tabled a resolution condemning generally the hijacking of civil aircraft and calling for states to prevent and punish such terrorist acts. While reaffirming the principle of state sovereignty and territorial integrity, it did not mention the Israeli action.[31] The draft resolution received only six votes in favour and two abstentions, while seven Council members elected not to participate in the vote.[32] But this vote, of course, does not

[26] Higgins (1963) 6.
[27] Brownlie (2004, p. 315) wrote:

> A minority of academics have asserted that, in the case of the Security Council, a failure to condemn a particular action by a State constitutes approval of the action concerned. This approach is much too simplistic. Everything depends upon the context and the precise content of the records of the debates. Failure to express disapproval of the conduct of a State may have a number of procedural and political causes unconnected with the issue of legality.

See also Wood (2019).

[28] Kreß and Nußberger (2018).
[29] S/PV.1939, 1 July 1976, p. 3; see also statement of Mauritania, p. 6, statement of Kenya, pp. 17–18.
[30] Ibid., pp. 13–14; see also statement of USA in S/PV.1941, 12 July 1946, p. 8.
[31] S/12138, 16 July 1976. [32] S/PV.1943, 16 July 1976, p. 18.

mean that the majority of Council members were of the view that hijacking planes is not illegal, and it cannot be taken as state practice or *opinio juris* in support of that proposition. Rather, as several Council members explained, while agreeing with the text of the draft, they did not vote in favour because it ignored the question of the legality of the Israeli operation.[33]

Conversely, a draft resolution co-sponsored by Benin, Libya, and Tanzania condemning the Israeli action and demanding that Israel pay compensation to Uganda was never voted on as its drafters knew that it was unlikely to pass.[34] Sweden's statement on its legal analysis and its potential vote on this resolution demonstrate what Higgins articulated thirteen years earlier:

> In our view, the Israeli action which we are now considering involved an infringement of the national sovereignty and territorial integrity of Uganda. We understand the strong reactions against this action, which cost the lives of many Ugandan citizens and led to heavy material damage. At the same time, we are aware of the terrible pressures to which the Israeli Government and people were subjected, faced with this unprecedented act of international piracy and viewing the increasing threat to the lives of so many of their compatriots ... My Government, while unable to reconcile the Israeli action with the strict rules of the Charter, does not find it possible to join in a condemnation in this case.[35]

Sweden articulated clearly that, regardless of its *legal* position, its intended vote on the draft resolution put forward by the three states would reflect its *political* position. It is not often that states articulate the variance between their political voting patterns and their legal positions with such precision.

In a more recent example, after heated discussions in the Council on 14 April 2018, a Russian draft resolution condemning air strikes in Syria conducted by the United States, France, and the United Kingdom against suspected chemical-weapons facilities as an act of aggression, received only three affirmative votes.[36] Nevertheless, during the Council deliberations, out of the eight Council members that voted against the draft resolution, only the United Kingdom expressed

[33] Ibid., statement of Soviet Union, p. 18, statement of Pakistan, pp. 17–18, statement of Guyana, p. 18, statement of Benin, p. 18, statement of Tanzania, p. 21.
[34] S/12139, 12 July 1976. [35] S/PV.1940, 12 July 1976, p. 14.
[36] S/2018/855, 14 April 2018.

a clear and coherent legal justification for the attacks.[37] Others, such as France, labelled them 'necessary' without explaining the legal underpinnings for such an assertion;[38] the Netherlands dubbed them 'understandable'.[39] Thus, out of the votes of fifteen Council members, legal value may be ascribed to the views taken by three states that voted in favour of condemning the attacks as 'acts of aggression' and to the clear legal position of the United Kingdom justifying the legality of the attacks, but not to the votes of the majority of Council members.

9.1.4 The Council Stimulates Legal Developments

The Security Council itself, through its action (or, less likely, through inaction), may stimulate developments in general international law (that is, customary international law and general principles of law). 'Responsibility to protect' is sometimes seen as an example.[40] Other examples are resolutions 794 (1992) and 814 (1993) on Somalia, in which the Council stated that those committing violations of international humanitarian law in the internal conflict would be held 'individually responsible for them'.[41] This was cited by the ICTY in support of the proposition that international law recognized that war crimes may be committed in non-international armed conflicts.[42] In the same vein, as discussed already, the Council has adopted several resolutions in support of the right of self-defence against non-state actors.[43]

Unlike the General Assembly, the Security Council has only rarely instigated the negotiation of a treaty. In 1989, however, following the Lockerbie disaster, the Council urged the International Civil Aviation Organization to intensify its work on devising an international regime for the marking of plastic or sheet explosives for the purpose of detection.[44]

9.2 The Security Council and the Sources of International Law

Article 38(1) of the ICJ Statute lists the sources of international law.[45] Although Article 38(1) originally dates from the 1920 Statute of the

[37] S/PV.8233, 14 April 2018, pp. 6–7. [38] Ibid., p. 9. [39] Ibid., p. 13.
[40] Higgins et al., (2017) 12.09.
[41] S/RES/794, 3 December 1992, para. 5; S/RES/814, 26 March 1993, para. 13.
[42] *Prosecutor* v. *Tadić* (1995), para. 133. [43] See Chapter 6.
[44] S/RES/635, 14 June 1989, para. 4. [45] See Chapter 1.

PCIJ, it was repeated virtually verbatim in 1945 in the ICJ Statute,[46] and has been reproduced in many other treaties. It is sometimes suggested that its list of the sources of international law is incomplete in light of contemporary international law.[47] An oft-cited 'omission' is binding decisions of the Security Council, but these derive their quality as law from an international treaty, the UN Charter.[48]

It is worth examining in a little detail the two main sources listed in Article 38(1) (a) and (b): treaties and customary international law.

9.2.1 Treaties

Writing some ten years ago, one of the authors of this book summed up the Council's relationship with treaties as follows:

> The Council has shown self-restraint, as indeed it should, in its approach to treaties, only 'interfering' to the extent necessary for the maintenance of international peace and security (as in the fields of terrorism and non-proliferation). And most such 'interference' can be readily explained and analyzed by having regard to the distinction between Council action that affects treaty obligations as such (as is the case under Article 103, though even then only to a limited extent), and Council action that imposes obligations set forth in a treaty (the provisions of a treaty), but not the treaty itself. In reality, 'Security Council treaty action' can be a useful tool in the challenging task of maintaining and restoring international peace and security, and should not be seen as an attack on the law.[49]

Over the years, the Security Council has engaged extensively both with 'the law of treaties' (the secondary rules mostly set forth in the VCLT) and with 'treaty law' (the rights and obligations found in treaties). This is to be expected given the central role that treaties play in contemporary international relations. The performance of treaties in good faith (*pacta sunt servanda*) has great importance for the maintenance of international peace and security. This is reflected in the preamble to the UN Charter itself ('respect for the obligations arising from treaties') and also in the preamble to

[46] The only textual change in 1945 was the inclusion in the chapeau of the words 'whose function is to decide in accordance with international law such disputes as are submitted to it'.
[47] For an account of this debate, see Thirlway (2019) 24–30. [48] Chapter 1.
[49] Wood (2011) 255.

the VCLT. The Security Council has an important potential role in securing compliance with treaties where non-compliance may threaten international peace and security. This is so not only in those cases, largely in the arms control and non-proliferation fields, where the Council's role is expressly recognized in the treaty.[50]

In addition to the effect of Council action on treaties (including by virtue of Article 103 of the UN Charter[51]), a comprehensive account would also consider the impact of treaties on the Council. For example, treaties may make express provision for Council action, as does Article 16 of the Rome Statute of the ICC, or even appear to encroach upon the prerogatives of the Council, as with the 2010 Kampala amendments to the Rome Statute (concerning the crime of aggression). But such matters are beyond the scope of this book, and in any event have been covered elsewhere.[52]

Some treaties, such as ceasefire agreements, call on the Council to act, for example by establishing a peacekeeping operation, and thus the Council assists in implementing the treaty.[53]

The Security Council often deals with agreements that are of uncertain status,[54] particularly when dealing with conflicts within a state; it could be interesting to see how far Council action has clarified or enhanced the status of such agreements.

There have been occasions when the Security Council has seemed to impose treaty obligations upon states which are not party to the treaty in question. But this is in appearance only. In fact, there is a basic distinction, observed in the practice of the Council, between the obligations set forth in a treaty, which are

[50] For example, NPT, Art. 10; Convention on the Prohibition of the Development, Production and Stockpiling of Bacteriological (Biological) and Toxin Weapons and on Their Destruction 1972, Art. VI; Chemical Weapons Convention 1993, Art. XII(4); Comprehensive Test Ban Treaty 1996, Art. V(4). See also Convention on the Prevention and Punishment of the Crime of Genocide, Art. VIII.

[51] Chapter 1. The provisions of Art. 30 of the VCLT (successive treaties) are expressly made '[s]ubject to Article 103 of the Charter'.

[52] Talmon (2009) 65–116; Wood (2011).

[53] See, for example, S/RES/1031, 15 December 1995, establishing IFOR, at the request of the parties to the 'Dayton Accords'; S/RES/1270, 22 October 1999, establishing the United Nations Mission in Sierra Leone (UNAMSIL), in order to implement the tasks enumerated for the Council in the 'Lomé Peace Agreement' between Sierra Leone and the Revolutionary United Front (annexed to S/1999/777, 12 July 1999, Art. XIV).

[54] S/RES/1031, 15 December 1995, with respect to the 'Dayton Accords'.

binding on the parties to the treaty by virtue of their participation in the treaty, and the obligations set forth in a treaty that may be binding on states and others for some reason outside the treaty, including because they are made so by mandatory action of the Security Council.

By resolution 1373 (2001), adopted shortly after 9/11, the Council imposed upon all states the terms of a treaty, though without any mention of the treaty itself: paragraph 1 required all states to comply with provisions corresponding to those in the International Convention for the Suppression of Terrorist Financing of 1999.[55]

In resolution 1593 (2005), by which 'the situation in Darfur since 1 July 2002' was referred to the ICC Prosecutor, the Council decided 'that the Government of Sudan ... shall cooperate fully with and provide any necessary assistance to the Court and the Prosecutor'.[56] Sudan had signed but not ratified the Rome Statute, but the Council nevertheless imposed upon it obligations to co-operate at least as comprehensive as those it would have if it had been a party.

In resolution 1718 of 14 October 2006, the Council demanded that North Korea 'immediately retract its announcement of withdrawal' from the NPT and that it 'return to the Treaty'; and at the same time decided that 'the DPRK... shall act strictly in accordance with the obligations applicable to parties under the Treaty on the Non-Proliferation of Nuclear Weapons and the terms and conditions of its International Atomic Energy Agency (IAEA) Safeguards Agreement'.[57]

Resolution 1757 (2007) concerned the Special Tribunal for Lebanon: in it, the Council decided that '[t]he provisions of the annexed document, including its attachment, on the establishment of a Special Tribunal for Lebanon shall enter into force on 10 June 2007'.[58] The 'annexed document' was the Agreement between the UN and the Lebanese Republic on the establishment of a Special Tribunal for Lebanon, which had been signed by the government of Lebanon and the UN, but which had not entered

[55] S/RES/1373 (2001), 28 September 2001, para. 1.
[56] S/RES/1593 (2005), 31 March 2005.
[57] S/RES/1718, 14 October 2006, paras. 4, 6.
[58] S/RES/1757, 30 May 2007, para. 1(a).

into force because the Lebanese government had been unable to notify the UN that the legal requirements for its entry into force had been complied with.

A further example was resolution 1929 (2010), by which the Council called upon Iran to act strictly in accordance with the provisions of the Additional Protocol to its Safeguards Agreement, which it had signed but not yet ratified.[59]

The Security Council has sometimes encouraged states to negotiate a treaty. For example, in resolution 635 (1989), the Council urged the International Civil Aviation Organization 'to intensify its work ... on devising an international regime for the marking of plastic or sheet explosives for the purpose of detection'.[60] This was a purely political action, though it is possible that the Council could require states to negotiate an agreement. The Council has requested states to enter into Status of Forces/Mission Agreements, and has sometimes required them to apply the UN Model Agreement provisionally, pending the conclusion of such agreements.[61]

Whether the Security Council may make a state a party to a treaty has remained a largely theoretical question since – perhaps out of respect for the principle of free consent that underlies the law of treaties – the Council has refrained from doing this.[62] The Council has frequently called upon states generally, and in some cases individually, to become or consider becoming parties to particular treaties, for example counter-terrorism conventions,[63] humanitarian and human rights conventions,[64] or the Additional Protocols to the Geneva Conventions specifically.[65]

[59] S/RES/1929, 9 June 2010, para. 5.

[60] S/RES/635, 14 June 1989. Resolution 635 was a joint Czechoslovak/United Kingdom initiative following the Lockerbie incident.

[61] See, among many examples, S/RES/1626, 19 September 2005, para. 9.

[62] The Council came close to making Lebanon a party to 'the Agreement between the United Nations and the Lebanese Republic on the establishment of a Special Tribunal for Lebanon', however, when adopting S/RES/1757, 30 May 2007. While it was careful to refer to the 'provisions' of the Treaty establishing the Tribunal rather than the Treaty itself, at the same time it decided that these provisions 'shall enter into force', the equivalent of ratification, rather than just deciding that they become binding on Lebanon.

[63] See, for example, S/RES/1371, 28 September 2001, para. 3(d).

[64] See, for example, S/RES/1265, 17 September 1999, para. 5.

[65] See, for example, S/PRST/2019/8, 20 August 2019.

9.2.2 Customary International Law

One author has suggested that the Security Council's 'more significant place [more significant than its direct law-making function] is in the formation of customary international law'.[66] That seems quite doubtful; it is necessary to approach any Council role in the customary law process with care. One cannot jump easily to conclusions based on what is said and done in a highly political organ like the Security Council. Having said that, there undoubtedly is some role for the Council in this sphere.

Article 38.1(b) of the ICJ Statute lists as a source of international law 'international custom, as evidence of a general practice accepted as law'. This is generally accepted as referring to the two-element approach, as set out in the case law of the ICJ and its predecessor the PCIJ in such cases as *Lotus*,[67] *North Sea Continental Shelf*,[68] and *Jurisdictional Immunities of the State*,[69] and as restated in the 2018 *Conclusions on the identification of customary international law*, with commentaries, which were adopted by the ILC in August 2018 and endorsed by the UN General Assembly in December of that year.[70]

Conclusion 2 of the ILC's Conclusions reads: 'To determine the existence and content of a rule of customary international law, it is necessary to ascertain whether there is a general practice that is accepted as law (*opinio juris*).' Conclusion 4 explains that practice refers primarily to the practice of states but that, in certain circumstances, the practice of international organizations also counts.[71]

[66] Ratner (2004) 593.

[67] *The Case of the S.S. 'Lotus', P.C.I.J., Series A, No. 10* (1927).

[68] *North Sea Continental Shelf*, Judgment, ICJ Reports 1969.

[69] '*Jurisdictional Immunities of the State*,' p. 139.

[70] A/73/10: Report of the International Law Commission on Its Sixty-Seventh Session (30 April–1 June and 2 July–10 August 2018), Chapter V. In resolution 73/203 of 20 December 2018, the UN General Assembly '[took] note of the conclusions on identification of customary international law ... with the commentaries thereto, [brought] them to the attention of States and all who may be called upon to identify rules of customary international law, and encourage[d] their widest possible dissemination'.

[71] Conclusion 4 (1) and (2) read: '1. The requirement of a general practice, as a constituent element of customary international law, refers primarily to the practice of States that contributes to the formation, or expression, of rules of customary international law. 2. In certain cases, the practice of international organizations also contributes to the formation, or expression, of rules of customary international law.'

Evidence of acceptance as law (*opinio juris*) of international organizations may likewise count.[72] Conclusion 12 makes special mention of resolutions of international organizations.[73]

The work of the Security Council may, depending on the circumstances, amount to relevant practice and acceptance as law (*opinio juris*) both of participating states and organizations and of the UN as such.[74] It is chiefly as an arena for state practice and *opinio juris* that the Security Council plays a role in relation to the formation and identification of rules of customary international law. Notwithstanding the limited representation in a Council with five permanent members and ten members elected for two-year terms, a significant number of states have contributed to this practice as Council members over the years.[75] But sometimes, with the adoption of a resolution or the issuing of a presidential statement, the practice or *opinio juris* in question may be viewed as that of the Council as such, that is, of the UN. It has been argued that Council action is a forum for channelling the practice of states, since the Charter is explicit that member states 'agree that in carrying out its duties under this responsibility the Security Council acts on their behalf'.[76]

In its *Kosovo* Advisory Opinion, the Court, after considering various resolutions condemning specific unilateral declarations of independence, said that '[t]he exceptional character of the resolutions enumerated above appears to the Court to confirm that no

72 Conclusion 10, commentary, para. 7.

73 Conclusion 12 provides:

> 1. A resolution adopted by an international organization ... cannot, of itself, create a rule of customary international law.
> 2. A resolution ... may provide evidence for determining the existence and content of a rule of customary international law, or contribute to its development.
> 3. A provision in a resolution ... may reflect a rule of customary international law if it is established that the provision corresponds to a general practice that is accepted as law (*opinio juris*).

74 While the contribution of the practice of international organizations as such remained controversial throughout the ILC topic, the great majority of ILC members and states supported it, provided that it was approached with suitable caution.

75 Fox et al. (2018) 707, noting that between 1990 and 2013, ninety-five member states have served as Council members.

76 Charter, Art. 24(1); see Fox et al. (2018) 707–12.

general prohibition against unilateral declarations of independence may be inferred *from the practice of the Security Council*'.[77] While a negative finding, this tends to suggest that 'the practice of the Council' might in other circumstances have led the Court to infer a rule of international law. More likely to be cited, however, is not the practice of the Security Council as such but the practice and *opinio juris* of states as expressed in Council proceedings.

A significant number of Security Council resolutions have expressly stated that they 'shall not be considered as establishing customary international law'.[78] Security Council resolutions were referred to by the ICTY Appeals Chamber in *Prosecutor* v. *Tadić* as evidence of *opinio juris* for rules of customary international humanitarian law governing internal armed conflict.[79]

Many other examples could be given. For example, in his Dissenting Opinion in the *Legality of Nuclear Weapons* Advisory Opinion, Judge Schwebel mentioned 'action of the United Nations Security Council' in a section entitled 'State practice'; he clearly considered acceptance by the Security Council as relevant to the identification of a rule of customary international law.[80]

77 *Kosovo* Advisory Opinion, at pp. 437–8, para. 81 (emphasis added).

78 See, for example, S/RES/2500, 4 December 2019, para. 15; S/RES/2383, 7 November 2017, para. 15; S/RES/2292, 14 June 2016, para. 9; S/RES/2184, 12 November 2014, para. 14; S/RES/2182, 24 October 2014, para. 21; S/RES/2146, 19 March 2014, para. 9; S/RES/2125, 18 November 2013, para. 13; S/RES/2077, 21 November 2012, para. 13; S/RES/2020, 22 November 2011, para. 10; S/RES/1950, 23 November 2010, para. 8; S/RES/1918, 27 April 2010, preamble; S/RES/1897, 30 November 2009, para. 8; S/RES/1851, 16 December 2008, para. 10; S/RES/1846, 2 December 2008, para. 11; S/RES/1838, 7 October 2008, para. 8; S/RES/1816, 2 June 2008, para. 9. In S/RES/2231, 20 July 2015, on the Iran nuclear issue, the Council '*[d]ecide[d]* that all provisions contained in the JCPOA [Joint Comprehensive Plan of Action] . . . should not be considered as setting precedents . . . for principles of international law' (at para. 27).

79 *Prosecutor* v. *Tadić* (1995) paras. 114–16 ('Of great relevance to the formation of *opinio juris* to the effect that violations of general international humanitarian law governing internal armed conflicts entail the criminal responsibility of those committing or ordering those violations are certain resolutions unanimously adopted by the Security Council.').

80 *Nuclear Weapons* Advisory Opinion, Dissenting Opinion of Vice-President Schwebel, at p. 311.

Conclusion

The Security Council is a highly politicized body, but that does not mean that the law is irrelevant to its work. As the principal organ of the United Nations with primary responsibility for the maintenance of international peace and security, it is of course bound by the Charter, from which its functions and powers derive.

The work of the Security Council is followed and scrutinized closely, for good reason given its extensive powers (in a limited – albeit expanding – field). But observers – whether practitioners or academics, and whether looking at the Council from within or without – should not advocate for what it should be doing, not doing, or doing better without a correct understanding of the legal framework within which the Council acts. Otherwise, states generally are unlikely to take their views seriously. This applies also to international lawyers who critique the Council.

We have sought in this book to make the legal nature of the Security Council more readily understood. To do so, we have sought to adopt a straightforward approach to the legal aspects of a very practical body, focusing on what concerns the main actors in international law, states. We have focused on the text of the Charter and how the Council and the member states have understood and applied the provisions relating to the Security Council in practice over the years.

Just as the ICJ is not the world's adjudicator, despite being dubbed the 'World Court', so the Security Council is not the international community's executive body. Its decisions may, at times, resemble those of an executive body, legislator, or judicial body, but, as we have seen, despite a natural inclination to categorize them within familiar legal constructs, they are none of these. As stated in the Charter, the Security Council is the UN organ with the primary responsibility for the maintenance of international peace and security. Its decisions are those that it itself deems necessary to achieve that purpose.

Its binding decisions are usually found in resolutions adopted under Chapter VII, though this is not out of legal necessity. When it seeks to adopt binding decisions, the Council often uses terms like 'decides' or 'authorizes' to convey binding obligations. Nonetheless, sometimes the Council may make binding 'demands' of parties and, on occasion, even seemingly non-binding language such as 'calling upon' states to take or refrain from action may be considered binding, having regard to all the circumstances. Thus, while the Council's practice provides some guidance as to when the Council creates binding obligations and for whom, a case-by-case approach, based on a careful reading of the Council's outcome documents in context, is always necessary.

Under the Charter, the Council can make recommendations or adopt decisions that are binding on member states. The Council's practice from its early days demonstrates that it is of the view that it can also impose binding obligations on other actors, an approach that finds support in the jurisprudence of the ICJ.

The Charter grants the Council wide discretion in its decision-making. The Council enjoys wide discretion in determining whether a situation is a 'threat to the peace', which allows it to move forward to adopt enforcement measures under Chapter VII. The Council has utilized its discretion to expand the scope of this term and apply it to a variety of situations. Similarly, the Council enjoys wide discretion in deciding what measures are necessary to maintain or restore the peace in such situations. This is true whether the Council is adopting provisional measures under Article 40, measures not involving the use of force under Article 41, or, if necessary, collective security measures involving the use of force under Article 42.

This wide discretion in determining the nature of the situation and deciding on the necessary measures to address it is not unbound by law. But, as lawyers, it is important to be precise: the law applicable to the Council is first and foremost the UN's constituent instrument, the Charter. Many also view the Council as subject to the small yet important set of *jus cogens* norms.

These limitations may seem weak. Indeed, in practice, as we have seen, it is hard to envisage a situation where it can reasonably be argued that the Council has exceeded its discretion and stepped beyond its legal powers, particularly its discretion in identifying a threat to the peace under Article 39 or adopting measures under Chapter VII.

At the same time, some judicial bodies, such as the ECtHR and the CJEU, have sought to constrain the Council, applying stricter legal limitations to its actions. But these approaches overlook the basic structure of international law in the UN era, that of the priority of obligations under the Charter, including for Council decisions and authorizations, over all other international obligations.

Understandably, to allow the Security Council – the composition of which reflects the power dynamics of 1945 – such a wide discretion may make judges, lawyers, diplomats, and students of the Council uneasy. But, fundamentally, the powers of the Council and its wide discretion set forth at San Francisco lie at the heart of the Council's very existence.

The Council's effectiveness and success in maintaining international peace and security and in preventing and stopping disasters and atrocities are dependent on these unique powers. Learning the hard lessons from the failure of the League of Nations, the Council was purposely granted in the Charter the mandate to go beyond that which states can do unilaterally: the extraordinary power to impose legal obligations on member states and the extraordinary powers to authorize the use of force, even when there exists no right of self-defence for a state. Combined with the priority given to Charter obligations over other international obligations, the Council can authorize and even oblige states to do what would otherwise be illegal, irrespective of their other obligations. And, as stated in Article 24(1) of the Charter, when the Council acts, it acts on behalf of all of the member states.

Though the Council has not infrequently failed the international community, the minimal legal constraints on the Council in terms of the timing of its actions, their scope, and their nature are precisely why it has been able to adopt innovative measures, adapt to new types of conflict and situations over the years, and match reality with equally unique measures. Without such discretion and flexibility, the Council could not have established the ICTY and the ICTR;

administered territory in order to protect local populations; authorized the use of force to end mass atrocities; ensured that all states appropriately criminalize acts of terrorism and the financing of terrorism, and so on.

This adaptability results from the open-ended nature of the text of the Charter and is reflected in the actual practice of the Council, rather than from wishful thinking and idealism, or criticism dressed up as law but in fact based on policy. But, it should be borne in mind, this approach necessitated by the Charter and carved out in practice also places legal limitations on the Council. For example, staying true to the nature of the Charter as a treaty among the member states, rather than a constitution of the international community, means that other international organizations are not necessarily bound by Council decisions. Thus, the ICC (as opposed to the states party to the Rome Statute) is not necessarily bound by Council resolutions aiming at carving out its jurisdiction over certain nationals.

Most importantly, as is often the case, politics are more important than the law. We have seen that, despite the limited legal constraints on the Council, the main 'check' on the Council continues to be political. The Council is, ultimately, entirely reliant on others to carry out its decisions. Its authority and effectiveness depend on whether states will carry out its decisions or not, notwithstanding their legal obligations under the Charter. This is, in reality, the ultimate test for the authority of the Council. That is how it should be. Member states gave the Council its extensive powers in the Charter and, ultimately, they are the ones that can determine how it exercises its powers.

The Council, we have seen, is at the heart of the UN collective security system and, for that purpose, enjoys extraordinary powers, including authorizing the use of force. There are only two exceptions to the prohibition on the use of force: collective security measures authorized by the Council and the inherent right of individual or collective self-defence against an armed attack. The law on the use of force develops in practice mostly on a case-by-case basis, and discussions in the Council, as well as Council decisions, play a role in that process. Generally speaking, in a field of law where action is so consequential, and disagreement on particular doctrines such as humanitarian intervention persists, the exceptions to the prohibition should be applied stringently. It may be better to accept the occasional breach to serve valid interests (such as the interventions in Kosovo in 1999 and Syria in 2018) than to relax the rules to such a degree that they invite abuse.

As with states, which are often inconsistent in their views and are reluctant to take principled positions for political reasons, so the Council – after all a political body – has been inconsistent and uneven in approaching instances of the use of force. Nevertheless, the Council has contributed to the development of the law in its field of operation, for example towards recognizing a right to self-defence against non-state actors, in the face of a threat of an imminent attack.

We have also examined, in the context of the use of force, the relationship embodied in Chapter VIII of the Charter between the Council and other international organizations. These cannot engage in the use of force against external threats or their own members except in collective self-defence or if authorized in advance by the Council. Interpretations or views in support of doctrines like *ex post facto* authorizations or consent-based regional collective security mechanisms (as some view Article 4(h) of the AU Constitutive Act) may well undermine the balance achieved in the Charter and the authority of the Council.

Undoubtedly, with these extraordinary powers allotted to the Council comes great responsibility. Has the Council been able to meet expectations and maintain international peace and security or restore it when need be? The answer to this question is inevitably dependent on the varying subjective expectations of each person. It can be said that the Council has been successful in implementing the mandate given to it by the member states in some instances, and failed miserably at other times. As more crises erupt and long-standing ones continue to linger, so will views of the Council continue to evolve.

The Council may be the organ with the primary responsibility for the maintenance of international peace and security and central to the UN collective security system, but it is by no means the only relevant actor. The current and future success of the system is dependent on the effectiveness of the UN as a whole, including the General Assembly, the Secretary-General, and the ICJ. With respect to the ICJ, and despite the various points for potential interaction envisaged in the Charter, it remains underutilized by the Council.

The success of the UN collective security system is also dependent on co-operation between the Council and the member states which implement its decisions, whether independently or through their membership in other international organizations, as recognized in Chapter VIII of the Charter.

But one thing is certain: without an effective Security Council, there cannot be an effective UN collective security system. And, with Security Council reform unlikely in the near future, it is incumbent upon us all to remember that it is the only Security Council we have. The common goal should be the effectiveness of the Council. We hope that this book contributes to that end.

Bibliography

For a bibliographical essay, see Luck (2006) 177–9. For other bibliographies, see Sievers and Daws (2014) 682–90; Simma (2012) *passim*.

Akande, D., 'The Security Council and Human Rights: What Is the Role of Article 103 of the Charter?', *EJILTalk!*, 30 March 2009, available at www.ejiltalk.org/the-security-council-and-human-rights-what-is-the-role-of-art-103-of-the-charter/.

Akehurst, M., 'Enforcement Action by Regional Agencies, with Special Reference to the Organization of American States', 42 *BYIL* (1967) 175–227.

Alvarez, J., *International Organizations as Law-Makers* (Oxford University Press, 2004).

Amvane, G., 'Intervention Pursuant to Article 4(h) of the Constitutive Act of the African Union without United Nations Security Council Authorisation', 15 *AHRLJ* (2015) 282–98.

Aust, A., 'The Procedure and Practice of the Security Council Today', in Dupuy (1993) 365–74.

Beckett, W. E., *The North Atlantic Treaty, the Brussels Treaty and the Charter of the United Nations* (Stevens & Sons, Ltd., 1950).

Bellamy, A., and Dunne, T. (eds.), *The Oxford Handbook of the Responsibility to Protect* (Oxford University Press, 2016).

Bellinger, J., 'The Security Council Resolution on Syria: Is It Legally Binding?', *Lawfare*, 28 September 2013, available at www.lawfareblog.com/security-council-resolution-syria-it-legally-binding.

Berman, F., 'The Authorization Model: Resolution 678 and Its Effects', in Malone (2004) 153–61.

Bethlehem, D., 'Principles Relevant to the Scope of a State's Right of Self-Defense Against an Imminent or Actual Armed Attack by Nonstate Actors', 106 *AJIL* (2012) 770–9.

Blokker, N., *Saving Succeeding Generations from the Scourge of War: The United Nations Security Council at 75* (Brill/Nijhoff, 2020).

Boon, K., 'The UN Security Council and Non-state Actors', 113 *Proceedings ASIL* (2019) 209–12.

Bowett, D., 'Collective Security and Collective Self-Defence: The Errors and Risks of Identification', in M. Rama Montaldo (ed.), *El Derecho internacional en un mundo en transformación: liber amicorum en homenaje al profesor Eduardo Jiménez de Aréchaga* (Fundación de Cultura Universitaria, 1994) 425–40.

Brownlie, I., 'Some Problems in the Evaluation of the Practice of States as an Element of Custom', in G. Arangio-Ruiz (ed.), *Studi di diritto internazionale in onore di Gaetano Arangio Ruiz* (Editoriale Scientifica, 2004) 313–18.

Butchard, P., *The Responsibility to Protect and the Failures of the United Nations Security Council* (Hart, 2020).

Byers, M., 'Book Review of T. Franck, Recourse to Force', 97 *AJIL* (2003) 721–5.

Byers, M., 'The Intervention in Afghanistan – 2001', in Ruys et al. (2018) 625–38.

Caron, D., 'The Legitimacy of the Collective Authority of the Security Council', 87 *AJIL* (1993) 552–88.

Chesterman, S., Johnstone, I., and Malone, D., *Law and Practice of the United Nations* (2nd ed., Oxford University Press, 2016).

Chinkin, C., 'The Legality of NATO's Action in the Former Republic of Yugoslavia (FRY) under International Law', 49 *ICLQ* (2000) 910–25.

Churchill, W., *The Second World War, Vol. I, The Gathering Storm* (Cassell and Company Ltd., 1949).

Cockayne, J., Brubaker, R., and Jayakody, N., *Fairly Clear Risks: Protecting UN Sanctions' Legitimacy and Effectiveness through Fair and Clear Procedures* (United Nations University, 2018), available at http://collections.unu.edu/view/UNU:6450#viewAttachments.

Conforti, B., and Focarelli, C., *The Law and Practice of the United Nations* (5th rev. ed., Brill/Nijhoff, 2016).

Corten, O., *Le droit contre la guerre* (2nd ed., Pedone, 2014).

Corten, O., and Koutroulis, V., 'The *Jus Cogens* Status of the Prohibition on the Use of Force: What Is Its Scope and Why Does It Matter?', in Tladi (2021) 629–67.

Costelloe, D., 'Peremptory Norms and Resolutions of the United Nations Security Council', in Tladi (2021) 441–67.

Cot, J.-P., Pellet, A., and Forteau, M., *La Charte des Nations Unies: Commentaire article par article* (3rd ed., Economica, 2005).

Crawford, J., *The Creation of States in International Law* (2nd ed., Oxford University Press, 2006).

Deeks, A., 'Threading the Needle in Security Council Resolution 2249', *Lawfare*, 25 November 2015, available at www.lawfareblog.com/threading-needle-security-council-resolution-2249.

De La Sablière, J. M., *Le Conseil de sécurité des Nations Unies. Ambitions et limites* (Larcier, 2015).

De Wet, E., *The Chapter VII Powers of the United Nations Security Council* (Hart, 2004).

De Wet, E., 'Regional Organizations and Arrangements: Authorization, Ratification, or Independent Action', in Weller (2015) 314–28.

De Wet, E., *Military Assistance on Request and the Use of Force* (Oxford University Press, 2020).

De Wet, E., and Wood, M. 'Peace, Threats to the', *MPEPIL* (2022).

Dinstein, Y., *War, Aggression and Self-Defence* (6th ed., Cambridge University Press, 2017).

Dugard, J., *Recognition and the United Nations* (Cambridge, Grotius, 1987).

Dupuy, R.-J., *The Development of the Role of the Security Council* (Hague Academy Workshop/Martinus Nijhoff, 1993).

Eckert, S., 'The Role of Sanctions', in von Einsiedel et al. (2016) 413–42.

Fijnaut, C., and Larik, J., *Humanitarian Intervention and Political Support for Interstate Use of Force* (Brill, 2021).

Fassbender, B., *The United Nations Charter as the Constitution of the International Community* (Nijhoff, 2009).

Fifoot, P., 'Functions and Powers, and Interventions: UN Action in Respect of Human Rights and Humanitarian Intervention', in N. Rodley (ed.), *To Loose the Bands of Wickedness: International Intervention in Defence of Human Rights* (Brasseys, 1992) 133–64.

Forteau, M., 'Rescuing National Abroad', in Weller (2015) 947–61.

Fox, G., Boon, K., and Jenkins, I., 'The Contributions of United Nations Security Council Resolutions to the Law of Non-international Armed Conflict: New Evidence of Customary International Law', 67 *Am U L Rev* (2018) 649–731.

Franchini, D., and Tzanakopoulos, A., 'The Kosovo Crisis – 1999', in Ruys et al. (2018) 594–622.

Franck, T., 'Who Killed Article 2(4)? Or: Changing Norms Governing the Use of Force by States', 64 *AJIL* (1970) 809–37.

Franck, T., *The Power of Legitimacy among Nations* (Oxford University Press, 1990).

Franck, T., *Fairness in International Law and Institutions* (Oxford University Press, 1998).

Franck, T., *Recourse to Force: State Action Against Threats and Armed Attacks* (Cambridge University Press, 2002).

Franck, T., 'Legality and Legitimacy in Humanitarian Intervention', in *Nomos 2006, Vol. 47: Humanitarian Intervention* (American Society for Political and Legal Philosophy, 2006) 143–57.

Frowein, J., and Krisch, N., 'Introduction to Chapter VII', in Simma (2002).

Gaja, G., 'The Impact of Security Council Resolutions on State Responsibility', in G. Nolte (ed.), *Peace through International Law: The Role of the International Law Commission* (Springer Verlag, 2009) 53–60.

Giegerich, T., 'Article 36', in Simma et al. (2012).

Goodrich, M., and Hambro, E., *The Charter of the United Nations: Commentary and Documents* (World Peace Foundation, 1946).

Goodrich, M., Hambro, E., and Simons, A., *The Charter of the United Nations: Commentary and Documents* (3rd ed., Columbia University Press, 1969).

Goodrich, L., and Simons, A., 'Preface to the Third Edition', in Goodrich et al. (1969).

Gowlland-Debbas, V., 'The Security Council and Issues of Responsibility under International Law', 353 *Recueil des cours* (2011) 187–443.

Gray, C., *International Law and the Use of Force* (4th ed., Oxford University Press, 2018).

Green, J., 'The Article 51 Reporting Requirements for Self-Defense Actions', 55 *Va J Int Law* (2015) 563–624.

Greenwood, C., 'Humanitarian Intervention: The Case of Kosovo', 21 *Finn Yearb Int Law* (1999) 141–75.

Hajjami, N., 'Que signifie l'expression 'prendre toutes les mesures nécessaires' dans la pratique du Conseil de sécurité des Nations unies?', 46 *RBDI* (2013) 232–55.

Hajjami, N., 'The Intervention of the United States and Other Eastern Caribbean States in Grenada – 1983', in Ruys et al. (2018) 385–95.

Hakimi, M., 'To Condone or Condemn? Regional Enforcement Actions in the Absence of Security Council Authorization', 40 *Vand J Transnat'l L* (2007) 643–86.

Hakimi, M., 'The *Jus ad Bellum*'s Regulatory Form', 112 *AJIL* (2018) 151–90.

Harrell, P., 'Modern-Day "Guarantee Clauses" and the Legal Authority of Multinational Organizations To Authorize the Use of Military Force', 33 *Yale J Int Law* (2008) 417–46.

Helal, M., 'The ECOWAS Intervention in The Gambia – 2016', in Ruys et al. (2018) 912–47.

Henderson, C., *The Use of Force and International Law* (Cambridge University Press, 2018).

Henkin, L., 'Kosovo and the Law of 'Humanitarian Intervention', 93 *AJIL* (1999) 824–8.

Higgins, R., *The Development of International Law through the Political Organs of the United Nations* (Oxford University Press, 1963).

Higgins, R., 'The Development of International Law by the Political Organs of the United Nations', *Proceedings ASIL* (1965) 116–24.

Higgins, R., *United Nations Peace Keeping: Documents and Commentary, Vol. II, Asia 1946–1967* (Oxford University Press, 1970a).

Higgins, R., 'The United Nations and Lawmaking: The Political Organs', 37 *Proceedings ASIL* (1970b) 37–47.

Higgins, R., *Problems and Process. International Law and How We Use It* (Oxford University Press, 1994).

Higgins, R., 'Some Thoughts on the Evolving Relationship between the Security Council and NATO', in *Boutros Boutros-Ghali Amicorum Discipulorumque Liber*, Vol. I, 511 (Bruylant, 1998).

Higgins, R., 'A Babel of Judicial Voices? Ruminations from the Bench', 55 *ICLQ* (2006) 791–804, reproduced in Higgins, *Themes and Theories* (2009) 1256–68.

Higgins, R., 'The United Nations at 70 Years: The Impact upon International Law', 65 *ICLQ* (2016) 1–19.

Higgins, R., 'The United Nations and International Law', in Higgins et al., *Oppenheim's International Law: United Nations* (2017a) 413–28.

Higgins R., Webb, P., Akande, D., Sivakumaran, S., Sloan, J. (eds.), *Oppenheim's International Law: United Nations* (Oxford University Press, 2017b).

ILA, Accountability of International Organizations, Final Report (Berlin, 2004), available at https://ila.vettoreweb.com/Storage/Download.aspx?DbStorageId=1058&StorageFileGuid=04c9caf1-2834-4490-9125-7d9ba3683246.

ILA, Committee on the Use of Force, 2010–18, *Final Report on Aggression and the Use of Force* (Sydney, 2018), available at ila-hq.org/images/ILA/DraftReports/DraftReport_UseOfForce.pdf.

ILC, Draft Articles on the Responsibility of International Organizations, *Yearbook of the International Law Commission*, Vol. II, Part Two (2011).

Informal Inter-Allied Committee on the Future of the Permanent Court of International Justice, Report, published in 39 *AJIL* (1945) Supp., 1–42.

International Commission on Intervention and State Sovereignty, Responsibility to Protect, Report, 2001, available at https://idl-bnc-idrc

.dspacedirect.org/bitstream/handle/10625/18432/IDL-18432.pdf?sequence=6&isAllowed=y.

Jenks, C., 'The Conflict of Law-Making Treaties', 30 *BYIL* (1953) 401–53.

Johnson, L., '"Uniting for Peace": Does it Still Serve Any Useful Purpose?', 108 *AJIL Unbound* (2014) 106–15.

Johnstone, I., 'When the Security Council Is Divided', in Weller (2015) 227–50.

Johnstone, I., 'The Security Council and International Law', in von Einsiedel et al. (2016) 771–92.

Joyner, D., 'Legal Bindingness of Security Council Resolutions Generally, and Resolution 2334 on the Israeli Settlements in Particular', *EJIL:Talk!*, 9 January 2017, with comments, available at www.ejiltalk.org/legal-bindingness-of-security-council-resolutions-generally-and-resolution-2334-on-the-israeli-settlements-in-particular/.

Kadelbach, S., 'Interpretation of the Charter', in Simma et al. (2012).

Keeler, C., 'The End of the Responsibility to Protect?', *Foreign Policy Journal*, 12 October 2011, available at www.foreignpolicyjournal.com/2011/10/12/the-end-of-the-responsibility-to-protect/.

Kendal, D., *Denmark and the Responsibility to Protect (R2P): How Denmark Can Further Contribute to the Prevention of Mass Atrocities*, paper commissioned by the Danish Ministry of Foreign Affairs (2013), available at http://um.dk/en/danida-en/partners/research/other//~/media/UM/English-site/Docu-ments/Danida/Partners/Research-Org/Research-studies/Denmark%20and%20the%20Responsibility%20to%20Protect%202013.pdf.

Kindiki, K., 'The Normative and Institutional Framework of the African Union Relating to the Protection of Human Rights and the Maintenance of International Peace and Security: A Critical Appraisal', in 3 *AHRLJ* (2003) 97–117.

Kioko, B., 'The Right of Intervention under the African Union's Constitutive Act: From Non-interference to Non-intervention', 85 *Int Rev Red Cross* (2003) 807–24.

Kirgis, J., 'Security Council Resolution 1483 on the Rebuilding of Iraq', 8 (13) *AJIL Insights*, 6 June 2003, available at www.asil.org/insights/volume/8/issue/13/security-council-resolution-1483-rebuilding-iraq.

Knoll, B., *The Legal Status of Territories Subject to Administration by International Organizations* (Cambridge University Press, 2008).

Kokott, J., and Sobotta, C., 'The Kadi Case – Constitutional Core Values and International Law – Finding the Balance?', 23(4) *EJIL* (2012) 1015–24.

Kolb, R., *L'article 103 de la Charte des Nations Unies* (Hague Academy, 2014).

Kreß, C., and Nußberger, B., 'Pro-democratic Intervention in Current International Law: The Case of the Gambia in January 2017', 4 *JUFIL* (2017) 239–52.

Kreß, C., and Nußberger, B., 'The Entebbe Raid – 1976', in Ruys et al. (2018) 220–33.

Krisch, N., 'Article 39', in Simma et al. (2012).

Krisch, N., 'Article 40', in Simma et al. (2012).

Krisch, N., 'Article 41', in Simma et al. (2012).

Kuwali, D., 'Article 4(h) + R2P: Towards a Doctrine of Persuasive Prevention to End Mass Atrocity Crimes', 3 *Interdiscip J Hum Rights Law* (2008) 55–85.

Kuwali, D., 'The End of Humanitarian Intervention: Evaluation of the African Union's Right of Intervention', 9 *AJCR* (2009) 41–62.

Kuwali, D., 'What Is "Intervention" under Article 4(h)', in D. Kuwali and F. Viljoen (eds.), *Africa and the Responsibility to Protect: Article 4(h) of the African Union Constitutive Act* (Routledge, 2014).

Lagerwall, A., 'Threats of and Actual Military Strikes Against Syria – 2013 and 2017', in Ruys et al. (2018) 828–54.

Lauterpacht, E., 'The Legal Effects of Illegal Acts of International Organizations', in *Cambridge Essays in International Law: Essays in honour of Lord McNair* (Cambridge University Press, 1965) 88–121.

Lauterpacht, H., *The Development of International Law by the Permanent Court of International Justice* (Longmans, Green & Co., 1934).

Lauterpacht, H., 'The Covenant as the "Higher Law"', 17 *BYIL* (1936) 54–65.

Lauterpacht, H., *Aspects of the Administration of International Justice* (Cambridge, Grotius, 1991).

Lamb, S., 'Legal Limits to UN Security Council Powers', in G. Goodwin-Gill and S. Talmon (eds.), *The Reality of International Law: Essays in Honour of Ian Brownlie* (Oxford University Press, 1999) 361–88.

Lemos, M., '*Jus Cogens* Versus the Chapter VII Powers of the Security Council: With Particular References to Humanitarian Intervention and Terrorism', 19 *Chin J Int Law* (2020) 1–52.

Lenaerts, K., 'The Kadi Saga and the Rule of Law within the EU', 67 *SMU Law Rev* (2014) 707–15.

Lentner, G., *The UN Security Council and the International Criminal Court: The Referral Mechanism in Theory and Practice* (Edward Elgar, 2018).

Lewis, D., Modirzadeh, N., and Blum, G., *Quantum of Silence: Inaction and* jus ad bellum, Harvard Law School Program of International Law and Armed Conflict (2019), available at https://pilac.law.harvard.edu/quantum-of-silence.

Lowe, V., Roberts, A., Welsh, J., and Zaum, D. (eds.), *The United Nations Security Council and War: The Evolution of Thought and Practice since 1945* (Oxford University Press, 2008).

Lubell, N., and Wood, M., 'The ILA's 2018 Report on Aggression and the Use of Force', 6 *JUFIL* (2019).

Luck, E., *UN Security Council. Practice and Promise* (Routledge, 2006).

Malone, D. (ed.), *The UN Security Council: From the Cold War to the 21st Century* (Lynne Rienner, 2004).

Malone, D. 'An Evolving UN Security Council', 47 *Indian J Int Law* (2007) 594–615.

Marauhn, T. 'North Atlantic Treaty Organization', *MPEPIL* (2016).

Matheson, M., *Council Unbound: The Growth of UN Decision Making on Conflict and Postconflict Issues after the Cold War* (United States Institute of Peace, 2006).

Mendelson, M., and Hulton, S., 'The Iraq-Kuwait Boundary', 64 *BYIL* (1993) 135–95.

Milanovic, M., 'Can UNSC Presidential Statements Be Legally Binding?', *EJIL:Talk!*, 15 April 2009a, available at www.ejiltalk.org/can-unsc-presidential-statements-be-legally-binding/.

Milanovic, M., 'The Human Rights Committee's Views in Sayadi v. Belgium: A Missed Opportunity', 1 *Goettingen Journal of International Law* (2009b) 519–38.

Milanovic, M., 'European Court Decides Nada v. Switzerland', *EJIL:Talk!*, 14 September 2012, www.ejiltalk.org/european-court-decides-nada-v-switzerland/.

Milanovic, M., 'Grand Chamber Judgment in Al-Dulimi v. Switzerland', *EJIL:Talk!*, 23 June 2016, www.ejiltalk.org/grand-chamber-judgment-in-al-dulimi-v-switzerland/.

Murphy, S., 'Assessing the Legality of Invading Iraq', 92 *Georgetown Law J* (2004) 173–258.

Nasu, H., *International Law on Peacekeeping: A Study of Article 40 of the UN Charter* (Martinus Nijhoff, 2009).

Neri, K., 'Security Council's Contribution to the Evolution of the Law of the Sea: Avant Garde or Self-Limitation?', in M. Ribeiro, F. Bastos, and T. Henriksen (eds.), *Global Challenges and the Law of the Sea* (Springer, 2020) 177–90.

O'Connell, M. E., Tams, C., and Tladi, D., *Max Planck Trialogues, Vol. 1: Self-Defence against Non-State Actors* (Cambridge University Press, 2018).

Oellers-Frahm, K., 'Article 94', in Simma et al. (2012).

Oellers-Frahm, K., 'Article 41', in Zimmermann et al. (2019).

Orakhelashvili, A., *Peremptory Norms of International Law* (Oxford University Press, 2006).

Österdahl, I., 'The Exception as the Rule: Lawmaking on Force and Human Rights by the UN Security Council', 10 *J Conflict & Sec Law* (2005) 1–20.

Paulus, A., and Leiß, J., 'Article 103', in Simma et al. (2012).

Peters, A., 'Article 25', in Simma et al. (2012).

Peters, A., (2021–) and Wolfrum, R. (2004–20) (eds.), *Max Planck Encyclopedia of Public International Law* (Oxford University Press, 2008–), available at www.mpepil.com/.

Popovski, V., and Fraser, T. (eds.), *The Security Council as Global Legislator* (Routledge, 2014).

Randelzhofer, A., and Nolte, G., 'Article 51', in Simma et al. (2012).

Ratner, S., 'The Security Council and International Law', in Malone (2004) 591–605.

Reinisch, A., and Novak, G., 'Article 48', in Simma et al. (2012).

Reisman, M., 'Editorial, Termination of the USSR's Treaty Right of Intervention in Iran', 74 *AJIL* (1980) 144–54.

Reisman, M., 'Humanitarian Intervention and Fledgling Democracies', 18 *Fordham Int Law J* (1994) 794–805.

Reisman, M., and Stevick, D., 'The Applicability of International Law Standards to United Nations Economic Sanctions Programme', 9 *EJIL* (1998) 86–141.

Roberts, A., 'Legality vs. Legitimacy: Can Uses of Force be Illegal but Justified?', in P. Alston and E. Macdonald (eds.), *Human Rights, Intervention, and the Use of Force* (Oxford University Press, 2008) 179–213.

Rosand, E., 'The Security Council as "Global Legislator": *Ultra Vires* or Ultra Innovative?', 28 *Fordham Int Law J* (2004) 542–90.

Russell, R., *A History of the United Nations Charter: The Role of the United States, 1940–1945* (Brookings Institute Press, 1958).

Ruys, T., Corten, O., and Hofer, A. (eds.), *The Use of Force in International Law: A Case-Based Approach* (Oxford University Press, 2018).

Sands, P., and Klein, P., *Bowett's Law of International Institutions* (6th ed., Sweet and Maxwell, 2009).

Sassòli, M., *International Humanitarian Law: Rules, Controversies, and Solutions to Problems Arising in Warfare* (Edward Elgar, 2019).

Schabas, W., 'Accountability for International Crimes – Special Tribunals and Referrals to the International Criminal Court', in J. Gesner and B. Stagno Ugarte (eds.), *The United Nations Security Council in the Age of Human Rights* (Cambridge University Press, 2014) 173–94.

Schermers, H., and Blokker, N., *International Institutional Law* (6th rev. ed., Brill, 2018).

Schweigman, D., *The Authority of the Security Council under Chapter VII of the UN Charter: Legal Limits and the Role of the International Court of Justice* (Kluwer, 2001).

Security Council Report, *Special Research Report No. 3: Security Council Transparency, Legitimacy and Effectiveness: Efforts to Reform Council Working Methods 1993–2007*, 18 October 2007, available at www.securitycouncilreport.org/atf/cf/%7B65BFCF9B-6D27-4E9C-8CD3-

CF6E4FF96FF9%7D/Research%20Report_Working%20Methods%2018%20Oct%2007.pdf.

Security Council Report, *Special Research Report No. 1: Security Council Action under Chapter VII: Myths and Realities,* 3 June 2008, available at www.securitycouncilreport.org/research-reports/lookup-c-glkwlemtisg-b-4202671.php.

Security Council Report, *Special Research Report No. 1: Security Council Working Methods – A Work in Progress?,* 30 March 2010, available at www.securitycouncilreport.org/atf/cf/%7B65BFCF9B-6D27-4E9C-8CD3-CF6E4FF96FF9%7D/Research%20Report%20Working%20Methods%202010.pdf.

Security Council Report, *Cross-Cutting Report on the Rule of Law,* 28 October 2011, available at www.securitycouncilreport.org/atf/cf/%7B65BFCF9B-6D27-4E9C-8CD3-CF6E4FF96FF9%7D/XCutting%20Rule%20of%20Law%202011.pdf.

Security Council Report, *Security Council Working Methods: A Tale of Two Councils?,* 25 March 2014, available at www.securitycouncilreport.org/atf/cf/%7B65BFCF9B-6D27-4E9C-8CD3-CF6E4FF96FF9%7D/special_research_report__working_methods_2014.pdf.

Security Council Report, *The Veto,* 19 October 2015, available at www.securitycouncilreport.org/research-reports/the-veto.php.

Security Council Report, *The Rule of Law: Can the Security Council Make Better Use of the International Court of Justice?,* 20 December 2016, available at www.securitycouncilreport.org/atf/cf/%7B65BFCF9B-6D27-4E9C-8CD3-CF6E4FF96FF9%7D/research_report_5_rule_of_law_2016.pdf.

Security Council Report, *Can the Security Council Prevent Conflict?,* 9 February 2017, available at www.securitycouncilreport.org/atf/cf/%7B65BFCF9B-6D27-4E9C-8CD3-CF6E4FF96FF9%7D/research_report_conflict_prevention_2017.

Security Council Report, *In Hindsight: The Security Council in 2019,* 31 January 2020, available at www.securitycouncilreport.org/monthly-forecast/2020-02/in-hindsight-the-security-council-in-2019.php.

Sheeran, S., 'The Use of Force in United Nations Peacekeeping Operations', in Weller (2015) 347–74.

Sievers, L., and Daws. S., *The Procedure of the UN Security Council* (4th ed., Oxford University Press, 2014), with updates at www.scprocedure.org.

Simma, B., 'NATO, the UN and the Use of Force: Legal Aspects', 10 *EJIL* (1999) 1–22.

Simma, B. (ed.), *The Charter of the United Nations: A Commentary* (2nd ed., Oxford University Press, 2002).

Simma, B., Khan, D.-E., Nolte, G., and Paulus, A. (eds.), *The Charter of the United Nations: A Commentary* (3rd ed., Oxford University Press, 2012).

Spiermann, O., 'Historical Introduction', in Zimmermann et al. (2019).

Stahn, C., 'Terrorist Acts as "Armed Attack": The Right to Self-Defense, Article 51(½) of the UN Charter, and International Terrorism', 27 *Fletcher Forum World Aff* (2003) 35–54.

Sthoeger, E., 'International Courts and Tribunals', in von Einsiedel et al. (2016) 507–26.

Suyash, P., 'The Primacy of Regional Organizations in International Peacekeeping: The African Example', 51 *Va J Int Law* (2010) 185–230.

Talmon, S., 'The Statements by the President of the Security Council', 2 *Chin J Int Law* (2003) 419–65.

Talmon, S., 'Security Council Treaty Action', 62 *RHDI* (2009) 65–116.

Talmon, S., 'Article 2(6)', in Simma et al. (2012).

Tavernier, P., 'Les déclarations du Président du Conseil de sécurité', 39 *AFDI* (1993) 101.

Thirlway, H., *The Sources of International Law* (2nd ed., Oxford University Press, 2019).

Tladi, D. (ed.), *Peremptory Norms of General International Law* (Jus Cogens*): Disquisitions and Disputations* (Brill, 2021).

Trahan, J., *Existing Legal Limits to Security Council Veto Power in the Face of Atrocity Crimes* (Cambridge University Press, 2020).

Traoré, S. B., *L'interprétation des résolutions du Conseil de sécurité des Nations Unies: Contribution à la théorie de l'interprétation dans la société internationale* (Helbing Lichtenhahn Verlag, 2020).

Tzanakopoulos, A., *Disobeying the Security Council: Countermeasures against Wrongful Sanctions* (Oxford University Press, 2011).

Tzanakopoulos, A., 'Theorizing or Negotiating the Law? A Response to Devika Hovell', 110 *AJIL Unbound* 3 (2016) 3–7.

Van den Herik, L., and Schrijver, N., 'Leiden Policy Recommendations on Counter-terrorism and International Law', 57 *NILR* (2010) 531–50.

von Einsiedel, S., Malone D., Stagno Ugarte, B. (eds.), *The UN Security Council in the 21st Century* (Lynne Rienner, 2016).

Walter, C., 'Article 52', in Simma et al. (2012).

Walter, C., 'Article 53', in Simma et al. (2012).

Weller, M., (ed.), *The Oxford Handbook of the Use of Force in International Law* (Oxford University Press, 2015).

Weller, M., 'The Iraq War – 2003', in Ruys et al. (2018) 639–61.

White, N., 'The UN Charter and Peacekeeping Forces: Constitutional Issues', 3 *Int Peacekeeping* (1996) 43–63.

Wilde, R., *International Territorial Administration* (Oxford University Press, 2008).

Wilmshurst, E., 'The Chatham House Principles of International Law on the Use of Force in Self-Defence', 55 *ICLQ* (2006) 963.

Wilmshurst, E., and Wood, M., 'Self-Defense Against Nonstate Actors: Reflections on the "Bethlehem Principles"', 107 *AJIL* (2013) 390–5.

Winkelmann, I., 'United Nations Charter, Amendment', in *MPEPIL* (2007).

Wippman, D., 'Pro-Democratic Intervention', in Weller (2015) 797–815.

Witschel, G., 'Article 108', in Simma et al. (2012).

Witschel, G., 'Article 109', in Simma et al. (2012).

Wolfrum, R., 'Legitimacy in International Law', *MPEPIL* (2011).

Wolfrum, R., 'Article 1', in Simma et al. (2012).

Wood, M., 'Security Council Working Methods and Procedure: Recent Developments', 45 *ICLQ* (1996) 150–61.

Wood, M., 'The Interpretation of Security Council Resolutions', 2 *MPUNYB* (1998) 73–96.

Wood, M., 'The Demonization of the Security Council', ILA Swedish Branch, 10 May 2004, available at www.sirmichaelwood.net.

Wood, M., Hersch Lauterpacht Memorial Lectures 2006, 'The UN Security Council and International Law', available at www.lcil.cam.ac.uk/press/events/2006/11/lauterpacht-lectures-2006-united-nations-security-council-and-international-law-sir-michael-wood.

Wood, M., 'Iraq, No-Fly Zones', *MPEPIL* (2010).

Wood, M., 'The Law of Treaties and the UN Security Council: Some Reflections', in E. Cannizzaro (ed.), *The Law of Treaties beyond the Vienna Convention* (Oxford University Press, 2011) 244–55.

Wood, M., 'The International Law on the Use of Force. What Happens in Practice?', 53 *Indian J Int Law* (2013) 345–67.

Wood, M., 'Self-Defence and Collective Security: Key Distinctions', in Weller (2015) 649–60.

Wood., M., 'Symposium on the Iraq Inquiry', 87 *BYIL* (2016a) 98–230.

Wood, M., 'The Interpretation of Security Council Resolutions, Revisited', 20 *MPUNYB* (2016b) 3–35.

Wood, M., 'The Use of Force Against Da'esh and the *jus ad bellum*', 1 *Asian Yearbook of Human Rights and Humanitarian Law* (2017a) 9–34.

Wood, M., 'Self-Defence Against Non-state Actors – A Practitioner's View', 77 *ZaöRV* (2017b) 75–7.

Wood, M., 'The Caroline Incident – 1837', in Ruys et al. (2018) 5–14.

Wood, M., 'Assessing Practice on the Use of Force', 79 *ZaöRV* (2019) 655–8.

Wood, M., 'Terrorism and the International Law on the Use of Force', in B. Saul (ed.), *Research Handbook on International Law and Terrorism* (2nd ed., Edward Elgar, 2020) 180–91.

Zacklin, R., *The Amendment of the Constitutive Instruments of the United Nations and Specialized Agencies* (Sijthoff, 1968).

Zacklin, R., *The United Nations Secretariat and the Use of Force in a Unipolar World: Power v. Principle* (Cambridge University Press, 2010).

Zaum, D., 'The Security Council, the General Assembly, and War: The Uniting for Peace Resolution', in Lowe et al. (2008) 154–74.

Zimmermann, A., 'Article 27', in Simma et al. (2012).

Zimmermann, A., Tams, C., Oellers-Frahm, K., and Tomuschat, C. (eds.), *The Statute of the International Court of Justice: A Commentary* (3rd ed., Oxford University Press, 2019).

Index

Index

Index

Made in United States
North Haven, CT
04 March 2024